Praise for *Mind If I Order the Cheeseburger?*

"With compassion, humor, and eloquence, Sherry Colb provides a clear and engaging account of what motivates vegans to eat and live the way we do. A must-read for anyone who has ever wondered (or been asked) 'Why do vegans think it is okay to kill plants but not animals?' or 'Why avoid dairy and eggs?'" **—Rory Freedman**, *New York Times* bestselling co-author of *Skinny Bitch*

"With crystal clear logic and an empathic voice, Sherry Colb has written a must-read source for anyone curious, skeptical, or downright antagonistic towards vegan living. This book is destined to be a classic of the emerging vegan oevre." **—Jonathan Balcombe**, Ph.D., author of *The Exultant Ark*

"A powerful, compelling, and thoroughly engaging defense of veganism from an absolutely terrific legal scholar." **—Gary L. Francione**, Board of Governors Professor of Law and Katzenbach Distinguished Scholar of Law and Philosophy, Rutgers University, author of *Introduction to Animal Rights: Your Child or the Dog?*

"*Mind If I Order the Cheeseburger?* is full of thoughtful analyses of some of the most common, perplexing, and often challenging reactions to vegans and veganism. Any vegan or vegetarian who has wished they'd had a more informed response to a question or challenge about their ideology—and anyone who wants to better understand some of the fundamental concepts of veganism—will benefit from reading Sherry Colb's in-depth exploration of the issues." **—Melanie Joy**, Ph.D., author of *Why We Love Dogs, Eat Pigs, and Wear Cows.*

"Sherry Colb's *Mind if I Order the Cheeseburger?* is a rare fusion of passion and logic, idealism and pragmatism, style and substance, and—in its measured confrontation of the most challenging questions vegans face—a revolutionary guide for advocates seeking to engage the ethics of eating animals through authentic dialogue rather than bombastic rhetoric. Colb's literary touch is something to behold. She writes in a way that will appeal to non-vegans and vegans alike, building bridges across an all too turbulent divide. This is food writing at its best and food writing as it should be: honest, inclusive, inspirational, and, more than you might imagine, timely." —**James McWilliams**, Professor of History, Texas State University, San Marcos, author of *Just Food* and *The Politics of the Pasture*

"Sherry Colb provides thoughtful, articulate, intelligent answers to the commonly asked questions faced by every vegan. Intertwining information, reason, and her own personal experience, Colb offers an invaluable aid both for those answering the questions and for those posing them. The perfect companion!" —**Colleen Patrick-Goudreau**, bestselling author and creator of *The 30-Day Vegan Challenge*

MIND IF I ORDER THE CHEESE-BURGER?

And Other Questions People Ask Vegans

SHERRY F. COLB

with a Foreword by Jeffrey Moussaieff Masson

LANTERN BOOKS • NEW YORK

A Division of Booklight, Inc.

2013
Lantern Books
128 Second Place
Brooklyn, NY 11231
www.lanternbooks.com

Printed in the United States of America

Library of Congress Cataloging-in-Publication Data

Colb, Sherry F., 1966–
Mind if I order the cheeseburger? : and other questions
that people ask vegans / Sherry F. Colb.
pages cm
ISBN 978-1-59056-384-7 (pbk. : alk. paper)—
ISBN 978-1-59056-383-0 (ebook)
1. Veganism. 2. Vegans. I. Title.
TX392.C685 2013
613.2'622—dc23
2013007504

Contents

This book is dedicated to my family
of humans and nonhumans,
Michael, Meena, Amelia, Sheyna and Cody,
for inspiring me to see the world from
multiple perspectives,
and to the memory of my mother,
Clara Colb (1920–2009).

Foreword

Jeffrey Moussaieff Masson

There are many good reasons to read this wonderful book. For one, it is extremely well written, clear, and accessible. Reading it is like having a good and intelligent friend standing next to you as you struggle with all the major issues that come up when you consider becoming vegan. More and more people are doing just that. Another reason to read the book is that Sherry Colb, a professor of law and a former law clerk to the legendary Supreme Court Justice Harry Blackmun, is both very good at reasoning, and very good at being reasonable. There is nothing fanatic about this book. This means it is hard to avoid engaging with her reasons suggesting we become vegan. By the time you have considered her views, it is hard to dissent. "Yes," you will say, "she is right." So why the hesitation, you may wonder? She will tell you.

If you are already a vegetarian and want to take the next logical step and become vegan, there are very good reasons to do so, and Colb reviews all of them. I often hear people say the equivalent of "Can [you] not see that cheese occupies an entirely distinct moral category from meat?" Milk and eggs seem worlds away, it is true, from the direct violence we see when we look at red meat. But is hidden violence any less violent for not being apparent? Not according to Colb. Her arguments are compelling.

She is not ponderous, however. She can be lots of fun, even while she tells us things we need to know. People say: Well, animals are not as complex as we are. In many ways, that is true, and she tells us those ways:

Unlike humans, other animals cannot—so far as we know—do calculus, organize a complex criminal justice system, plan for retirement, or write a novel. Such differences mean that when we organize a human society, we would not want to allocate important responsibilities to nonhuman animals. We would not hire chickens to treat our illnesses or sheep to teach us English, and we would not appoint fish to serve on the federal (or state) bench.

Nicely put.

She also lets us know that when it comes to suffering, pain, and sorrow, none of those abilities matter. She makes it all so clear and easy to understand. "Of course," I found myself exclaiming over and over as she made her points.

She is not a prig, not somebody who thinks anyone who is on the other side, who eats meat and is not an animal rights activist, is simply obtuse or stubborn or ignorant. She suggests something far more subtle at work here, and it is enlightening: "[T]he incentive of one side of the debate to resist hearing the merits of the other side—out of a fear, subconscious perhaps, of having to alter one's life in a fundamental way—can easily impede full engagement in the discussion. The stakes in such a discourse can be high." True, we are not talking about simply deciding what color dress to wear today, but how we should live our lives, how much consideration we need or should give to other animals who share this planet with us.

But she accords humanity to the other side as well, and I have not seen anyone else make this excellent point in quite the same way: "Just as vegans value the lives and experiences of nonhuman animals, however different those lives may be from our own, so we must understand and empathize with the feelings, associations, and anxieties of non-vegan humans."

She does not let anyone off the hook either. She has the terrific phrase, "a state of ethical slumber," and follows by speaking of the anesthetization of the human conscience. You may try to wriggle your way out of that one in vain!

You will be hard pressed to meet an argument that she has not already anticipated. She ably thinks through problems such as why vegans avoid harming animals but are seemingly indifferent to the suffering of plants. Is there a difference? She is very good at getting us to see what we already know intuitively. When I was reading chapter 1, I could not help thinking about how those of us who live with companion animals know their horror at being hurt. Should you, by mistake, step on your dog's tail, for example, how she will look at you in terror, then realize you meant no harm and forgive you. (A cat, not so much). Think, then, of the horror of those animals who are sent to slaughter. There is no greater violation than that of the integrity of one's own physical boundaries, for people *and* for animals.

Eggs, surely, you might wonder, how can that involve suffering? Well, you have to hear her out: She knows that you do not viscerally experience the connection between buying a dozen eggs and suffocating a one-day-old baby chick. But she shows how intimately connected they are, and why you cannot eat eggs without being directly involved in large-scale murder. Sorry, her job is not to comfort you in your denial.

I defy anyone to read chapter 4 without coming away changed. (Every sentence is worth quoting.) I did not know, for example, that "[o]ther cows in a herd, if permitted to do so, will often spend more time with and comfort the mother who has just lost her baby." Lost her baby! See how she puts things? It is not abstract for her; she is talking about the real world, whether ours or the world of the mother cow grieving her lost child.

Think about it: a dairy farm exists so that humans can take the milk of cows. To get that milk, you need pregnant cows. Pregnant cows give birth and then lactate to feed their calves. The females who are born to the cow are inducted into the same life as their mother. They will spend the rest of their lives giving milk. But what do you do with the males? After all, half her babies will be boys. What happens to them on a dairy farm? They are killed. She gives us a heartbreaking image of the innocent little guys, only a few days old, when they may still have an umbilical cord attached to them, attempting to suckle on the workers' fingers as they are readied for slaughter. They are not aware of the betrayal that awaits them.

Or consider what she tells us about the chickens who appear to be adults, because they are designed to grow very quickly so that we spend less on them before we kill them for dinner when they are still but weeks old. They utter the "peep" sounds we associate with baby chicks, because they are in fact still babies. I didn't know this, and it breaks my heart to learn it. But learn it I must.

Sometimes she uses a phrase that is stunning in its implications. We might never have admitted it to ourselves, but once she brings it to our attention, there is no way of weaseling out of it. Here is an example: "we admit that by consuming the animal, we have taken what was his most valued possession and converted it to our own use." Of course, we have taken the very life of the animal. What is more valuable than life? And what could be more cruel than converting the life of another being into a mere meal? How do we escape this logic? I think it is airtight. And then it becomes clear that when we observe animals on a farm, what we are seeing are captives, basically a prison population, no matter how we try to dress it up to make it seem harmless. There is nothing sweet about death row. Colb's use of language throughout the book does not permit us to wallow in a false sense of ignorance.

I cannot imagine anyone reading this book without undergoing a transformation. I think she has accomplished something really quite remarkable.

Introduction

Apeaceful revolution has begun, and it starts with what we eat.

This revolution calls on every one of us to stop and think about what we know in our hearts: There is a wide chasm between what we believe animals deserve and how we conduct our lives. The men and women actively calling for enlightened change for animals—a change borne of passion and compassion—are vegan.

Vegan? What is that? For some, the word evokes a bleak and inexplicable asceticism akin to culinary celibacy. For others, vegans are those who disparage traditions and customs that make life meaningful and sacred to many people. Yet others think of "vegan" as a trend or adolescent phase that young people inhabit as they figure out who they are. But from the perspective of those who call themselves "vegan," what does the word mean to them, and what values do they cherish?

Vegans avoid participating in violence toward animals. This means they refuse to purchase and consume animal flesh, dairy, eggs, and other products of animal slaughter and exploitation, such as wool, leather, and fur. In her daily choices, the vegan thereby freely chooses not to contribute to the carnage and suffering associated with the breeding and slaughter of animals. Her daily life expresses her commitment to compassion and non-violence, and her interaction with her world is one of caring.

Veganism is currently on the rise. As of December 2011, an estimated five percent of Americans were vegetarians, and roughly half of those were not eating dairy products or eggs.[1] Millions of people in this country already adhere to a vegan diet, even if they do not use this word to describe themselves. And the public has taken note. Vegan cookbooks have sprouted in abundance, including popular titles such as *Skinny Bitch in the Kitch* by Rory Freedman and Kim Barnouin, *Veganomicon* by Isa Chandra Moskowitz and Terry Hope Romero, *The Candle Cafe Cookbook* by Joy Pierson and Bart Potenza, and *The Kind Diet* by Alicia Silverstone.

Beyond the growing ranks of vegans, even larger numbers of people are trying to limit their consumption of one or more categories of animal products. Vegetarians avoid eating the flesh of any animal (including mammals such as pigs and cows, birds such as chickens and turkeys, and fishes such as salmons and tunas). "Pescetarians" avoid mammal and bird flesh. And still others, calling themselves "flexitarians," try to reduce their intake of various animal-based foods. Call them what you will; the fact remains that more and more Americans are rethinking their choices about how to fill their shopping carts and their bellies.

Why? Many meat eaters question the decision to stop consuming animals. To an even greater degree, because everyone is more or less familiar with vegetarians, people wonder why a vegan chooses to avoid products like dairy and eggs. Aren't these foods nutritionally vital? And what is the harm in them? And finally, why, as we face the stresses and difficulties of modern life, should anyone look for *more* ways to deny herself the joys of eating?

People are increasingly curious about the answers to these and other questions and find themselves saying: "Do you mind if I ask you something?" when they encounter a vegan "in the flesh." Or, in a more challenging mood, some might ask: "Are you really *serious* about this?" It can be daunting for a vegan to explain her way of life at a holiday dinner or at a restaurant in the company of friends. In a culture where meat, dairy, and eggs are the currency of the realm, veganism can seem like a foreign and suspicious coin.

Conversations between vegans and non-vegans can sometimes devolve into the sort of counterproductive name-calling (with the vegan as "Nut Job" or "Martyr," and the non-vegan as "Corpse-muncher" or "Murderer") that is both toxic and inimical to mutual understanding. This book offers the vegan side of a mutually respectful conversation instead.

The Simple Case For Veganism

The affirmative case for becoming a vegan has three parts:

- Health
- Environment, and
- Animals.

Health: Animal-based foods contribute to the astronomical rates of heart disease, cancer, and diabetes in the United States and elsewhere in the developed world. Heart disease, for example, is currently the leading cause of death in this country and a major source of disability as well. Though scientists previously believed that animal fat was the main culprit, epidemiological and laboratory experimentation have identified animal protein as another important contributor to the epidemic of cardiovascular illness in our population.[2]

Dairy products (such as cheese, in which animal protein is highly concentrated) are particularly harmful to health, even as the population largely views them as "healthy" in the wake of successful dairy industry advertising. As T. Colin Campbell, Professor Emeritus of Nutritional Biochemistry at Cornell University, amply documents in his book *The China Study* and elsewhere, the primary protein in dairy—casein—is among the most important known human carcinogens. The foods that both omnivores (consumers of flesh, dairy, and eggs) and ovo-lacto vegetarians consume thus leave them vulnerable to the heart disease, cancer, and diabetes that are prevalent in the West, and that have begun increasingly to appear in other populations that emulate the Western diet. Translation: Eating animal products (even those that are low in fat, such as skim milk and lean meat) increases our risk of life-threatening and debilitating sickness.

Environment: The environmental impact of animal agriculture has slowly but surely made its way into the public consciousness. In 2006, the United Nations Food and Agriculture Organization issued a report called "Livestock's Long Shadow." It identified animal agriculture as playing a significant role in global warming as well as in air and water pollution.[3] The report concluded that "the livestock sector . . . is one of the largest sources of greenhouse gases and one of the leading causal factors in the loss of biodiversity, while in developed and emerging countries it is perhaps the leading source of water pollution." In 2009, the World Watch Institute published an article by Robert Goodland, retired lead environmental advisor at the World Bank Group, and Jeff Anhang, research officer and environmental specialist at the World Bank Group's International Finance Corporation.[4] The authors concluded that livestock and their byproducts account for an astounding 51% of worldwide greenhouse gas emissions. The article proposes the replacement of meat and dairy foods with plant-based alternatives as a critical part of alleviating the existing and accelerating environmental crisis we face.

Then, in 2010, the United Nations Environment Programme's (UNEP) International Panel of Sustainable Resource Management concluded that a global shift away from the consumption of animal products (with an emphasis on meat and dairy) is vital to saving the world from hunger, fuel poverty, and the worst impacts of climate change.[5] Translation: Meat and dairy pose a clear and present danger to our global environment.

Animals: Most people are at least abstractly aware of the fact that animals bred and raised for slaughter suffer terribly. Videos like "Meet Your Meat" (narrated by Alec Baldwin and directed by Bruce Friedrich) and other readily-available footage of animals being farmed for their flesh illustrate the pain and death we support by consuming slaughterhouse products. This is why, when a person says "I'm a vegetarian for the animals," meat eaters may need little in the way of explanation. Not surprisingly, as Americans become increasingly aware of the problem, more and more of them are abandoning meat diets in part because they do not wish to add to the horrendous levels of animal misery and death.

What many people do not know is that animals "raised" for dairy and eggs suffer just as much as, or more than, the "meat" animals do, and all endure the same slaughterhouse horrors in the end. Dairy cows—like other mammals, including humans—produce milk only when they are pregnant and give birth. Every time a pregnant cow gives birth to a calf, farmers take her[6] calf away from her (so that her breast milk can be pumped into containers for human consumption). Both the cows and their calves vocalize and otherwise exhibit extremely high levels of distress when farmers take the babies away from their mothers.[7] Dairy farmers then send male calves (who will never produce milk), and many female calves as well, to veal facilities that will have the calves slaughtered while they are still babies.[8] Farmers do not typically raise the calves to adulthood for meat, because dairy cattle lack the genetically "desirable" meat characteristics of beef cattle (a different breed) and therefore are not worth the expense of feeding and raising.[9] After several rounds of subjecting a cow to inseminations, pregnancies, births, and the taking of her children, when the cow's milk production drops off, the farmer sends her to slaughter as well, to become some variant on hamburger meat or dog food.[10]

Like cows and their calves, hens are naturally very caring and protective mothers to their chicks.[11] At some level, our language appears to acknowledge this fact by using the metaphor of a "mother hen" to describe over-protective human mothers. When allowed to nurture her young, she and her baby chicks stay close to one another, and the first sign of danger sends the chicks running for cover under their mother's feathers,[12] behavior that our language again acknowledges with the metaphor of seasoned professionals taking novices "under their wing."

Even before a baby chick hatches out of his shell, he and his mother exchange vocalizations with each other.[13] In modern farming, however, very few hens have the chance to nurture their chicks or even to sit on their eggs to incubate them prior to hatching. Once a hen lays her eggs, the eggs that are meant to hatch are ordinarily removed and placed in an artificial incubator at a hatchery.[14]

Egg-laying hens produce equal numbers of male and female chicks.[15] Because the male chicks will never be able to lay eggs, a farmer will sort them from the females within a day of their hatching and kill them.[16]

Veal-farming of male calves and "disposal" of male chicks are regular, routine industry practices for disposing of unprofitable but inevitable reproductive byproducts of the dairy and egg industries.[17]

When we look closely at the behavior of cows and chickens, however, we see that these creatures exhibit strong emotional attachments to other animals, including—for the lucky few animals saved from farms—the humans who rescued them.[18] And as both ethologists (who study animal behavior) and most people who share a home with a dog or a cat can confirm, the capacities to love, to think, to suffer, and to grieve are not unique to our species but are in fact common to the countless beings who live and die on the farms that produce the meals that people consume.[19] What distinguishes us from other animals is that we have the power to spare them suffering and death at human hands simply by changing our definition of such terms as "breakfast," "lunch," and "dinner."

Strangely, the most controversial of the three main reasons for veganism is also the most obvious one: *the desire to refrain from hurting and killing animals.* The ethical vegan chooses not to consume animal products because she views animal agriculture as violence that she does not want to support with her dollars. She considers it unjust to breed and hold animals captive and to subject them to unimaginable suffering and slaughter to satisfy her appetite for animal products.

In a system of supply and demand such as ours, the consumer effectively votes with her dollars for the production of whatever she buys. Because consuming animals and their products is unnecessary and indeed threatens human health and global survival, the ethical vegan concludes that it simply cannot be justified. In short, vegans wish to change our consciousness, our culture, and our ways of consumption.

The Questions That Follow

There's no doubt about it. Vegans sometimes make people feel uncomfortable. Non-vegans may view the vegan as an outsider who has rejected their cultural ways, or as a follower of an implausible and peculiar belief system. In response to the emergence of ethical vegans, individuals in the animal-consuming majority, often curious and sometimes defensive, have tended to pose a variety of questions to vegans that they meet. Many of the questions imply that to accept the position of ethical vegans would require us to endorse immoral, illogical, or even crazy conclusions. Such questions may thus seem to invite people to reject ethical veganism.

This book is founded on the premise that it is useful to take the questions posed by non-vegans seriously and to answer them well, because they represent non-vegans' attempt to engage in a dialogue with vegans.

It is important for everyone to acknowledge that there is an emotional side to both support for, and resistance to, the idea of animal rights. For this reason, the book offers readers the opportunity to examine their own and others' motivations. Such an examination allows us to see that some questions posed to vegans may be premised on the assumption that the non-vegan lifestyle is morally neutral (and thus in no need of examination or alteration). The questions could accordingly, at least in part, reflect the desire to rationalize a deeply-entrenched set of practices that may have pre-existed any encounter with vegan ideas.

At the same time, most ethical vegans at one time shared mainstream assumptions about animal rights and the consumption of animal products, and therefore can at times become too easily frustrated and defensive when encountering the ideas of others who stand by the familiar ways of thinking. Like hyper-patriotic immigrants to a new country, vegans may sometimes find it challenging to engage in civil discourse with those who regard the new country as presumptively illegitimate or even threatening.

Because most meat eaters and vegetarians (and vegans) grew up consuming the products of animal agriculture, the notion that such consumption raises ethical questions can understandably appear threatening. The questions posed in each chapter of this book are therefore not simply intellectual queries but may also, on occasion, represent the omnivore's psychological weapons drawn in self-defense. The questions thus demand a combination of intellectual clarity and psychological insight. They call for a clear-eyed understanding of the emotional conflicts that they reflect and a commitment to open, honest, and compassionate communication.

From the perspective of an ethical vegan, one basic but unstated assumption frequently appears to hover over questions posed by non-vegans: that non-vegans are detached judges of reality, while vegans are people with an "agenda." Ethical vegans do, of course, have an agenda—to offer an alternative way of living that may better reflect the value of compassion that most of us already cherish than current predominant practices do. In reality, however, there is a competing (if perhaps not entirely conscious) agenda in play when vegans and non-vegans argue with one another. What we might call "The Omnivore's Agenda" aims to perpetuate the comforting idea that there is nothing amiss in the meals that most people feed themselves and their families every day. This observation is not an indictment so much as it is a statement of facts that we need to recognize before we can consider the possibility of meaningful discussion.

One need look no further than to children's stories about happy animals on the farm (in reality, a place where animals are brought into existence to be slaughtered) to recognize the power of "The Omnivore's Agenda." The adult omnivore may continue to embrace comforting fairy tales about happy cows and humane, necessary slaughter as an adjunct to the dietary and other practices that define an important part of his life. Simply by living in accordance with her values—values of nonviolence shared broadly by the surrounding society—the ethical vegan disrupts the fairy tales.

Let a robust and informed dialogue begin, so we can all come to better understand one another and our world.

1

WHAT ABOUT PLANTS?

When a non-vegan encounters a vegan and wants to engage in dialogue, one of the most common questions he will pose concerns what vegans are willing to eat and otherwise use: plants. The plants exchange might go something like this:

Non-Vegan: Have you tried the lasagna? It's delicious!

Vegan: Well, I'm vegan, so I don't eat animal products such as meat, eggs, or dairy.

Non-Vegan: Really? Why not?

Vegan: Because producing animal products requires humans to inflict suffering and death on animals. I don't want to participate in that. That's why I became vegan.

Non-Vegan: Interesting, but you do eat plants?

Vegan: Yes. I definitely eat plants! Plant-based food gives me so many options, and the food is amazing. I make an incredible vegan lasagna!

Non-Vegan: Hmmm. You do know that plants have to die for you to eat them, right? Don't you think that plants have a right to live too?

This is the point at which the conversation between vegan and non-vegan might break down. From the perspective of many ethical vegans, the "What about plants?" question sounds absurd. Does the omnivore *really* believe in plants' rights? More likely, the vegan assumes, the omnivore is suggesting that granting rights to animals is as ridiculous as granting rights to plants. But perhaps the non-vegan sincerely wants to hear the vegan's answer to this seemingly-rhetorical question.

For a non-vegan (which most existing vegans were, before we decided to become vegan), the idea of living without animal products is quite foreign. It is natural for a person who is relatively unfamiliar with veganism to try to understand what it is about eating and otherwise consuming animal products that the vegan rejects. One possibility that leaps to mind is that animals must die for people to eat, wear, or otherwise use them. If the problem is killing, however, then the non-vegan may reasonably wonder how one avoids the fact that plants also die for people to eat, wear, and use them.

A commitment to *all* life, then, could appear to entail human starvation. So the vegan might seem to be acting in an inconsistent and untenable fashion. The non-vegan, observing this potential inconsistency, wants to bring it to the vegan's attention and find out whether, in fact, there is a principle at work besides the preservation of all life. This is a fair question to ask.

The inquiry is appropriate for another reason as well. In the past (and to a great extent, even now), animal activists have tended to focus their condemnation on some kinds of animal exploitation while ignoring (or even condoning) other kinds. For example, some animal activists have emphasized how terrible fur is, boycotting stores that sell fur and even harassing women wearing fur coats. As a young person, I was opposed to fur, and I believed that opposition to be the appropriate stance for someone who cared about animals. When I expressed my views to people who wore fur, however, they asked me why I ate meat. Here again, the question was a fair one, and I did not have a real answer to it. People then suggested that I just liked the cute animals best and therefore extended moral rights on the basis of this preference. They argued that this was not a plausible basis for a moral distinction. They were right.

People, of course, are free to decide to consume only the less "cute" animals and spare the most adorable ones. If that is the line they choose to draw, however, then there is not much reason for anyone to try to emulate them, because their decision is a morally arbitrary one. Given the animal rights movement's history, it is therefore not surprising that an omnivore encountering an ethical vegan would wonder, "What arbitrary line is *this* animal advocate trying to draw?" The living/nonliving line presents itself as one possibility. If this were in fact the operative distinction, then it would seem that a vegan could not justify eating plants, according to her *own* values, and that, accordingly, adopting her values would make it impossible to live an ethical life, vegan or otherwise. This alone would strike most people as a good reason to reject ethical veganism. "Aha!" some might say. "We've shown the absurd consequences of the vegan argument and can thus ignore it."

Animals Are Sentient

A vegan must therefore be prepared to answer the plants question respectfully and to explain to the non-vegan why the animal/plant distinction is a meaningful one. What, then, distinguishes plants from animals? One important answer is *sentience*, the capacity of an organism to experience the world around her. If an animal has perceptions and experiences, then that animal is sentient.

To be sentient generally means that a living creature is able to experience pain and pleasure. We do not need much scientific study, for example, to know that under this definition, a dog is sentient.[20] Anyone who has had occasion to live with a dog (with the rather notorious exception of René Descartes)[21] can attest to the fact that a dog can feel pain, fear, affection, anger, and other states that reflect the ability to perceive and to experience the world. Those who study animal behavior more broadly find overwhelming evidence that not only dogs but all vertebrates—including mammals, birds, reptiles, and fish—and many invertebrates as well—including octopi and squid—have the capacity to suffer.[22]

Our recognition of sentience in other living beings helps explain why many people avert their eyes in the face of animal suffering or when they see a dead animal on the road. That recognition explains too why many non-vegans would likely decline an invitation to bear actual witness to the cruelty involved in bringing a chicken to our dinner plates. These actions reflect a laudable compassion and empathy in people, worthy of nurtur-

ance. Uprooting a plant, or tearing fruit from a tree, ordinarily fails to
prick our consciences in quite the same way, even if we admire the beauty
and benefits that plants bestow on our world.

Animals who have a brain and a nervous system—like we do—who
appear to find some things pleasant and some unpleasant, who produce
chemicals that block the effects of pain and anxiety—like we do—and
who otherwise behave in the ways that we behave when they are frustrated, curious, confused, injured, or mistreated, thereby give us every
reason to conclude that they too are sentient, just as we are.[23] I suspect that
most people do not doubt the sentience of the animals we use, though
some neo-Cartesians have tried to argue that pain is impossible without
language or some other human capacity.[24]

Most of us know that animals suffer, but some philosophers suggest
that the capacity to suffer, to experience an internal state (of pain, pleasure, or fear) is not enough to entitle someone to rights (including the
right not to be hurt, killed, and eaten).[25] According to some, one needs to
be able to use language or tools or plan for the future or otherwise show
advanced, human-like cognition before acquiring an entitlement not to be
subjected to the infliction of pain or death. But are these other capacities
morally relevant?

Unlike humans, other animals cannot—so far as we know—do calculus, organize a complex criminal justice system, plan for retirement,
or write a novel. Such differences mean that when we organize a human
society, we would not want to allocate important responsibilities to nonhuman animals. We would not hire chickens to treat our illnesses or sheep
to teach us English, and we would not appoint fish to serve on the federal (or state) bench. No one who supports animal rights believes that we
should send nonhuman animals to public schools, permit them to vote
in elections, or require employers to consider them as job applicants. The
right to have such opportunities—to obtain an education, to vote, and to
be considered for employment—are distinctively human in nature, and
they will likely remain that way so long as humans occupy the planet.

Most of us, however, do not think of these special, human capacities
as necessary to triggering the moral obligation to refrain from killing or
torturing other human beings. If I were to ask you "Why don't you kill
your next-door neighbor?" the answers you would give me would likely
have nothing to do with your neighbor's ability to use language, to plan

for the future, or to do complex equations. Your answer, instead, might go something like this:

First, my next-door neighbor has done nothing to hurt me and does not threaten my life or my well-being in any way. I should not kill someone innocent who does not pose a threat to me or to others. Second, my next-door neighbor is able to experience his life and the physical pain, pleasure, love, and loss that are part of that life. I would not want to deprive him of the joy and the emotional experiences that are his, by taking away his life.

Your next-door neighbor might be an infant, one who cannot yet talk, but this would not defeat your obligation to refrain from killing him. You should not kill an infant, because that infant does not threaten you and is capable of experiencing joy and sorrow, pain and pleasure. The infant does not have moral agency, the ability to conform his conduct to moral norms. Furthermore, the infant does not understand the idea of death, beyond his visceral readiness to fight, however ineffectually, against an attack on his life. And the infant cannot contemplate in linguistic terms the joy he feels when he is held by his parents, well-fed, warm, and comfortable.

Yet none of these incapacities diminishes the infant's entitlement to be free of violence and to be free to experience his life. The infant's simplicity does nothing to reduce his interest in not being killed or tortured. Indeed, his cognitive incapacities may heighten our outrage at learning of his murder or of torture that someone has inflicted on him.[26] It is his vulnerability to distress that triggers moral outrage, not his intellectual quotient. It is his sentience.

In response to the undeniable intuition that we should not harm an infant, some people might suggest that the reason we extend moral consideration to infants is that infants will someday be the sorts of beings who can use language, solve complex equations, and plan for the future. When we refrain from harming an infant, in other words, we do so out of respect for what he will one day be able to do, rather than out of respect for who he is right now.

This suggestion proves quite counterintuitive, however, when we examine its implications. To rest our moral obligations to infants on what they will one day become would be to say that infants are not actually entitled in their own right to be free of human violence—to say that we have obligations only to the cognitively sophisticated beings that they will one day become. If so, then it would follow that if we knew a particular infant was suffering from a disease that would kill her before she became old enough to speak (or to make moral choices or to do whatever one must do to qualify for rights), or if we knew that someone else was going to kill her at an early age, then we would have no obligation to refrain from torturing her or utilizing her in painful experiments in the meantime, because she would no longer be a potential rights-bearer.

Yet we know this to be nonsense. If a human baby's entire life will take place without her ever having the special abilities that distinguish normal human adults from nonhuman animals, we are obligated to treat that baby with great kindness and to protect her from pain and distress, perhaps to an even greater extent than we would be for a healthy baby who can survive into adulthood. And we similarly recoil from the notion of exploiting mentally enfeebled humans who will live through adulthood without the potential of ever becoming moral agents.

It is the fact that an individual is capable of distress that makes us feel an obligation to that individual to avoid causing him or her distress. The experience of observing suffering or even of imagining ourselves inflicting suffering on another human being triggers moral impulses in normal humans. Indeed, we label as pathological the failure to experience such impulses. A similar process is at work when we observe suffering in animals. Many of us, for example, would swerve our cars to avoid hitting a duck, a goose, a turtle or some other nonhuman animal walking across our path on the road, where we would not swerve to avoid hitting a bunch of grapes or a tulip.

Why avoid the first but not the second group of obstacles? Because our own moral intuitions tell us that we ought to avoid inflicting pain and terror on someone who is capable of experiencing these states. Our intuitions simultaneously tell us that running over a fruit or other plant, because it does not appear to cause the plant pain or any other consciously aversive state, does not trigger the same obligation to avoid doing so as harming the sentient animal does (although running over a plant might be wasteful, in the way that destroying someone else's inanimate property is wasteful).

Vegans and non-vegans alike can readily accept the difference between *something* that is alive and *someone* who is sentient, and most of us attempt to act accordingly, to a greater or lesser extent. That is why many people naturally feel outrage when they read about or see someone committing cruelty against a dog or a cat.[27] And many people are likewise horrified when they read about or see cruelty inflicted on farmed animals, such as cows, calves, chickens, or pigs. As Jeremy Bentham put it almost two centuries ago, "a full-grown horse or dog is beyond comparison a more rational, as well as a more conversable animal, than an infant of a day or a week or even a month, old. But suppose the case were otherwise, what would it avail? The question is not, Can they *reason*? nor, Can they *talk*? but, Can they *suffer*?"[28] A moral imperative thus begins with a concern for those who can experience suffering, those—in other words—who are sentient.

Some writers have assumed that cognitive endowments determine the extent to which a particular animal is sentient and, therefore, the degree of an animal's interest in avoiding pain or death.[29] There is no reason, however, to credit this assumption. I will here quote several writers who have addressed the matter more eloquently than I could do. An Anglican priest, Humphrey Primatt, put it aptly over two centuries ago:

> Superiority of rank or station exempts no creature from the sensibility of pain, nor does the inferiority render the feelings thereof the less exquisite. Pain is pain, whether it be inflicted on man or on beast; and the creature that suffers it, whether man or beast, being sensible of the misery of it whilst it lasts, suffers *Evil*; and the Sufferance of evil, unmeritedly, unprovokedly . . . is *Cruelty* and Injustice in him that occasions it.[30]

And further, Primatt added:

> A *Brute* is an animal no less sensible of pain than a Man. He has similar nerves and organs of sensation; and his cries and groans, in case of violent impressions upon his body, though he cannot utter his complaints by speech or human voice, are as strong indications to us of his sensibility of pain, as the cries and groans of a *human* being, whose language we do not understand.[31]

Much to the same effect, Emeritus Professor of Animal Husbandry John Webster has more recently said: "People have assumed intelligence is linked to the ability to suffer, and that because animals have smaller brains they suffer less than humans. That is a pathetic piece of logic."[32] In his book *Animal Welfare: Limping Towards Eden*, Webster stresses that "[t]he nature and extent of the cognitive abilities of animals is a fascinating topic of research . . . . However, it would be a mistake to infer that the capacity of an animal to suffer is proportional to the extent of its cognitive ability (its intelligence)."[33]

Is Killing Animals Okay?

What about death? Can killing an animal be harmless? Some philosophers—including Jeremy Bentham and Peter Singer—have taken the position that causing suffering to animals raises moral questions, but that killing them painlessly does not.[34] Singer contends that humans (and perhaps some of the other "higher" animals) have life plans that include preferences for a far-reaching future, while the "lower" animals do not. He asserts that it is immoral to frustrate the "higher" animals' life plans (by killing them and thus cutting short their plans) in a way that it is not immoral to kill those who lack the capacity to form such long-term plans.

Only an emotionally disengaged philosopher could readily accept the idea that the capacity for life plans is necessary to qualify for rights against being killed. Outside the world of such philosophers, how many of us live planned lives? Are the lives of those of us who do not have long-term plans or who feel unable to engage in long-term planning less valuable lives, more disposable lives, than those of people who can and do plan their futures in advance?

And why is the mere *possibility* of assembling a life plan so valuable and important? When some philosophers elevate the *capacity* to create such a plan, it would seem to follow logically that one need not even *exercise* the planning capacity to be worthy of moral consideration. Somehow, the capacity itself is enough to distinguish between those whose lives may be destroyed and taken for reasons of culinary taste and fashion without moral consequence, and those whose lives matter enough to prohibit their killing.

If the ability to plan had any bearing on the moral question, we might note that nonhuman animals do in fact have momentary plans—to find a mate, to groom their children, to seek out food and water, to find and maintain shelter, to try to avoid pain and death—and we frustrate those plans when we slaughter nonhumans. Moreover, infant humans and mentally disabled humans—individuals who are fully entitled to be free of murder, even though they cannot use language—are similarly incapable of long-term planning. Yet no moral consequences either do or ought to attach to that incapacity.

So if long-term planning does not justify a right against murder, then what does? It is easy to explain why we and other sentient animals have an interest in not being tortured. When we and other animals experience pain, we suffer, and we can readily say, "I hate the experience of suffering, so I would want to avoid causing another to have that experience." Oddly, the interest in not being murdered is in some ways harder to explain.

We, the living, have never been dead, and—apart from speculation about an afterlife—we have no evidence that being dead is an unpleasant (or pleasant) state in which to be. Whether human or nonhuman, once a creature has died, we have no reason to think that he or she will experience pain or distress. And importantly, for the "life plan" approach that Singer takes, there is no basis for concluding that someone who has died suddenly and painlessly will actually *experience* frustration of his life plan, however long- or short-term that plan might have been. Once death has occurred, in other words, the deceased—whether human or nonhuman—no longer suffers, from pain, from distress, or from a life interrupted and a life plan thereby frustrated.

It is for this reason—that death does not cause the dead individual to suffer—that the philosopher Epicurus took the position that death is not truly a harm to the individual who dies: "Death, therefore, the most awful of evils, is nothing to us, seeing that, when we are, death is not come, and, when death is come, we are not. It is nothing, then, either to the living or to the dead, for with the living it is not and the dead exist no longer."[35]

Perhaps Epicurus was right, and death is not a harm. If one believes this to be true, however, then it is true not only of nonhuman animals (against whom "painless" killing might now be morally permissible) but for human animals as well (who would also be permissibly vulnerable to "painless" killing), because neither of them suffers anymore once death has arrived.

Yet most of us believe that killing another person *does* inflict a harm against that person, quite apart from any suffering involved in the actual murder. Indeed, our law holds murder to be the most serious of harms that one human being can inflict on another. In the United States, murder is the only crime that one individual commits against another that is subject to the death penalty.[36] The idea that killing others is harmless is therefore counterintuitive, notwithstanding the fact that once someone has died, she no longer exists in the world and can therefore no longer suffer pain, distress, loss, or the fact that her plans have been frustrated.[37] There are several likely reasons for our deeply held intuition that killing another, in and of itself, represents a harm.

First, killing a living being generally leaves behind others to suffer his loss. This "collateral" effect of murder is well understood. For nonhuman animals, this effect is pronounced as well. The animals who lose their lives on farms are highly social beings who vocalize and evidence emotional distress when their loved ones are torn from their side for shipment to slaughter.[38]

The suffering that mother cows and their baby calves experience when separated from one another on dairy farms provides just one example.[39] A second example of animal grief is the prolonged bereavement in baboons who lose a close relative and show the same hormonal changes as humans experiencing a loss.[40] Another way to think about the "collateral" harm of killing is that neither human nor nonhuman individuals exist in a vacuum, and killing them therefore virtually always has an impact on more individuals than just the one who dies. There are the ones who cared about the now-deceased, and even the killer herself may be profoundly affected by the experience of taking a life.

A second basis for our intuition that killing inflicts harm is that in the real world, killing another almost always causes suffering to the one who is killed, prior to death's arrival. This is certainly true of nonhuman animals at the slaughterhouse, notwithstanding the "Humane Methods of Slaughter Act."[41] Animals at a slaughterhouse are ordinarily terrified and miserable and vocalize their distress in a manner that leaves little room for doubt about their suffering.[42]

From an evolutionary perspective, the capacity to suffer serves the purpose of motivating the suffering individual animal to escape and later to avoid circumstances that caused him injury and threatened to end his life prematurely and thereby eliminate or diminish his opportunities for reproduction. The capacity to feel pain, in other words, confers a survival advantage, an advantage that those who cannot feel pain—those who suffer from congenital analgesia, for example—miss.[43]

Because sensation and emotion—pain and fear—function as means of protecting individual beings from death, it is easy to see that accomplishing death without simultaneously causing fear and suffering is quite challenging. Stated differently, neither we nor our non-human cousins are built to die prematurely without experiencing pain or distress. Add to this natural state of affairs the need, in the case of slaughtered animals, to maintain the edibility of their flesh and byproducts (a need that eliminates the option of simply putting the animal to sleep with a barbiturate injection), and add the enormous number of animals who must be killed at a great speed to satisfy consumer demand, and the notion of humane slaughter becomes quite implausible.

Third, even apart from indirect harm to others (who will miss the deceased) and from the pain and terror that being killed virtually always entails, we intuit that killing someone is an independent harm inflicted against that individual. We do not accept the idea, for example, that it is harmless for you to sneak into someone's home and painlessly kill that person, even if he has no family and no friends, and even if he never saw it coming. That person was entitled to continue living, and you unjustly took that away from him.

Though it is difficult to explain precisely what harm we do to someone when we kill him, given that he is no longer around to experience the harm, most of us strongly and intuitively believe that we should not kill people.[44] And what makes us believe we should not do so—the fact that people have lives that belong to them and that they experience living—is not unique to humans. Nonhuman animals live and experience their lives too, and when we kill them for our purposes, we steal something precious from them, something that we have no right to take. We instinctively understand that the right not to be tortured goes hand in hand with the right not to be murdered, and neither of these rights has anything to do with the capacity to use language, to make a life plan, or to do other things that only humans (and that not even all humans) are able to do.

What If Plants Were Sentient?

In a variation on the "What About Plants?" question, posing the dilemma of why ethical vegans draw the line where we do, science writer Natalie Angier wrote an article that appeared in the *New York Times* in 2009, titled "Sorry, Vegans: Brussels Sprouts Like to Live, Too."[45] The article discussed new research suggesting that plants have active and sophisticated methods of resisting predators and disease. Angier argued in the article that because plants escape predators in a sophisticated manner, it follows that they "like to live too," just as animals do.

If plants "liked" to live, the reasoning goes, then it would follow that killing them would raise the same sorts of moral questions that killing an animal does. Vegans directly fund the killing of plants, while omnivores (and vegetarians as well) directly fund the killing of animals. Therefore, all of our consumption habits are equally unethical, Angier implied, and no one can claim the moral high ground.

If accepted, her conclusion might make the choice between different foods or clothing seem to be arbitrary. It would bring us back to the arbitrary distinctions that some animal advocates have drawn between fur and leather or between eating some kinds of animals (such as cows) and eating other kinds of animals (such as chickens or fishes): are vegans simply discriminating against plants?[46]

Angier herself decided not to eat pigs, she tells us, when a scientist reportedly told her that pigs' teeth most closely resemble our own. Angier apparently does, however, eat chickens, ducks, fishes, and other animal products. If her choice is arbitrary—and she does not deny that it is—so, then, is the choice of the plant eater, she argues.

The premise of Angier's argument is an important one, because it both acknowledges and shares the sentience foundation of ethical veganism: The morality of killing a living thing depends on whether that living thing actually has experiences in the world. Conversely, if plants are unable to feel or experience their lives, then killing a plant does not inflict a moral harm against that plant (though it may immorally deprive other humans and animals *of* the plant, in the same way as stealing a car would immorally deprive another human of that car).

Angier thus recognizes that eating a carrot, which has been uprooted, appears, at least on the surface, to be quite different from eating a hen whose throat has been cut and who has then been bled (or gassed or electrocuted) to death. Consciousness and the capacity to have experiences matter in Angier's argument. But, Angier says, if it turns out that plants do have experiences, then this apparent moral difference between them and animals might be illusory. And of course, she has a point. If a plant turned out to have experiences, then eating a plant might actually represent an act of violence against that plant.

By suggesting that we can infer that plants want to live because they have sophisticated chemical means of survival, Angier attributes consciousness to plants. Only a being who has subjective experiences like pain and pleasure can *want* something. But does a sophisticated immune system evidence consciousness?

The fact that plants are well-adapted to survive does not indicate that they are conscious beings—"someone" rather than "something." Angier seems to assume that a plant could not successfully detect the eggs of a predator and produce chemicals to destroy the eggs or summon a super-predator to devour them without "feeling" something in the process. Is she right about this?

We may find an answer by considering our own immune systems. When a harmful micro-organism enters our bodies, if we are healthy, we will produce a very sophisticated cascade of immune responses. We will make astonishingly specific antibodies that target the invading micro-organisms and, if successful, devour the threat and simultaneously prepare for fighting off similar threats in the future.

When this complex process takes place, if it is effective, we typically have no sensory experience of it at all.[47] We do not hear, see, smell, taste, or touch either the invader or the defender. It all goes on inside our bodies and outside our consciousness.[48] If plants can mount similarly sophisticated immune responses, then there is no more reason to think that plants are therefore conscious than there is to think that our own immune systems' resistance to germs evidences or reflects our own consciousness.

Plants lack a brain and a central nervous system, the means by which many animals (including mammals, birds, and fishes) experience pain, pleasure, and emotion. Furthermore, there is little else to suggest that plants have subjective experiences. Some people nonetheless believe that plants may be sentient, and none of us can completely rule out this possibility. Perhaps Angier is among those convinced that when she eats a potato, she thereby contributes to the suffering of the potato plant. Let us assume that she holds this view in good faith, as some others do. What follows from that assumption?

If Angier believes that plants suffer, then it would be her obligation to minimize her contribution to the suffering and death of plants. Eating farmed animals and their secretions, however, *maximizes* the hypoth-esized plant-suffering many-fold, in addition to inflicting pain and death directly on animals.

Breeding animals requires us to grow plants to feed those animals. In fact, an overwhelming majority of the grains and other plants we currently grow in the United States goes to feed the many billions of animals peo-ple consume every year.[49] If we consumed the plants and grains directly instead and stopped breeding and slaughtering animals, we would spare the lives of most of the plants we now kill "for" the animals (not to men-tion sparing the animals themselves). Stated differently, eating farmed ani-mals kills many more plants than eating plants does, a colossal inefficiency the impact of which—on our planet and on human starvation—we will examine in more detail in chapter 8. Even if plants wanted to live, then, it would still make moral sense to consume plants directly rather than consuming farmed animal products. If we permit ourselves to cause harm when we must do so to survive, we ought to minimize the harm that we cause in those circumstances. It may sound contradictory, but eating a plant-based diet is more plant-friendly than eating a diet based on farmed animals.

At this time, although we cannot know with certainty that plants have no consciousness, we also have little reason to believe that plants suffer or otherwise experience the world around them. Eating an apple, a carrot, or a bowl of rice and pinto beans therefore seems unlikely to contribute to the suffering of plants. We still, of course, ought to treat such foods as the earth's scarce resources and respect the fact that others need food as well. We can express that respect for our fellow sentient earthlings by eat-ing a vegan diet, which helps eliminate the need to feed plants to farmed animals, an inefficient way of feeding people.[50] In addition, becoming vegan embraces a life of nonviolence. It represents a choice to refrain from causing pain and death to those who, like human beings, experience the world around them, crave food and shelter, and fear pain, from which they—and we—can and do suffer.[51] Unlike plants, the sentience of which remains, at best, a possibility, we know that cows, chickens, fishes, and other animals are sentient,[52] and our nonviolent impulses thus rightly extend first to them.

WHAT ABOUT PLEASURE IN EATING?

One notable feature of animal rights debates is that those on opposing sides generally eat different things. This may seem unimportant, but it is crucial.

Think of it: if two economically comfortable people engage in a private debate, for example, about whether a minimum wage is a good thing or not, they may become quite heated. They may even agree never to speak of the topic with each other again. Nonetheless, it is likely that neither one feels threatened in her practical everyday life activities by the prospect of the other person being correct.

If the *government* raises, lowers, or repeals the minimum wage, that may have important effects for individuals, but no individual's views about the minimum wage will change government policy. Very few people will feel obliged to change their day-to-day activities tomorrow if they decide that they were mistaken about the minimum wage (or, for that matter, about a whole array of issues about which people have heated debates with family and friends). Changing one's worldview can be challenging on its own, even when no practical consequences follow. But animal rights debates add an additional layer of challenge: they implicate how the people in the conversation choose to live their lives.

Potential Anxiety in Considering Veganism

If you are persuaded that humans should refrain from inflicting death and suffering on sentient animals, then you may feel obliged to reconsider your next meal, whether it is breakfast (no more eggs, dairy cheese, cow's milk), lunch (no more fish, chicken, turkey), or dinner (no more beef, lamb, butter). That prospect might seem overwhelming. For this reason, the incentive of one side of the debate to resist hearing the merits of the other side—out of a fear, subconscious perhaps, of having to alter one's life in a fundamental way—can easily impede full engagement in the discussion. The stakes in such a discourse can be high.

Thus, it is very important for vegans to address, explicitly, the emotional resistance that many people may feel in considering an argument that asks them to engage in what understandably looks to them like self-deprivation. For instance, it is common to hear refrains such as:

- "Food is what gives me pleasure, so I cannot *seriously* consider walking away from the food that I love";
- "The way you eat is deprivation, and you cannot *legitimately* expect anyone else to choose to eat that way";
- "I could never make the great *sacrifices* that you do!";
- "*What* do you eat, anyway?!";
- "You *must* miss [fill in the blank], right?";
- "Do you ever *cheat*?"

Before responding to these statements and questions, I want to unpack some of the underlying, unspoken, emotional messages. The most important one is this: "I feel threatened by your suggestion or implication that I ought to give up delicious foods. It isn't fair for you to put me in this position." A person who feels threatened with deprivation is ordinarily a less receptive audience. From the non-vegan's perspective in this exchange, the vegan is inviting the non-vegan to give up fun, joy, and satisfaction. Most people hearing this invitation will send along regrets and avoid further contact with the apparently puritanical vegan.

Some vegans may feel at times like responding that it does not matter whether their interlocutor really enjoys a particular set of foods and would miss it terribly. Vegans might assert, perhaps with outrage, that there is a more important principle at stake here—the rights of sentient beings not to be made to suffer and die. How can anyone make his own pleasure a higher priority than that?

I find this response understandable but unfortunate. It is understandable because for an ethical vegan, the idea that anyone would rank the joys of dairy ice cream or steak as more important than the torture of cows and calves may be disturbing. The response is nonetheless unfortunate, for two reasons.

First, it does not grapple with human nature—we are not simply moral or immoral individuals; we are also pleasure-seekers and pain-avoiders. If we believe that embarking on a particular way of living will result in feelings of hunger and deprivation, we will be driven to avoid doing so. Indeed, we will probably struggle to construct the underlying conduct in which we currently engage as morally innocuous and legitimate rather than even consider altering our actions under the circumstances.

In the case of non-vegan consumption, moreover, the non-vegan debater will find many allies in this endeavor, because at least 97% of the population is eating the way that he does[53] and may be eager to offer or to accept any seemingly-plausible argument that permits them to continue to do so with a clear conscience. Just as vegans value the lives and experiences of nonhuman animals, however different those lives may be from our own, so we must understand and empathize with the feelings, associations, and anxieties of non-vegan humans.

The second thing that makes some vegans' "Why are you focused on pleasure when lives are at stake?" reaction to non-vegans' concerns about self-deprivation unfortunate is that there is a much more responsive and accurate *answer* to non-vegans' worries about missing out on the pleasures of life: the worries are unfounded. One need not "give up" pleasure to become vegan. Eating as a vegan is not very difficult and does not entail any major sacrifice. Much to my own surprise, the most difficult thing about becoming vegan has been the frustrating ubiquity of animal flesh and secretions. I no longer crave such foods, and I find the sights and smells of them disturbing and simultaneously difficult to avoid in our present society. To say this differently, I find it easy to be vegan but somewhat difficult to live in a world that is not yet vegan.

If you are a non-vegan, then you may be thinking that I am either deluding myself or have forgotten how incredibly delicious meat, dairy, and eggs truly are. Trust me; I am doing neither. While most non-vegans have never been vegan (or have "tried" being vegan by eating what they've always eaten *minus* the main course, a counterproductive way to proceed), almost every vegan has been non-vegan.[54] What this means is that most non-vegans can only imagine what it would be like for them to be vegan, whereas the vegan can actually remember what it was like for her to be non-vegan. And yet, against all societal odds, he lives, thrives, and continues to enjoy food.

This difference—between imagining life as a vegan and living that life—is important, because people are astonishingly inept at figuring out what circumstances might lead them to become or to remain happy.[55] Just consider how many people take well-paying jobs at great distances from where they live, imagining that a long commute will not detract measurably from their quality of life and that a high salary will add tremendously to it. As it turns out, however, the opposite appears to be true, and the long commute diminishes quality of life more than the extra money enhances it.[56] In other words, it is all too easy to fail to see the obvious, to miss how much we sacrifice in the name of so little. And when it comes to food, it is truly non-vegans rather than vegans who have no idea what they are missing.

I remember well the feeling that I could never become vegan. I had already acknowledged to myself and others that becoming vegan felt like the right thing for me to do, so I called myself "an aspiring vegan." I was convinced, however, that I would miss the various foods that I had grown so accustomed to eating and that the so-called "alternatives" could not measure up. I viewed veganism in the way that so many non-vegans do—as a commitment to deprivation, one that I did not yet have the willpower and stamina to undertake.

Then one day, I decided to do it. I emailed a vegan friend of mine and said I was thinking about becoming vegan and wanted his favorite web sites for easy and delicious recipes. He wrote back in short order, and my new vegan life began. I am not a person who can easily give up pleasures. I, like so many women in the United States, did my share of attempted "dieting" as a young adult, and I was never good at it. I have always enjoyed food—in particular, rich, creamy, hearty, and delicious food—too much to diet. Deprivation is not, as it were, my cup of tea.

The day that I went vegan, I began collecting rich, decadent (and easy, because I am not a chef) vegan recipes. I now have a treasure trove of printed-out web recipes and cookbooks, and the dishes that my husband and I prepare from them give me more pleasure than any food that I ate before I became vegan. I have prepared and happily eaten sweets like baklava, glazed doughnuts, lemon coconut cake, chocolate peanut-butter squares, chocolate fudge, chocolate chip cookies, chocolate-cherry brownie cookies, creamy rice pudding (using coconut milk or almond milk), and rugelach, and all were as good as or better than the desserts I consumed as a non-vegan. And because I am sometimes more inclined to the savory, I have fried fantastic potato latkes (using quick-cooking oatmeal in place of eggs), baked delectable spinach pies and lasagnas (using a wonderful tofu ricotta recipe), and cooked cream of mushroom soups (with homemade pine-nut cream) that were creamier and more delicious than any dairy cream soup I had ever eaten.

Of course, *sensible* eating is important for everyone. Hence, a health-oriented vegan would surely point out here that one should eat a more whole-foods-centered diet than what I describe above, including lots of fresh fruit, vegetables, greens, rice, beans, and other grains. I agree. However, I point out the fatty, salty, sweet foods that I have eaten as a vegan not to be a role model of healthful eating (a subject for the next chapter) but to clarify that vegans do not have to "compromise" on the sumptuousness of their food. There is an important difference between becoming vegan, on the one hand, and giving up decadent and delicious food, on the other. Veganism is not deprivation, by any stretch of the imagination.

A vegan author, educator, and cooking instructor who is also a friend said it very well, explaining that what we crave when we yearn for decadent food is fat, salt, sugar, texture, and fragrance.[57] Non-vegans may believe that only animal-based foods can satisfy these cravings, but they are mistaken. We can achieve all of the pleasurable food-induced states with exclusively plant-based ingredients and indeed, most of people's positive associations with animal-based foods are truly the result of cooking (needed to alter the natural, mucus-like texture of flesh) and plant-based seasoning.[58] If pleasure is your life principle, you can still lead a very satisfying life as a vegan.

Why the AA Analogy Doesn't Work

To illustrate the public perception of veganism, let me describe an experience I had almost two years ago. It was during the summer, and I had just returned to work after attending an annual conference about vegan living and animal rights called "Vegetarian Summerfest." During the conference, a vegan chef directed meal preparation for several hundred guests and supplied us with an abundance of tasty meals, including a variety of desserts, three times a day, for almost a week. In addition to the meals, the conference offered many welcome sessions about nutrition, ethics, cooking, and baking, along with hikes and other activities.

I felt a bit dejected upon returning home from the conference—I had felt so free, for a few days, from having to see the products of animal misery and slaughter all around me. I had been temporarily relieved of having to hear people talk about living creatures as though they and their reproductive secretions were simply commodities to be purchased and consumed. One of my non-vegan colleagues suggested that perhaps I felt like someone returning from an AA (Alcoholics Anonymous) meeting or retreat to join a group of people, all of whom were drinking alcohol.

The suggestion rang false at the time, but I was not immediately able to identify why. In retrospect, I think it gave me a telling indicator of what non-vegans imagine it is like to be a vegan, and I figured out why it did not accurately capture my feeling, upon "reentry" into the animal-eating world.

Begin with the analogy to an AA meeting. What happens at an AA meeting? People who have acknowledged an addiction to alcohol meet to support one another in each one's efforts to resist the temptation to consume alcohol. They work together to avoid entering an almost inescapable downward spiral, away from sobriety. What the AA meeting shares with a vegan festival or conference is one thing only: the gathering of people who are committed to a project and who understand one another's experiences better than the ordinary cast of characters in each of their individual lives does. In other words, what the two meetings share is the opportunity to be part of a community.

An important motivation for people in AA to attend meetings, how-ever, is also the craving for alcohol, particularly in stressful situations. Going to meetings helps people to avoid drinking in part by allowing them to see and hear the voices of others who can testify to the destruction that alcohol can and will bring to their lives if they succumb. To compare an AA meeting to a vegan conference is to imagine that vegans crave ani-mal products and need to be protected from a self-destructive impulse.

Like some alcoholics watching people drink alcohol, then, the vegan—on this account—seeks community to help fortify her willpower so that she does not "fall off the wagon" and eat animal products. Non-vegans imagine that the vegan sees a steak or egg salad and pines for it in the way that an overweight person trying to lose a few pounds might pine for doughnuts or cake while exerting willpower and ordering tea instead.

That does not, however, describe what it is like to be vegan. I do not crave animal products. When I look at a dessert menu, I am tempted by the vegan desserts, whether a vegan apple crumble with coconut-based ice cream on top or a vegan chocolate mousse. The desserts are as delicious and creamy as their non-vegan analogues.[59] As was always true for me, I often find myself ordering dessert, even though I know I will later wish I had ordered the tea (just as anyone trying unsuccessfully to avoid rich food may later wish), so that has not changed. And when a restaurant provides no vegan desserts, I may go ahead and buy or bake myself some-thing sweet later. I am not worried that I will "fall off the wagon" and eat a non-vegan dessert.

The AA analogy is thus flawed, first, because vegans who join a com-munity do not generally crave and worry about succumbing to the temp-tation to eat animal products, while people who attend AA meetings attend in part because they *do* crave and think about alcohol and want to help themselves avoid giving in to cravings. This is not to disparage AA at all. For many, it is an important vehicle for remaining sober. Once a vegan becomes familiar with the many, varied, and scrumptious foods of all sorts that she can eat, however, she does not need to restrain herself from "indulging" in animal products, because she no longer regards such products as an irreplaceable or even desirable indulgence.

Like the cuisine of a different country, exclusively vegan dining is mys-terious to many non-vegans. They accordingly project popular inaccura-cies and misconceptions onto such dining.

Another flaw in the AA analogy is the suggestion that like people who suffer from alcoholism, vegans are distinct in some important way from their non-vegan counterparts. Unlike someone who would identify herself as an alcoholic, for example, a non-alcoholic can choose to drink a glass of wine or a beer without risking a cascade into excessive drink. What this means is that non-alcoholics have a biological capacity that alcoholics may lack—the capacity to ingest a small amount of alcohol without experiencing a compulsion to drink more. For an alcoholic to be around people who drink, while they are drinking, can accordingly be challenging because the alcoholic worries—with reason—that he may be tempted to take a drink, since he will likely be offered one, after which he may find it extremely difficult to stop.

Vegans, by contrast, are not biologically distinct from non-vegans. The body of a vegan is not built in such a way that the vegan finds it especially difficult (or easy) to resist the consumption of animal products, such that once he has a small amount, he will be unable to stop. The body of a non-vegan is, conversely, not distinctly designed to consume animal products in moderation. Indeed, a look at health statistics shows that it is the non-vegan diet that inclines people toward over-consumption (even when vegans are actually eating more food than non-vegans are).[60] The rates of obesity, type 2 diabetes, heart disease, and other illnesses connected with uncontrolled, excessive dietary intake are much higher among non-vegans than they are among vegans.[61] Vegans do not look with envy either at the products that non-vegans consume or at non-vegans' biological makeup. Quite the contrary, we are happy, healthy consumers.

If the AA analogy is inapt, then how do I explain my dejection upon reentry into non-vegan society? Here is my reasoning. It is a wonderful treat for me to be around people who have joined in the project of withdrawing support from violence against animals. It is a joy to share meals and conversation with others who know and understand that it is neither harmless nor innocuous to eat a turkey sandwich or a cow's milk yogurt. I feel truly at home with them.

Returning from such a place to a venue where violence towards animals is the accepted norm is, well, disheartening. In a sense, it feels like leaving a place of racial equality, peace, and harmony to enter the antebellum period in American history when people imagined that the enslavement of African Americans was acceptable, normal, natural, and just.[62]

Pining to return to a vegan paradise is simply a way of dreaming about a time of peace, when we no longer inflict great suffering and death on our innocent, feeling, fellow earthlings.

When people draw the common analogies between vegans and those who give up cigarettes, alcohol, or rich food, they betray their image of the vegan as a recovering patient who must forgo a pleasure that she craves. Several vegans have told me about how some friend or co-worker began describing a meal that he had recently eaten but then suddenly exclaimed something along the lines of "Oops! I'm sorry to be talking about that kind of food. I know you can't eat that."

The reality, of course, is that the vegan "can" eat whatever she wants to eat. Unlike the alcoholic who declines a glass of wine, the vegan is not physiologically addicted to animal flesh or secretions or at risk of a "relapse" if she consumes animal products, in the way that an alcoholic is, if he drinks a glass of wine. When someone describes a meal that he enjoyed and that contained animal products, a vegan will have one of two likely reactions: she may find the description disturbing—this is how I feel when I notice someone eating a roast beef or egg salad sandwich. An analogy for this sort of reaction is the feeling you might have if you previously enjoyed the food at a particular restaurant, but you then learned that the restaurant's workers use toilet brushes to wash the dishes, and that the food accordingly has traces of feces and fecal bacteria on it. The reaction is one of aversion, not of yearning.

The vegan may, alternatively, imagine the foods that she would eat instead—this is what I sometimes try to do if someone describes an apple pie that he very much enjoyed; I think about the cinnamon fragrance, sweetness, and flaky texture of a vegan apple pie (which are, in fact, not very different from the non-vegan pie's fragrance, taste, and texture). The one reaction that vegans do not have is the one which many non-vegans appear to anticipate—envy or craving for the "forbidden fruit."

Animal-based foods are not luxurious or wonderful. They are simply what most people are used to eating, and when we are used to eating something, we might imagine that other food must pale by comparison. A relative of mine once told me that he would miss all of the animal-based food that he eats, if he were to become vegan. I assured him that he would not miss it and that I do not miss it. He replied that he is different from me, because he really enjoys those foods, so he *would* miss it. My response

to him, and my response to (understandably) skeptical non-vegans reading this book is this: I have had the experience of being a non-vegan and of
believing that I would miss dairy, eggs, and animal flesh terribly. I enjoyed
eating those foods too—before becoming conscious about animals, I was
aware of no reason not to consume them, since they were what everyone
else appeared to be eating. And then I went vegan, and I was pleasantly
surprised.

My relative responds to my claim by saying that I do not "realize" that
I feel deprived, because I have been deprived for so long. Like someone
who has lived without pleasure for years, he imagines, I no longer know
what I am missing. This hypothesis, however, is misguided. I do not live
on an island of veganism. Most of the people around me are non-vegans
(and I would even add that "some of my best friends are non-vegans").
This means that I am not insulated from animal products. I see them,
smell them, and hear about them on a daily basis. And this exposure does
not make me want to eat what I see, smell, and hear about. It instead
induces only one sort of yearning—a yearning for a time when every person has finally decided to withdraw support from the slaughter, pain, and
captivity of animals. Then this violence can stop, and in the process, everyone will realize how truly easy it is to participate in bringing an end to
the slaughter. Saintly sacrifice is not required, though self-reflection and
self-education are.

WHAT ABOUT HUMAN HEALTH?

By the time we reach adulthood, most of us have received an enormous amount of misinformation about nutrition in the form of conventional wisdom. One example is the old food pyramid, which suggested that animal products were a crucial part of a healthful diet.[63] When I was in my twenties, I remember encountering vegetarians (I had yet to meet a vegan) and thinking that it must be difficult for them to do all of the "protein combining" that I thought was necessary to thrive without meat. No longer recalling where I had heard such a thing, I—like most people—had uncritically absorbed the idea that animal products were the easiest and best way to get the nutrients that I needed. I accepted the message that living without animal products was risky and complicated.

This message turned out to be false. And while the food pyramid was recently replaced with a plate, the misinformation remains rampant, even among otherwise well-educated people.

Do Vegans Get Enough Protein?

Perhaps the most common and pervasive misconception about veganism and nutrition is captured in a single question that every vegan will likely encounter at one time or another: "Where do you get your protein?" Many non-vegans believe that meat, poultry, fish, dairy, or eggs are necessary sources of protein and that vegans must therefore struggle mightily to ensure that they are not protein-deficient. This belief is not only inaccurate but potentially quite dangerous.

In truth, it is easy for vegans to eat enough protein. Consider just a few of the many rich, plant-based sources of protein: spinach, broccoli, tofu, lentils, peas, whole-wheat bread, potatoes, corn, oatmeal, and brown rice.[64] Most people would probably be surprised to learn that broccoli—a food that many may assume has *no* protein—has approximately twice as much protein per calorie as a steak.[65] Even I was surprised to learn this when I was doing research for this book, and I have been vegan for years.

Joel Fuhrman, M.D., is one of a small group of medical doctors who have brought about major improvements in patient health by emphasizing nutrition in the prevention and treatment of chronic disease. Other such doctors include Neil Barnard, Caldwell Esselstyn, Michael Greger, John A. McDougall, and Dean Ornish, several of whom have advised and inspired former President Bill Clinton to start eating a plant-based diet and reverse the progression of his own heart disease. Dispelling myths about animal products and protein, Dr. Fuhrman writes:

> [P]lant foods have plenty of protein, and you do not have to be a nutritional scientist or dietitian to figure out what to eat and you don't need to mix and match foods to achieve protein completeness . . . . [On a natural plant-based diet,] [w]hen your caloric needs are met, your protein needs are met automatically.[66]

The assumption that we must eat animal products to get adequate protein is not only mistaken; it can be dangerous too. By focusing on eating "enough" protein—a goal that vegans meet effortlessly by satisfying their appetites—we miss the fact that it is quite possible (and, indeed, much more likely) for us to eat *too much* protein.

When we consume more protein than we need, we do not store it for later use, in the way that we store excess carbohydrates—including the carbon-and-hydrogen compounds within the protein—as fat.[67] Instead, we excrete the nitrogen-and-hydrogen compounds found in the protein through our urine. In doing so, in turn, we expose our livers and kidneys to a large amount of nitrogenous waste.

Dr. Fuhrman cogently explains that "animal protein places a detox-ification stress on the liver and the nitrogenous wastes generated are toxic. These metabolic toxins (about fourteen of them) rise in the blood-stream and accompany the rise in uric acid after a meal rich in animal protein."[68] The protein reality of today is that "[m]ost Americans are protein-toxic . . . . [T]hey are toxic because their body detoxification sys-tem struggles under the excessive nitrogen load [along with the burden of other unhealthful foods]."[69]

In other words, a vegan diet easily satisfies our protein needs, and a diet heavy in animal protein can poison our bodies.

The protein myth may be especially persistent among bodybuilders. At the outset, it is important to note that bodybuilding is itself a pursuit that places extreme stress on human organ systems. Competitive bodybuilders often maintain diets "low in carbohydrates and high in protein and cal-ories, meticulously timed with arduous workout schedules."[70] The goal is to have large muscles and small amounts of body fat, "which may require cycles of adding weight, then chiseling away fat to make muscles pop like He-Man's."[71]

But success at bodybuilding requires neither the flesh nor the secretions of animals. Indeed, a growing group of vegan bodybuilders is demonstrat-ing that one can achieve the same results on a vegan diet. The website veganbodybuilding.com has more than 5,000 registered users.[72] A recent article describes a vegan bodybuilder who can "bench-press nearly twice his [body] weight."[73] Vegan bodybuilders are thus able not only to get enough protein but to win bodybuilding competitions as well.[74]

Do Vegans Get Enough Calcium?

Having addressed the most common misconception about vegan diets— the protein myth—we turn to a close second. Upon learning that I am vegan and therefore do not eat or drink dairy foods, people frequently ask, "But where do you get your calcium?" As with protein, the answer is both simple and surprising in its ramifications for our health. People concerned about calcium typically worry most about bone health and, for women, about the threat of osteoporosis, a disease that thins bone tissue and reduces the mineral density of bone, resulting in fractures.

A substantial proportion of American women over the age of fifty has osteoporosis,[75] which results in fractures of the hip, wrist, or spine in many sufferers.[76] Severe osteoporosis can be debilitating and terrifying, as I know from my late mother's experience. My mom had osteoporosis, and when she was in her eighties, her bones were so weak that she would sometimes suffer "spontaneous fractures." Without any noticeable precipitating trauma, one of her bones would break.

How can osteoporosis be prevented or mitigated? Calcium is one of the important minerals present in bone tissue that diminishes in the osteoporosis patient. Dairy products contain calcium. Encouraged by ubiquitous dairy advertising,[77] many Americans understandably conclude that a diet rich in dairy products must be necessary and effective protection against osteoporosis. These conclusions, however, turn out to be inaccurate.

First, plants provide plenty of calcium. To give an incomplete list, the following foods are rich in usable calcium: green vegetables such as broccoli, kale, collard greens, and romaine lettuce; beans; tofu; sesame seeds; cauliflower; and oranges.[78] Dairy consumption is not necessary for obtaining adequate calcium and avoiding osteoporosis.

Indeed, the populations that consume the most dairy have much *higher* rates of osteoporosis than those in countries that consume very little dairy.[79] My family experience sadly confirms the general pattern. In addition to taking prescription medication to maintain her bone density, my mother ate at least one and often several daily helpings of low-fat cheese, and she regularly drank calcium-rich skim milk. But the fractures just kept accelerating.

Part of why dairy consumption does not protect people from osteoporosis may be that calcium absorption alone does not assure bone health; healthy bones must *retain* their calcium as well. If bones lose calcium, then they are at least as vulnerable to fracture as they would be if they had never had the calcium in the first place. Animal protein (present in dairy as well as in virtually all other animal products) has been shown to cause bones to excrete their calcium, which then exits the body in the person's urine.[80]

Why would animal protein cause bones to excrete their calcium? One hypothesis is that ingesting animal protein (but not plant protein) causes the blood to become acidic, which triggers the release of calcium from bones to help neutralize the acid in the blood.[81] A 1992 study of hip fractures and food, for example, found a significant correlation between consuming animal protein and suffering hip fractures.[82] Leaving all animal products out of one's diet in favor of plant-based foods thus allows us to nourish our bodies with adequate calcium that, significantly, our bones may be better able to successfully retain.

One need not worry that removing meat, dairy, and eggs from one's refrigerator will threaten one's health. The Academy of Nutrition and Dietetics (AND, formerly known as the American Dietetic Association) has published its finding that "vegetarian diets" (which it defines as including completely vegan diets)[83] can be "healthful, nutritionally adequate, and may provide health benefits in the prevention and treatment of certain diseases," adding that such diets are "appropriate for individuals during all stages of the life cycle including pregnancy, lactation, infancy, childhood, and adolescence and for athletes."[84] The AND is the largest organization of food and nutritional professionals in the United States. It is a conservative group that has partners within the animal-food industries,[85] relationships that ought to resolve any concern that the AND would be biased *against* the consumption of animal products.

Can Pregnant Women Be Vegan?

It is worth emphasizing the portion of the AND's finding that confirms the appropriateness of a vegan diet for "all stages of the life cycle, including pregnancy . . . infancy, childhood, and adolescence." When the topic of veganism arises, people become most worried and alarmed about pregnant women and infants leaving animal products behind.[86] Believing that animal products supply the body with necessary nutrients unavailable in plant foods, people sometimes say to the pregnant woman or new mother, "You can eat whatever you like when you're the only one whose health is on the line, but the same does not hold true when a baby's health and life are at stake."[87] For a pregnant woman (or those who love her), hearing such dire warnings can be very frightening.

Medical doctors, who typically have no special training or expertise in nutrition,[88] have generally absorbed the same nutritional myths as the rest of us have. And doctors can wield enormous influence over patients' eating habits. For our part, patients are reluctant to challenge a doctor's advice regarding what many assume is part of a medical professional's expertise. To make matters worse, uninformed writers produce misleading articles that further scare people away from nourishing their babies and children on a highly nutritious, plant-based diet.[89]

On top of ignorant comments from uninformed doctors, family, and friends, an interesting additional factor can enter the picture during pregnancy—cravings. In worrying over the pregnant vegan, family and friends will sometimes cite the fact that the woman craves steak or ice cream as proof that her baby's health would benefit from her eating those or other animal products.[90]

On its face, this argument from cravings is somewhat peculiar, because we ordinarily treat our cravings with a healthy dose of skepticism. Consider the following hypothetical example. Suppose I consider my cravings the best evidence of what I ought to eat. I might then start each day with a freshly deep-fried and glazed donut or two, followed by a handful of chocolate hazelnut cups and a cookies-and-cream vegan milkshake. For lunch, I might turn to savory snacks and eat a bag of potato chips with a vegan onion dip and a pine-nut-cream-based cream-of-mushroom soup, along with a soft pretzel. If I were to say to you, "I feel like having some chocolate bars for dinner," would you honestly reply, "Then you had better eat some chocolate bars, because your craving is your body's way of telling you that you are not getting enough chocolate"?

It is at least in part by following these very sorts of cravings that a *majority* of American adults in 2009 found themselves overweight or obese, resulting in a greater likelihood of receiving a diagnosis of high blood pressure, high cholesterol, diabetes, or heart attack than their non-overweight counterparts.[91] *The Pleasure Trap* by Douglas J. Lisle and Alan Goldhamer nicely explains how processed foods (especially ones in which refined sugars and fats are concentrated in small-volume food products) induce health-threatening cravings.[92] In nature, where we find whole foods and no refined foods, we do not see much animal obesity, even when food is plentiful.[93] Our companion animals, however—to whom we feed processed foods—suffer obesity and related ailments, just as we do.[94] In a world of processed food and ubiquitous animal products,[95] cravings can pave the way to a hospital bed, and we generally seem to understand this reality.[96]

When a woman is pregnant, however, we tend to believe that her cravings reflect a deep bodily wisdom about her own and her growing fetus's nutritional needs. If she wants to eat meat, then she must have a need for meat, we conclude. The pregnant woman, however, is as subject to the sorts of misguided cravings as the rest of us are. A pregnant woman needs more calories than her non-pregnant analogue, as does a lactating woman.[97] Because animal-based foods are more calorie-dense than plant-based foods (in part because animal products contain virtually no fiber), it is understandable that a high caloric need would result in cravings for animal products, just as a shortage of calories might have done for our ancestors.

Yet today, calories are available in abundance in the plant kingdom. In times of scarcity, it might have been adaptive for a pregnant woman to eat a calorie-dense food such as meat whenever she could, because of her increased caloric need. Now, however, the people who consume the most animal-dense diet, also known as the Western diet,[98] have ready access to adequate calories in the form of plant foods. Indeed, obesity rather than caloric inadequacy has become a growing problem for pregnant women,[99] and obese women suffer greater pregnancy complications, including higher rates of pre-eclampsia, diabetes, and the need for C-sections, than their non-obese counterparts.[100] Some doctors have even begun to advise their obese pregnant patients to try *not* to gain weight during pregnancy.[101]

Another plausible account of a pregnant woman's cravings for meat is that when a woman is pregnant, she needs additional minerals like iron for herself and her baby. If she is used to getting her iron from meat, she might accordingly crave meat (if we assume that there is some wisdom to her cravings). She can, however, obtain all of the iron she needs from green, leafy vegetables such as spinach, collard greens, and kale. She would, in fact, have to eat 1700 calories of sirloin steak to get the amount of iron that she can obtain from just 100 calories of spinach.[102] Her need for iron therefore seems poorly addressed by her meat cravings, a reflection of familiarity rather than deep bodily wisdom.

Beyond our ability to explain the origins of pregnant women's cravings without treating the cravings as nutritionally sound biological directives, it is useful to remember that we can also understand some cravings to reflect hormonal fluctuations. It is therefore reassuring to learn, when it comes to assessing cravings for animal products, that a healthy pregnancy is fully compatible with a vegan diet, no matter what the pregnant woman might crave. This should not surprise even the most committed non-vegans, because non-vegan pregnant women have been known to crave all sorts of unhealthful foods, including things that are not even food, like chalk and paint chips![103]

Our modern world makes some of our inherited biological urges less than adaptive to our physiological health. Most of us understand that in conditions of plenty, we should generally treat our cravings as, at best, unreliable guides to diet. We need to extend that understanding to pregnancy cravings as well.

Getting Enough Vitamin B12 and Vitamin D

When embarking on a vegan diet, there is one nutritional supplement that you will almost certainly need to take: vitamin B12. This vitamin is an important part of maintaining healthy nerve cells and red blood cells, and it is also necessary to the body's manufacture of DNA (all cells' genetic material).

Though it is found in abundance in animal products, vitamin B12 is not itself an animal product. It is made by bacterial organisms that live in healthy soil and in the intestines of animals. As T. Colin Campbell explains, "[a]t one point in our history, we got B12 from vegetables that hadn't been scoured of all soil."[104] In the United States, however, because of pesticides, herbicides and other unnatural treatments, "most of our agriculture takes place on relatively lifeless soil."[105] As a result of that, we may no longer be able to reliably acquire vitamin B12 from plant-based food.

For people who prefer not to take vitamin tablets, many foods are fortified with B12, including soy milks, rice milks, almond milks, breakfast cereals, and nutritional yeast, a tasty product that can be sprinkled on spaghetti and tomato sauce for a cheesy flavor.

Another useful supplement for people (especially vegan but also non-vegan) who spend very little time outside in the sunshine is vitamin D, a compound also found in a number of fortified foods, such as soy milks, rice milks, and margarines. For someone like me who lives in upstate New York, vitamin D supplements are a must (and likely would be even if I were not vegan).

You do your health no harm by becoming vegan. To understand only that a vegan diet is entirely consistent with human health, however, is to miss the enormous health benefits that become available on a vegan diet, provided the vegan diet consists primarily of healthful vegan food, including fruits, vegetables, legumes, nuts, and whole grains, rather than primarily or exclusively of vegan junk food such as vegan donuts, cinnamon buns, ice cream, chocolate bars, and potato chips. Eliminating animal flesh (such as beef, poultry, and fish) as well as animal secretions (dairy and eggs) from one's diet, in other words, is not just safe; it can affirmatively benefit your health.

Preventing Cancer, Heart Disease, and Diabetes

Some of us believe that we are unalterably destined to become sick (with breast cancer, high blood pressure, or heart disease, for example), because we have genes that increase the odds of our developing such illnesses. As T. Colin Campbell explains in *The China Study*, however, we neglect the following wisdom to our own detriment: "Genes do not determine disease on their own. Genes function only by being activated, or expressed, and nutrition plays a critical role in determining which genes, good and bad, are expressed."[106]

In the course of his research, Campbell came to the conclusion that human beings can obtain the nutrients we need from plant-based foods.[107] More startling—to him as well as to much of his audience—he found that animal-based food is not only unnecessary to human health; it can be affirmatively harmful.

Campbell discovered through extensive, painstaking epidemiological and experimental study that an animal-based diet increases our risk of heart disease, obesity, several common cancers, and diabetes, while eliminating animal products from our diet promotes health and protects children and adults against disease.[108] Yet many educated and intelligent people remain in the dark about these findings, now the subject of a documentary film called *Forks Over Knives*.

Responding to the fatalistic resignation of people who believe their genes will determine their future health, no matter what they do, Campbell's work demonstrates that people with very similar genetic profiles become ill at very different rates, depending on their diet in general and on the amount of animal foods they consume, in particular. Comparing the prevalence of Western ailments—heart disease, several common cancers, and diabetes—in different countries, Campbell found that "one of the strongest predictors of Western diseases was blood cholesterol."[109] Comparing rural China, where people have until recently consumed very little animal protein and far more plant-based food, to the United States, where the standard diet is animal-protein-heavy, Campbell observed that decreasing blood cholesterol levels corresponded with a decrease in "cancers of the liver, rectum, colon, lung, breast, childhood leukemia, adult leukemia, [and cancers of the] childhood brain, adult brain, stomach, and esophagus."[110] At the time of Campbell's study, "the death rate from coronary heart disease was *seventeen times higher* among American men than rural Chinese men."[111] He also found that "[t]he American death rate from breast cancer was *five times higher* than the rural Chinese rate."[112]

The China Study itself (which comprises only part of the research described in Campbell's book) was not, however, dedicated to comparing the population of rural China to that of the United States. Instead, it studied the diet and death rates of a group of 880 million Chinese citizens for over thirty years.[113] The in-depth regional study found that even modest differences in the rate of animal protein consumption (where everyone was consuming far less than people do, on average, in the United States[114]) correlated with significant and consistent variations in cancer rates.[115] Because ethnic backgrounds of people within China are quite uniform throughout the country, genetic differences could not account for greatly differing death rates. Yet counties with the highest rates of some cancers (and the highest rates of animal protein consumption) had rates of cancer *over 100 times greater* than counties with the lower rates of the same cancers (and correspondingly lower rates of animal protein consumption).[116] By contrast, within the United States, where many different ethnic groups reside, the difference in cancer rates between some parts of the country and others is at most threefold.[117]

In addition to cancer, heart disease as well varies with the ingestion of animal-based foods. Cardiovascular disease (including malfunctions of the heart and the circulatory system) represents the number one cause of death in the United States.[118] A study of heart disease death rates for men aged 55 to 59 years of age in twenty countries found a statistically significant correlation between the ingestion of not only animal fat but also of animal protein and the rate of death from heart disease.[119]

In an article entitled *Is the Present Therapy for Coronary Artery Disease the Radical Mastectomy of the Twenty-First Century?*[120] Caldwell B. Esselstyn, Jr., M.D. identified the virtual nonexistence of coronary artery disease in plant-based cultures, including rural China. He noted, however, that "plant-based cultures that adopt Western, animal-based nutrition promptly develop coronary artery disease."[121] In his own 20 years of clinical experience treating patients suffering from advanced cardiovascular disease and prescribing a vegan, whole-foods, low-fat diet, Esselstyn found that he was able not only to arrest but in some cases to reverse the course of their disease, a feat that no modern medical treatment—neither bypass surgeries, nor stent, nor medication—has ever achieved.[122] Esselstyn discovered as well that in following his program, "[p]atients lose weight, blood pressure normalizes, and type 2 diabetes improves or resolves, as do angina, erectile dysfunction, and peripheral vascular and carotid disease."[123]

In addition to careful epidemiological and clinical study, an interesting "natural experiment" emerged that further supports the connection between animal-protein-heavy diets and heart disease. A natural experiment occurs when an external event precedes a dramatic change that cannot plausibly be attributed to independent factors. In an article that appeared in the medical journal *Lancet* in 1951, Axel Strom and R. Adelsten Jensen described their observation that cardiovascular disease deaths in Norway plummeted between 1939 and 1945, during the time that Germany occupied Norway, only to climb back up afterward.[124] In occupying the country, Nazis deprived the Norwegians of their livestock and diverted them to Germans.[125] After 1945, however, when the war ended, regular meat and dairy consumption resumed, bringing death rates from stroke and heart attack close to their pre-war levels again.[126]

Apart from drastically diminishing the consumption of animal products, it is hard to imagine how Nazi occupation would have been therapeutic for the heart-health of the Norwegian population or how it might have led people to feel less stress on their cardiovascular systems. The dramatic change—in both directions—is also not plausibly described as a mere coincidence.[127]

The third "disease of affluence" to which animal products appear to contribute, after some cancers and cardiovascular disease, is type 2 diabetes. Until recently, this illness was called "adult-onset diabetes," but it has become almost as common among children as adults, so the old name no longer fits.[128] Diabetes involves the dysfunctional metabolism of sugar in the blood. Diabetes patients have difficulty both in converting the sugar from food into usable blood sugar and in managing blood sugar itself by storing it on a temporary or long-term basis for later use. As a result, blood sugar levels rise to dangerous heights in people with diabetes, who therefore often require medication to maintain a functional lifestyle. Even with medications, however, diabetes is the leading cause of blindness in adults, the leading cause of end-stage kidney disease, and a reliable correlate of amputation, nervous system disease, high blood pressure, heart disease, and stroke.[129] Medication has yet to make living with diabetes either easy or safe.

But diet can make an enormous difference. Researchers who examined four countries from Southeast Asia and South America found that the country with the highest rate of diabetes consumed a diet "high in calories, animal protein, fat and animal fat," while countries with low rates of diabetes ate a diet "relatively lower in protein (particularly animal protein), fat and animal fat."[130]

In one of several clinical interventions, with similar results, a group of scientists prescribed a low-fat, plant-based diet and exercise to a group of patients suffering from diabetes. Of forty patients who took medications for their diabetes at the beginning of the program, thirty-four were able to discontinue all of their medication in less than a month following the introduction of exercise and changes in their diet.[131]

In short, even conservative, conventional experts in nutrition acknowledge that a vegan diet is entirely consistent with human health and well-being. And a wealth of research, epidemiological and experimental as well as clinical, suggests that eliminating animal products from our diets can dramatically reduce our susceptibility to heart disease, the number one killer in the United States, several common cancers (including breast, prostate and colon cancers), and type 2 diabetes, all of which cost Americans dearly both in the quality of their lives and in medical expenses.[132]

We do not need animal products to be healthy and well, and such products may in fact seriously threaten our health. To the question "What About Human Health?," the answer is plain: "Protect and guard it by becoming vegan."

WHY NOT JUST BE VEGETARIAN?

Many people, including me, have spent years giving little or no thought to how our decisions about food, clothing, and other consumer items bring misery and slaughter to nonhuman animals. In the time before I "woke up" to the violence in which I was participating every day, I considered myself a person who would never hurt an animal. Like others, I was disturbed and even outraged when I heard accounts of animal abuse, but I tended to confine my scrutiny to those animals who never made their way onto my plate: dogs, cats, whales, and baby seals, for example. In being largely oblivious to the equally grotesque and far more pervasive violence solicited by my own food choices, I was very much a product of my society.

There were always a few people around me, however, who intuitively understood the connection between what they ate and their commitment to compassion toward animals. They were vegetarians. The word "vegetarian" is somewhat misleading, because people generally use it to refer to someone who refrains from eating the dead bodies of animals but who does consume eggs and dairy. Eggs and dairy are not "vegetables," of course, so to be more precise, we would use the term ovo-lacto vegetarian or lacto-ovo vegetarian, but either one is a mouthful, so I shall use the familiar word "vegetarian" here interchangeably with "ovo-lacto" or "lac-to-ovo" vegetarian, the way speakers commonly use the term.

Many people I encounter have been vegetarian for decades; that is, since long before I had any awareness of the ethical dimensions of my food choices. When I meet such a person, I know that I am in the presence of someone whose awakening long preceded my own and whose empathy for animals helped shape his or her life at a time when I was happily and obliviously eating cows, chickens, and fishes (along with cows' milk and chickens' eggs), without understanding that I was participating in animal cruelty.

Realizing that not everyone was as oblivious as I was, I feel humbled by long-time vegetarians. Many of them figured out that farming animals was violent long before I did. Not without reason, then, some vegetarians (and many omnivores) wonder why I or anyone else would go beyond refraining from eating and wearing the muscles, organs, and skins of slaughtered animals. Why also eschew such products as eggs and dairy?

After all, people have said to me, these products need not involve killing or hurting anyone. Am I aspiring to some sort of holiness or purity? Can I not see that cheese occupies an entirely distinct moral category from meat? Even omnivores in my circles have sometimes tried to show respect for my choices at meals by consuming dairy and eggs instead of flesh. Why would I reject the apparently logical distinction that they and vegetarians draw?

Animal Flesh Versus Animal Products

First, I want to acknowledge the logical pull of the distinction between flesh, on the one hand, and dairy and eggs (and other such animal products), on the other. If we are asked to imagine the origins of each of these products, respectively, we arrive at very different pictures. As a thought experiment, let us imagine the living origins of a steak, a slice of bacon, a chicken breast, or a fish fillet. In doing so, I think of a cow or a pig or a chicken having her throat cut at a slaughterhouse. I think of a fish flailing about, suffocating, or being beaten, hacked to death, or skinned alive. Because the animals' flesh is made up of corpses after slaughter, the violence involved is difficult to deny.

Now imagine the living animals from whom our eggs and cheese come. Many of us immediately think of a contented hen laying an egg in a comfortable barn and a cow standing placidly while someone gently squeezes milk from her udders. By contrast to slaughterhouse images, we can think about the laying of eggs and the milking of cows without feeling uncomfortable. While we instinctively know that taking children to a slaughterhouse would be traumatic, we have no such worries about bringing children to a family farm where they can see hens and the eggs that they lay, and where cows might be milked out in the open.

Unlike at even the "nicest" slaughterhouse, we can easily imagine cows and chickens laying eggs and giving milk without offering resistance and without the need for violent force. This peaceful and easy image can make it seem like eggs and milk are truly a world away from meat.

To equate the consumption of meat with the consumption of dairy and eggs thus seems counterintuitive. If I am prepared nonetheless to claim, as I do, that the distinction between these products is an illusion, I must offer a response to the strong intuitive appeal of the distinction. I must explain why the production of dairy and eggs for sale is inherently violent, just as the production of meat is inherently violent. It is inadequate, in other words, to point out—as, for example, books like *Eating Animals* by Jonathan Safran Foer have pointed out—that concentrated animal feeding operations, also known as "factory farms," produce eggs and dairy in a particularly cruel and inhumane manner.

I must respond specifically to the image that many of us have of the possibility of a contented hen or cow producing her natural products on a peaceful farm. I need to show that even when we witness this picture of bucolic serenity and bliss, animals are and must be injured and slaughtered in the background, outside the range of the camera's lens. I aim to explain why the calm that might seem to prevail for the laying hen and the dairy cow on even an exceptional farm cannot exist without an accompanying storm of terror and bloodshed.

To understand the hidden violence that does and must pervade the production of eggs and dairy for human consumption, it is useful to note an obvious but also somehow hidden fact about the animals who make eggs and milk inside their bodies: they are all female. Only hens—female chickens—lay eggs, and only cows—female cattle—(or other female mammals, like sheep and goats) produce milk. Though we may think of them as human food, eggs and dairy are reproductive secretions that only females produce.

Why should the female-specific source for these products matter? One reason is that birds (such as chickens) and mammals (such as cows) reproduce males and females in roughly equal proportion. A farmer who wants to earn money from a biological product that comes from only female animals must bring such females into existence through breeding, a process that will on average yield one non-productive baby male for every useful baby female hatched or born.

In the U.S. egg industry (which responds to the enormous demand of U.S. consumers), this comes to a total of 250 million rooster chicks a year who hatch along with the 250 million baby hens bred to lay the nation's eggs.[133] And every year in the United States, more than 9 million cows are used for milk production, and these dairy cows, on average, give birth two or three times before they are slaughtered at the age of four or five.[134] Approximately 4 million calves are born to U.S. dairy cows annually, and half of them are male.[135]

Farmers who bring these animals into existence for egg or dairy production must find something to do with the males, of whom only a very tiny fraction are needed for further breeding.[136] It would be financially ruinous to nurture and care for the males for the length of their natural lives while receiving nothing of value in return. Especially as females become less productive and have to be replaced with younger offspring, a farmer who hopes to remain solvent cannot sustainably feed and house all of the resulting male animals for the duration of the natural life of each, all without any prospect of recovering his costs. Even family dairy farmers do not, after all, operate animal sanctuaries.

When farmers breed animals to produce eggs or milk, they must therefore find a way to use or dispose of the equal numbers of males who come into the world at the same time. Before the advent of modern farming innovations that exist now, in "factory" and "family" farms alike, a male animal hatched or born from a hen or a cow, respectively, would be raised and slaughtered for meat. Some of the males might be put to work as "beasts of burden" for a period, if the farmer needed them to pull heavy loads, but their strength would eventually wane and no longer support such work.[137]

At that point, like all of the other male animals who could not "pay their way" in eggs or milk, they would have to do so in flesh and skin. Egg- and dairy-farming have therefore never been the "no-kill" enterprises pictured when we imagine hens laying eggs in a barn or cows being milked in a shed. Because the production of eggs and dairy selectively utilizes female animals, it has always and necessarily involved the slaughter of the males.

The Suffering Inherent in Dairy

Dairying, even before modern developments, has also carried with it an additional cruelty that I never contemplated until someone specifically brought it to my attention. Like most people in this country, I grew up drinking and eating dairy foods without for a moment imagining that suffering or slaughter lay behind these products. I felt virtuous when I frequented ovo-lacto vegetarian restaurants and ordered egg salad or a grilled cheese sandwich.

Many of us assume that milk is as innocuous a product as an apple or a handful of pumpkin seeds, because we have absorbed this message repeatedly from a very early age. Children's books portray female cattle as naturally producing milk, in the way that humans naturally perspire. The toy cows among children's "farm animal" games typically have distended udders, as though being filled with milk is the natural and constant state for this animal's mammary glands, much as it is natural for our hearts to be filled with blood. This impression of dairy cattle remains with most of us into adulthood, in part because standard textbooks in high school and college biology do little to correct it.

Cows, however, are not born producing milk. Like other female mammals, including human women, female cattle produce milk as a complex hormonal response to pregnancy and birth. Producing milk, also called lactation, is a process by which a mammal provides easily digested food for her baby directly from her body. A mother animal's milk contains the perfect balance of fat, sugar, protein, and micro-nutrients for a newborn baby of her species, along with specialized immunity to the pathogens to which her environment, and thus her nearby infant's environment, exposes both of them. In humans, for example, studies confirm that babies who breastfeed enjoy numerous benefits over babies who drink formula, no matter how "fortified" the formula might be.[138]

Lactating, however, is not a cost-free proposition for the mammalian mother. Any woman who has nursed a baby knows that her appetite increases during lactation, to drive her to consume sufficient calories to make baby food inside her body, an energy-intensive enterprise. A mother needs to take in many more calories than usual when she is producing milk.

In nature, making milk in the absence of a pregnancy and birth would unnecessarily divert enormous amounts of energy and other nutrients needed by the female animal. It would represent a very wasteful and costly process of a sort that would be unlikely to evolve in any animal. And as it turns out, young female cattle, whom farmers call "heifers," come into the world like other mammals, eager to drink their mothers' milk but unable to produce their own. A dairy farmer who wants to get milk from a cow (or a sheep or a goat) must first impregnate the cow, and that is precisely what the farmer does. Dairy farmers regularly and forcibly place each dairy cow into what is sometimes called a "rape rack," a device on which animals are restrained while they are inseminated.

Once the baby calf (or lamb or kid) is born, he will contentedly nurse from his mother, and she will, just as serenely, stand protectively over her baby as he suckles. Like other mammals, including humans, cows produce hormones during labor and delivery that ordinarily cause them to bond intensely with their newborns. The natural maternal bonding in cattle, as in other mammals, causes both cow and calf to feel pleasure and comfort in each other's company and alarm and distress in separation.[139]

If left to her own devices, the mother cow would nurse her baby for nine to twelve months.[140] And as dairy farmers accordingly acknowledge,[141] cows suffer tremendously when farmers take their calves away from them shortly after birth. Cows bellow, sometimes for days on end, and behave in ways that plainly exhibit desperation and misery, including a lack of interest in eating and a tendency to pace around the area where they last saw their calves.[142]

Other cows in a herd, if permitted to do so, will often spend more time with and comfort the mother who has just lost her baby.[143] Moreover, cows, who are ordinarily gentle animals, become highly agitated and potentially violent when forcibly separated from their calves.[144] None of this is especially surprising when we consider that overpowering feelings for one's baby are a deeply hard-wired feature of the mammalian brain and nervous system.[145]

After the farmer removes a baby calf from his mother, the mother's milk will be expressed by hand or machine to become the many dairy products that human consumers demand. To ensure a richer supply of milk, the dairy farmer will impregnate his cows again soon, a process that will end, as always, in misery for the mother cow, as she sees one after another of her babies torn from her side. Once she no longer produces enough milk to satisfy consumers' demand and thereby pay her way, the farmer will send his cow to slaughter, like each of the male calves to whom the cow has given birth.[146] She may, in fact, reach the slaughterhouse with the last of her calves still living inside her body, if she is like the many dairy cows who arrive at the slaughterhouse pregnant.[147]

Though a cow could live to be 20-25 years old,[148] the dairy cow of today (even from family farms)[149] typically arrives at the slaughterhouse by the time she is between four and seven years old, "spent" from a regimen of repeat pregnancies and virtually constant forced lactation. A significant portion of the nation's hamburger meat comes from the flesh of these slaughtered "spent" dairy cows.[150]

The suffering and slaughter of cows in dairy is accordingly not a result of "factory farming," though the latter has further intensified the process. Suffering and slaughter are instead inevitable features of consuming a product that mother animals produce for their babies. A dairy farmer cannot make a living from this work unless he subjects a cow to pregnancy, removes her calf from her side, and then slaughters the mother cow once her milk production diminishes. These are each unavoidable aspects of dairy farming.

"Disposable Male Babies"

Beyond the suffering and slaughter that our demand for dairy requires, a modern innovation has brought a whole new kind of violence into the world of cattle and, as I shall explain, of chickens as well. The innovation arose from breeding programs selecting for animals whose bodies allow farmers to maximize production of one particular product, whether that product be eggs, dairy, or flesh.[151] Such specialization extends to factory, organic, and family farms alike, because farmers, however large or small, purchase and breed these "optimized" animals. The overwhelming majority of the chickens we now use for meat are thus genetically distinct from the chickens we use for eggs,[152] and most of the cattle we use for beef are genetically different from the cattle we use for dairy.[153] These distinctions have resulted in a phenomenon we might call "disposable male babies."

In using the phrase "disposable male babies," I refer to the fact that we have bred into existence several domesticated animals whose only economically valuable members are females. Specifically, the males among "layer" breeds and "dairy" breeds cannot lay eggs or lactate. But neither are they the most desirable source for meat, by contrast to their "beef" and "broiler" counterparts who are bred to grow quickly and provide a large amount of muscle flesh for consumers before the animals can even reach maturity. Because the males in the dairy and egg industries offer little or no economic value to the farmer, both layer-breed roosters and male dairy calves (and many females as well) are killed even earlier in their lives than they would be in the flesh industries, since there is no profit to be made in feeding and housing them for an extended period of time.

Male dairy calves, sometimes called "veal calves,"[154] are slaughtered when they are anywhere from a few days old (when many still have an umbilical cord and attempt to suckle on the workers' fingers while being readied for slaughter)[155] to a few months old,[156] depending on the sort of meat desired. Over the years, the plight of male dairy calves has received considerable publicity in this country, and some consumers have responded by boycotting veal.[157] In boycotting, however, many of these consumers are unaware that veal is simply a byproduct of the dairy industry.

The production of veal is an attempt to find an economically profitable use for the male babies whom a cow must deliver before she can begin lactating or to increase her milk yields for human consumption. So long as people buy milk, cheese, and other dairy products, in other words, farmers will have male calves to dispose of, whether or not we call the slaughtered calf "veal" and whether or not we eat his body for dinner.

To understand why a veal boycott will not protect calves (from cruelty or from slaughter) so long as we continue to consume dairy products, consider the fate of male chicks in the egg industry. Like cattle, chickens are now bred in two varieties. "Broilers" are chickens raised and slaughtered for meat, and "layers" are kept for the eggs that they lay. Chickens from the two breeds are very different from each other, as one can readily see in photographs.[158]

A "broiler" chicken grows rapidly to reach full size by the age of six or seven weeks old, at which time he or she is slaughtered.[159] People who have visited chicken slaughter facilities have reported that although the birds are large, many still utter the "peep" sounds we associate with baby chicks, because they are in fact still babies.[160] The speedy growth of "broiler chickens" allows farmers to pay to house and feed each one for only a relatively short time before his or her slaughtered body will be profitable at market.

Layer hens do not grow this quickly, but they lay an astonishing number of eggs. A wild female Red Junglefowl, a member of the species from which domesticated chickens originated, lays fewer than 20 eggs each year.[161] By contrast, the contemporary layer hen lays close to 300 eggs every year, a process that causes many hens to experience a painful uterine prolapse in which the almost daily, powerful uterine contractions necessary to lay so many eggs push part of the hen's uterus outside of her vagina.[162]

Because shells are made of calcium leached from their bones, the production of so many eggs also leads layer hens to suffer extreme osteoporosis at a young age.[163] One retired farmer described the bones of layer hens as having the consistency of potato chips.[164] When the layer hen reaches the age of approximately two years old, her body is ravaged from producing almost 600 eggs, and she is considered "spent," at which time she is likely to be slaughtered or thrown into a garbage bag to suffocate.[165]

What about the roosters? Male "layer" chicks are considered virtually worthless in the egg industry.[166] They are not genetically programmed to grow to full size by the time they reach six or seven weeks old, the way that broiler chickens are. And they are also incapable of laying eggs, as female layers do.

This reality makes it necessary for the hatcheries that sell layer hens to egg farmers, including suburban owners of "backyard" chicken coops, to separate the males from the females, as a wheat farmer would separate the wheat from the chaff, so that farmers receive only the product they want: hens. Because it is challenging to distinguish between male and female newly-hatched chicks, the expertise of "chicken-sexing" has developed,[167] through which a person who masters this skill can separate males and females into separate bins with great speed. Chicken sexers then throw the male chicks, live and fully conscious, into a meat grinder or a plastic bag or into a chamber in which they will be exposed to lethal levels of gas.[168]

This death is the fate of male chicks in the egg industry, because these baby roosters represent an economically worthless byproduct.

None of what must happen to layer hens and their male offspring is apparent on any of the egg cartons you will find at a supermarket or farmer's market. Some cartons might even carry labels such as "humanely raised," "organic," or "happy hens,"[169] avoiding any reference to the rooster chicks. When we buy eggs from any source, however, we pay for the continued, cruel killing of male layer chicks.

By consuming eggs, we demand as well that farmers persist in selectively breeding hens whose reproductive systems are built to exhaust and betray them, leaving uterine prolapse and severe osteoporosis in their wake. And none of this turns on whether the eggs we consume come from "factory farms," "family farms," or the backyards of our well-intentioned but perhaps uninformed friends and neighbors.

We can now see why boycotting veal cannot effectively protect male dairy calves from slaughter. On a farm, male calves come into existence as a low-value byproduct of inducing cows to lactate. If consumers become unwilling to purchase the calves as veal but continue to consume dairy products, then the calves simply become even more like the male layer chicks at the hatchery, brought into an unwelcome existence and promptly killed in a manner that minimizes financial expense.

Both male layer chicks (half of the birds at the hatchery) and male dairy calves (half of the calves born to the dairy industry) are inevitable victims of egg and dairy consumption. Their victimization will accordingly continue so long as ovo-lacto consumption does. Consuming a cheese omelet, no less than eating a steak and chicken wings, thus entails the infliction of suffering and death on living, breathing, feeling animals, even if we manage somehow to avoid altogether the flesh, dairy, and eggs that come from "factory farms," the source for virtually all of the animal products consumed in this country.[170] The world of intensive animal-agriculture simply increases the suffering that animals already experience when we breed and raise them for their flesh or secretions.

Reproductive Slavery

One aspect of egg and dairy production, beyond the killing and the suffering that both require, independently disturbs me as a woman. It is the use of female animals as reproductive slaves. Whatever one's position might be on the question of abortion, discussed later in chapter 7, it is clear to virtually everyone that pregnancy and birth place a strain on the female of the species.

Consider that no religion requires people to have as many children as they possibly can. Catholicism allows for the use of the rhythm method of contraception (updated versions of which are called "Fertility Awareness Methods").[171] Judaism allows for the use of female contraception, once the couple has met the commandment of being fruitful and multiplying by having two children.[172] The Bible describes the travails of labor as difficult enough to qualify as a curse on women for Eve's transgression in the Garden of Eden: "Unto the woman he said, I will greatly multiply thy sorrow and thy conception; in sorrow thou shalt bring forth children."[173] Other religions permit limits on human reproduction as well.[174]

For other female mammals, the birthing process and its aftermath may be less arduous than for human females, but it is nonetheless demanding. And for birds, the process of laying eggs is difficult as well.[175] This is in part why the birds found in nature lay eggs at only a fraction of the rate of domesticated chickens. And it may help explain why the wild relatives of dairy cows produce far less milk than dairy cows do.[176] Genetic mutation and selective breeding played an important role in bringing about the animals whose systems maximize economic productivity without regard to the needs of the animals.

As reproductive slaves, "laying" hens and "dairy" cows must undergo the travails associated with reproduction almost constantly, at a great cost to their physical integrity and welfare. Laying hens are often so worn out by the time they are two years old that even the slaughterhouses do not want them.[177] The hens that do make it to slaughter most commonly become ingredients in soup, processed meats, or animal feed.[178] And "spent" dairy cows regularly arrive at the slaughterhouse with recent fractures, many of them nearly unable to walk.[179]

Because of their uniquely female capacities, capacities that they share with human women, we exploit laying hens and dairy cows every moment of their lives and then slaughter them or throw them away when their reproductive productivity diminishes. I feel sad to think that for three years, as an ovo-lacto vegetarian, I consumed the products of female-targeted reproductive exploitation, cruelty, and slaughter, and that I did so in the name of compassion and concern for animals.

One Meal at a Time

Given the truth about eggs and dairy, why do many of the people who have "woken up" to the violence we inflict on domesticated animals choose nonetheless to consume these products? I was an ovo-lacto vegetarian before becoming vegan, and I suspect that most other vegans were as well.[180] It may be because the relation between animal-killing and beef, chicken, and fish is intuitively clear to us in a way that the relation between animal-killing and eggs and dairy is not. As a result, many ovo-lacto vegetarians, like their omnivorous counterparts, are unaware of the inextricable link between eggs and dairy, and suffering and slaughter.

Even after we learn about this link, moreover, our behavior can lag behind our awakened conscience. We may not change our actions immediately when we decide that changing is the right thing to do. We are creatures of habit and socialization, and it takes energy for us to act in a different way and to stop emulating the people around us when we plan our meals and fill our wardrobes. For this reason, the decision to become vegetarian today, and vegan tomorrow, is not difficult to understand.

Many people are inclined to proceed in steps, and once a person becomes vegan, the preceding stages of her life become an important part of her story, a story she can share with others as inspiration. I first heard of an alternative "stages" approach to becoming vegan from Gary Francione.[181] He suggests that if someone feels unable or unwilling to become vegan all at once, she can move away from animal products one meal at a time. Vegan breakfast for a week, then vegan lunch too, etc.

As a stepping stone to veganism, though, I can appreciate the attraction of vegetarianism. Different people adjust to new ways of living differently, and because vegetarianism is relatively "mainstream," it may feel like a practical interim choice. My own worry about ovo-lacto vegetarianism, however, is that because it *is* so mainstream, many practitioners of it may become stuck there and never graduate to veganism.

As a final destination, however, ovo-lacto vegetarianism contributes enormously to the suffering and slaughter of chickens and cows, and, for many people, it may actually increase the sum total of animal products in their diet. Out of the well-meaning but mistaken sense that one is "helping" animals by being ovo-lacto vegetarian, one may also become less receptive to learning about the well-hidden but unavoidable violence involved in producing eggs and dairy.

To avoid feelings of guilt and remorse about the ways in which we choose to live, many of us develop rationalizations for what we do. When I was still consuming flesh, I remember telling myself that it must be morally unobjectionable to eat as I did, because nearly everybody I admired and knew to be kind and compassionate ate the same way. If eating meat were bad, I reasoned, then these people would either not be eating meat or would have to be classified as "bad."

Because I strongly rejected the idea that my role models and friends were bad, and because they did eat meat, I concluded that eating meat must be fine. I regret that this conclusion managed to quiet any rare pangs of conscience for a long time. Because most of us are "asleep" to the inescapable violence of animal products, I found no shortage of reinforcement for my desire to believe that I could continue living as I did without violating my own values of compassion towards animals.

An omnivore who becomes an ovo-lacto vegetarian because of the animals, however, has woken up from the moral slumber that afflicts most of us. She has likely encountered and taken in the truth about the cows, pigs, chickens, turkeys, fishes, and other animals who inhabit our earth and who have the same kinds of physiological and emotional experiences that we have. She has perhaps learned of the large numbers of chickens and pigs on a slaughter assembly line who remain fully conscious when thrown into boiling water or sliced into parts,[182] or of the terror that cows exhibit at the slaughterhouse.[183] After the ovo-lacto vegetarian's awakening, moreover, she changed the way she lived in an effort to have her actions reflect her deeply held values.

I greatly admire the decision of vegetarians to stop eating animal flesh as a response to their discoveries and their awakened conscience. Having made this switch, and believing it to be a serious boycott of animal slaughter, they may understandably find it frustrating and discouraging to hear that consuming eggs encourages the mass grinding-alive or suffocation of every male rooster who hatches from an egg, and that consuming dairy conveys the demand for slaughter as plainly as consuming veal does. And learning about the misery of the dairy cow who loses every baby to whom she gives birth, only to be slaughtered by the age of four, can be over-whelming for someone who imagined that there is all the difference in the world between meat and dairy.

It is not surprising that people who have committed to eating con-scientiously will feel frustrated upon discovering that the line they drew between meat, on the one side, and eggs and dairy, on the other, makes lit-tle sense. They might have the following reaction: "I have already changed. What do you want from me now?!"

I think it is fair to place some responsibility for this unpleasant feeling of betrayal at the feet of animal advocacy groups that issue campaigns to "go vegetarian."[184] The groups that advocate this step, moreover, may do so while fully aware of the violence that eggs and dairy entail.[185] When you have changed your life with the encouragement and support of an animal advocate, it can be disillusioning to find out that the changes they advised drew meaningless distinctions and, worse, that the advocates knew the truth but altered their message in the patronizing belief that you could not "handle the truth."

Such an experience might induce cynicism, followed by a desire to return to sleep, this time looking to the fact that so many kind and com-passionate people are ovo-lacto vegetarians as proof that it *must be* a mean-ingful and coherent way to resist violence against animals. Cooking dairy cheese lasagna for Thanksgiving instead of turkey thus comes to seem like a meaningful resistance to violence, while the reality of the dairy cow's suffering and slaughter fades from our consciousness.

Still, even as I understand the resistance that my ovo-lacto vegetarian friends might feel when reading this chapter, I would urge them to reflect on the concerns that brought them to vegetarianism in the first place. Doing so, they will come to see that they are *already* committed to vegan-ism, in principle if not yet in practice.

And what about people who are only beginning to think about moving towards more compassionate choices in their role as consumers? I think Gary Francione's advice is sound: People can consider getting to veganism by eliminating all animal products, including eggs and dairy, one meal at a time. If you decide, however, to begin your transition by becoming an ovo-lacto vegetarian, please think of it as a first step on the road to vegan-ism, and not a destination.

5

MIND IF I ORDER THE CHEESEBURGER?

On many an occasion, when dining with a non-vegan friend or acquaintance, my meal companion has asked me whether I would object if he ordered meat, dairy, or eggs off the menu. I do not always know what motivates the question, but I suspect it is usually pro forma. The inquiry, "Mind if I order the cheeseburger?" sounds a little like the question, "Will you excuse me for a moment while I call my husband?" The speaker makes his inquiry out of politeness.

The question seems accordingly to call for a tolerant response that recognizes that different people have distinct values and that what appeals to the vegan does not necessarily appeal to the non-vegan. Some might imagine that just as it would be inappropriate in most social settings for a Christian to try to pressure a Muslim, a Jew, or a Buddhist to act on Christian teachings, so too the only right answer to the non-vegan's polite question is to be equally permissive. "Of course I don't mind," people may expect the vegan to say. "We'll each eat what we are accustomed to eating." Why not let a thousand flowers bloom?

Can a vegan mind her friend's ordering the cheeseburger without creating the impression that she is judgmental or intolerant? Perhaps not, but it is worth exploring why the seemingly innocent, polite inquiry is so fraught for many vegans. The religious analogy is not entirely off base because the ethical vegan does share something with members of a religious group: the strong belief that some actions that people may lawfully take are nonetheless harmful and best avoided. For a vegan, as for a religious person, different approaches to the consumption of animal products are not equally valid: one approach (veganism) is best, and others (different versions of non-veganism) fall short. This is one reason it is awkward for an ethical vegan to confront the question, "Mind if I order the cheeseburger (or omelet or chicken sandwich)?"

The honest answer, for many vegans, may be "Yes, I mind." Ethical vegans, like members of any ethically-oriented group with respect to some questions, reject the view that the behavior at issue, consumption of animal products, is "not for me but fine for you" in the way that a career in dentistry or seven hours of sleep might be great for some people but a bad choice for others. Many vegans view the consumption of animal products simply as harmful, period, because it inflicts suffering and death on animals, and these vegans would therefore prefer to avoid implicitly affirming animal-product consumption by saying, "Go ahead." Doing so may, for some vegans, even feel like complicity, in the way that encouraging a friend to cheat on his examination might feel like participation to a student who opposes academic dishonesty.

Sharing Fundamental Beliefs and Values

Despite the resemblance between an ethical vegan and a practicing member of a religious group, vegans and non-vegans are in some ways quite distinct in their relationship to one another from members of different religious groups. When one religion uniquely prohibits a practice, the followers of that religion lack common ground with members of a different religion regarding that practice. Imagine a Catholic, for example, saying to a Muslim, "You should take communion because that is how you can honor Jesus, the son of God, turning into flesh to redeem the world from sin."

Although Islam regards Jesus as a prophet, it does not affirm the Christian view that he was the Son of God. Accordingly, the Muslim feels no drive to honor Jesus's divinity through communion. For the Catholic to insist on the Muslim's taking communion would therefore appear intolerant because it would presume to impose on another person specifically Catholic beliefs about reality and, accordingly, about morality.

Ethical vegans, by contrast, hold a set of underlying beliefs about reality that fundamentally resemble the beliefs of the non-vegans whom they know. Vegans and most non-vegans share many of the same beliefs, including most significantly the view that unnecessarily inflicting suffering and death on animals is something we should not do.

Non-vegans typically empathize with an animal when they learn of his or her suffering. Non-vegans similarly reject harmful treatment of animals and generally feel discomfort or even revulsion when they have occasion to consider the reality of what happens to animals at a slaughterhouse. I have never, for example, heard a non-vegan say, "The reason that I eat/wear/otherwise use animal products is that I believe that animal suffering and death are morally unimportant, innocuous events." Many a non-vegan lives with a dog or a cat whom he views as a member of his family, worthy of affection, empathy, and life.

Because vegans and non-vegans share the basic values that underlie veganism, it makes sense for a vegan to encourage non-vegan friends to give veganism a try. The vegan perspective is that the values that we all already embrace as a human society point to veganism as a more peaceful and morally consistent way to live. Vegans observe that institutions that surround the production and consumption of food and clothing actively disguise the truth about what happens to the animals we use, precisely because that truth would deeply offend so many consumers, vegan and non-vegan alike.

One need not accept any supernatural claims about reality or make any new leaps of faith to embrace ethical veganism, even if one has shared in non-vegan living up until that point. Like others I know, I became vegan as an adult, not because my values changed but because I came to understand much of what I did in my daily life as falling short of reflecting those values. I had also learned facts about such products as meat, dairy, eggs, and wool, of which I had previously been ignorant.

I came to appreciate the fact that my own consumption of animal products amounted to participation in cruelty to animals. I understood at the same time that the social institution of animal consumption is larger than the individuals who participate in that institution by producing and consuming its products. I therefore needed to become mindful of my routine, automatic actions in a way that I had not previously been.

From my perspective, the consumption of animal products is like other practices that most people once considered legitimate but that most of us now understand to be wrong, such as human slavery, race and sex discrimination, and spousal abuse. Kind, moral, and good people have always participated in practices embraced by the dominant culture. That is why we can admire people from earlier times whose views on some issues would strike people today as deeply racist or otherwise reprehensible. As historian James Oliver Horton explains, for example, even abolitionists who fought against the institution of human slavery were generally racist, judged by today's standards:

> We should never make the mistake of assuming that to be a white abolitionist was to be a believer in racial equality. Because there were lots of white abolitionists who did not believe in racial egalitarianism. They believed in abolishing slavery. They believed that slavery was a moral evil. They believed that slavery was wrong and needed to be destroyed, but that did not mean that they necessarily believed that whites and blacks could live together as equals.[186]

Ethical vegans today are similarly able to appreciate both that consumption of animal products is unjust and that good and kind people nonetheless participate in that practice. The problem of violence against animals thus arises not because many people are bad. It arises instead out of social traditions and institutions that prevent us from fully appreciating the implications of our actions and of the values that most of us already hold dear.

In interacting with non-vegans, a vegan must choose a style that fits both her personality and her sense of her own comfort level, strengths, and challenges. The reason that ethical vegans may feel uneasy when a meal companion asks, "Mind if I order the cheeseburger?," is that for some, the question seems to compel a choice between alienating her meal companion, on the one hand, and potentially betraying her strongly held values, on the other.

This sort of issue arises in numerous situations, and it poses some subtle challenges. When it is *not* mealtime, and the subject does not spontaneously arise, will I actively seek opportunities to let people around me know that I am vegan? When it *is* mealtime, will I react to what people around me are eating? Are there good times and bad times to provide people with information about veganism? And finally, are there non-vegans in my life from whom I can ask that at least when they are with me, they consume exclusively vegan food?

What We Can Learn From the Gay Rights Movement

Different vegans will answer each of these questions differently. I find one useful analogy to be the challenges that gay people face in deciding exactly how "out" to be with the people around them. The analogy is helpful, because the gay rights movement has made tremendous progress in a short period of time and therefore provides relatively recent examples of how best to navigate the sorts of encounters that commonly confront the new vegan in a non-vegan world.

Less than three decades ago, the U.S. Supreme Court held that our Constitution permits states to enact and enforce criminal laws prohibiting consensual sodomy, specifically endorsing the selective application of such laws to same-sex couples.[187] Now, not only has the Supreme Court properly repudiated that 1986 decision,[188] but as of this writing, nine states and the District of Columbia have recognized same-sex marriage, and several of the states that have yet to do so have extended to same-sex couples the opportunity to enjoy marriage-like benefits and the option of becoming spouse-like "domestic partners."[189] Discrimination against gay people persists, of course, but the current state of affairs in this country would have been almost unimaginable just three decades ago.

The successes of the gay rights movement may provide important lessons for other movements that wish to change the status quo in a substantial way, particularly if there are similarities between members of the respective movements. I believe that the movements for gay rights and for animal rights share an important quality: They each have proponents, gay people and vegans, who must go out into the world every day and make choices about how "gay" or how "vegan" to be in their self-presentations in public and private spheres.

We must understand at the outset that there is an important dis-analogy between proponents of the two movements: Gay people and others within the LGBT community have suffered extreme violence, murder, legalized bullying, and social exclusion. Vegans have not. Disclosing one's sexual orientation has been and, for many, remains a potentially dangerous proposition, not simply a socially awkward one.

In suggesting parallels between the two movements, I would therefore also emphasize that vegans are a step removed from the violence that they protest (violence against nonhuman animals) and thus have far greater freedom than LGBT people have (and have historically had) to press their case without fear of violent reprisal. Unlike ethical vegans, then, a gay person is in the position of protesting injustice even as he or she is simultaneously the target of that injustice. Accordingly, it is even more miraculous and inspiring that the gay rights movement has proven to be as successful as it has.

Once we recognize the important differences between the two groups, we can appreciate important parallels as well. Both a gay person seeking to end anti-gay oppression and violence and the vegan seeking to end the torture and slaughter of non-human animals must make strategic choices about when and how to make their case and when and whether, instead, to blend in and permit others to assume that the person in their midst is comfortable with the way things are and lives and loves (and eats) in the way that the majority does.

Unlike one's membership in a racial group or one's sex, one can in many contexts decide to obscure one's sexual orientation as well as one's veganism. Though women have sometimes successfully "passed" as male,[190] and some African Americans have successfully passed as whites,[191] these cases are exceptional. By contrast, when gay people and vegans either hide their identities completely or avoid standing out, others will assume that they are straight and non-vegan, respectively. The default setting, in other words, for both gay people and vegans, is generally "passing," unless and until they consciously decide to present their identities to others.

The ability of gay people and vegans to camouflage their identities and even to conform to the majority's practices is no secret. People who are religiously committed to heterosexuality strongly encourage gay people to make precisely this "choice."[192] Indeed, the ability of gay people to defy their own sexual orientations helps explain how opponents of same-sex unions are able to maintain the paradoxical position that they oppose gay relationships but do not discriminate against gay people. They argue that they extend to gay people the same right that they extend to straight people—the right to marry someone of the opposite sex, as though this option is remotely the same one for a gay person as it is for a straight person.

Similarly, some people encourage vegans to "cheat" on their veganism and consume animal products. An example that comes to my mind is the menu at a restaurant I have visited, on which one of the items was called "cheatin' vegan nachos," a dish that contained dairy cheese and was therefore in no sense vegan. The name "cheatin' vegan," however, specifically addressed vegans and invited them to consume food produced in ways that violate their values.

We can see the disrespect implicit in extending such invitations to vegans if we imagine a menu of beverages including one alcoholic drink labeled "cheatin' Muslim Martini" or "cheatin' Mormon Margarita." Because vegans make a choice about whether they will live in a way that affirms their values, friends and acquaintances who are ambivalent about that choice can try to humorously undermine it in ways that we would recognize as disrespectful were it directed at practitioners of a religious faith instead of at vegans. Ethical vegans make a choice that we will start consuming vegan food, wearing vegan clothing, and otherwise withdrawing support from the violence of animal-derived products, to the extent that we can. Once we make this choice, vegans routinely face the question "Why are you vegan?," while non-vegans virtually never have to explain why they are not. It might even be considered rude for a vegan to ask a non-vegan why he chooses to participate in the violence of animal agriculture by consuming its products. Knowing of this disparity, it may take some courage to "come out" to others as a vegan, though the risks—to be clear—are not generally to personal safety, as they have been for gay people.

Like coming out to one's family as gay, announcing that one has become vegan can also generate family conflicts. Family members may have a difficult time accepting the change and may resist it either overtly or by "forgetting" that the food that they prepared contains animal products.

In the United States, as in the rest of the developed world, most people have very few, if any, interactions with living farmed animals. This reality permits consumers to close their eyes to the consequences of their choices—contributing to the suffering of animals through their consumption of animal products, which drives the animal-based food and clothing industries. The invisibility of farmed animals enables people to imagine that they are not even really making important purchasing choices at all.

Vegans pose a challenge to this kind of unawareness. A non-vegan may find it unsettling to come face to face with a vegan who appears to be healthy and happy. The experience could lead him, for the first time, to recognize, and then to question, the choice to consume animals and the products derived from animals.

Very few of us grew up close to someone who has departed from these practices, so the encounter may be disorienting. Deep down, I think, most of us occasionally feel a twinge of conscience about what we do to animals, but we are strongly encouraged to ignore and suppress those feelings when they arise. Bringing up such suppressed feelings, simply by being an "out" vegan, can therefore be discomfiting to non-vegans.

The resulting discomfort, whether subtle or overt, can resemble that of a person who is in fact attracted to people of the same sex but fails to acknowledge his attraction even to himself. This person, whom some might call a dormant or "latent" gay person, can feel threatened or angry when interacting with an openly gay person.[193] The visibility of openly gay people makes it difficult to avoid facing the fact that not everyone is attracted to members of the opposite sex and that heterosexuality is therefore not inevitable. For some number of people, this experienced threat to their heterosexual identity may play a significant role in explaining their homophobic behavior.[194]

An encounter with an ethical vegan may similarly awaken non-vegans to a truth that is, at some level, known but not openly acknowledged: the truth that one is participating daily in the suffering and death of animals—and that there is another way to live.

For the gay man or the lesbian who makes the decision to have same-sex relationships and who is open about that decision, the choices do not by any means end there. He or she must decide to whom to "come out" and, once out, to what extent to "flaunt" his or her sexual orientation. One can, for example, be openly gay but never say or do anything to call attention to this feature of one's identity. Or one can instead make a point of mentioning one's partner in casual conversation or of bringing him or her to public events and holding hands. One can also decide whether to bring up issues of concern to the LGBT community and whether to invite others to join in the conversation or in activism.

The person who decides to become vegan likewise faces additional choices about how she will express her veganism. She can stay in the closet. One woman I know stated that she purchases and consumes only vegan food but either pretends to eat what others are eating or claims that she is not hungry when shared meals occur. At a barbecue, for example, she would discreetly place only fixings like lettuce, tomatoes, pickles, and ketchup on a bun so that people would not know that she was actually avoiding the hamburgers. In this way, she did not risk making others feel uncomfortable or drawing attention to her commitments regarding animals. Once she knows someone well, she added, she confides to him or her that she is vegan.

This "closeted" approach to veganism mirrors the way in which most gay men and lesbians once conducted their lives. Rather than have people judge them or physically hurt them, they carefully selected, as some still do, the people to whom to confide their true identities. Such an approach was completely understandable for gay people in the past, because they risked blatant discrimination and even physical violence if they disclosed their sexual orientation. An unintended consequence, though, was that the decision to remain in the closet may have served only to entrench the false and destructive notion on the part of many that being gay is very unusual or deviant.

I suspect that most ethical vegans do not conceal that they are vegans in the way that the woman eating fixings on a bun at the barbecue did. As discussed above, vegans do not face the kinds of threats that have motivated gay people to remain closeted. However, while a vegan may safely and comfortably be "out" in the sense of letting people know that she is vegan, she may otherwise attempt to play down any differences between her own and non-vegans' consumption choices. A vegan who does so resembles gay men and lesbians who "cover." Gay people who "cover" disclose the fact that they are gay but try to blend in by not acting "too gay" when in the company of straight people.[195] People might say of a gay person who covers that "I don't think of him as gay; he doesn't seem gay at all." Vegans similarly might consider whether and how much to have people around her "think of her as vegan."

Returning to the question, "Mind if I order the cheeseburger?," it might seem that the analogy between gay people and vegans breaks down here. If a straight man were to ask a gay man with whom he is dining, "Do you mind if I have a relationship with a woman?," the gay man would be unlikely to say, "Yes, I mind; I prefer that everyone have only same-sex relationships." Gay men and lesbians do not typically object to a heterosexual's choosing to be with someone of the opposite sex. Vegans, by contrast, would like the whole world to become vegan.

On a different level, however, gay people advocating gay rights *are* asking people to change themselves in an important way, even though no one has to change his sexual orientation. Gay and lesbian activists are and always have opposed dishonesty and self-delusion about sexual orientation. They have claimed, convincingly, that many of the people who have lived and who currently live as heterosexuals are in fact denying their true orientation.[196]

People like this have an obligation to themselves, and also to others, to embrace their authentic identities. In addition to demanding equality and pluralism, gay rights advocates have therefore also challenged the notion that heterosexuality is simply an inevitable and natural trait.[197] This idea may be particularly challenging for people invested in denying their own sexual orientation but also for a parent who might be invested in denying the sexual orientation of her child or of others whose heterosexuality may, for whatever reason, be important to her.

Ethical vegans face related, though in some ways far less daunting, challenges. By living as they do, they implicitly communicate to others a critique of the status quo and of the way that most people live. Vegans suggest—without necessarily saying anything explicitly—that people ought to examine and reconsider their consumption decisions, rather than accepting the widespread notion that eating animals and animal-derived products is inevitable, necessary, or natural for human beings.[198]

Despite increasingly compelling evidence that animal protein is unnecessary and even unhealthful for human beings, at both the individual and the global levels, many non-vegans insist that people were simply meant to eat animals.[199] The parallel within the gay rights struggle has been the claim by anti-gay advocates that people were simply meant to be straight and that anything else is "unnatural."[200]

Acknowledging that opposite-sex attraction is not inevitable does, of course, have quite different implications from acknowledging that animal-product consumption is not inevitable. If you learn that one can be attracted to people of the same sex, it does not follow that you therefore either are or ought to be attracted to people of the same sex. If you are, then that is fine, and you can live accordingly. If you are not, then that too is fine, and you can just as legitimately live accordingly. And if those close to you are (or are not) gay, your job is to support and accept those people rather than inflict harm on them by denying the truth of who they are.

When we acknowledge, by contrast, that consuming animal products is unnecessary to human health and happiness, it follows not only that it is fine to choose to consume only vegan products but that it is *not fine* to choose instead to consume animal products. When we learn that it is unnecessary to breed, harm, and slaughter animals for our use, in other words, it follows that we ought not to participate in that exploitation by consuming the products of animal industries. This is why an ethical vegan minds not only when a non-vegan asks for "permission" to order a non-vegan meal. She minds as well, though in a different way, when the non-vegan orders that meal at all, with or without the vegan's blessing.

The Vegan at the Dinner Table

The ethical vegan facing a table of people eating non-vegan food today is a little like the gay person forty years ago facing a table of people making homophobic comments, people who are otherwise fond of the particular gay person at the table. In both contexts, individuals who are otherwise compassionate people nonetheless say and do things that hurt others, because the zeitgeist has not yet moved beyond this sort of statement or conduct. As a result, in both contexts, the dissenter, whether a vegan or a gay person, must decide how to handle the tension between wanting to dine companionably with colleagues, friends, or family, on the one hand, and feeling upset by socially accepted but harmful actions, on the other.

There is no simple solution to the problem of these competing pressures. Some gay people might have joined their families for the holidays, for example, and overlooked the offensive comments and jokes that people used to (and that some people still do) make as a matter of course. Others might have chosen to avoid such family gatherings whenever feasible. And still others would get together with family and then seek out opportunities to educate people about issues of gay liberation and equality, even without prompting. Though many Americans have become more conscious about issues of sexual orientation, there is still ample opportunity for gay people to decide how "in your face" to be about standing by their principles.

A related set of dilemmas faces the ethical vegan. Most of the other people at her workplace will likely be non-vegan and will accordingly drink coffee with cows' milk rather than coconut, almond, or soy milk in common areas. Most will eat lunches of cows' yogurt rather than soy or almond or coconut yogurt, and meat or fish sandwiches rather than rice and beans, vegetable wraps, or nut-based burgers. An ethical vegan cannot function effectively at work if she is unable to overlook, ignore, or resign herself to the presence of these foods. Nor, if one is to help others understand what lies behind innocuous-looking animal-based food, can one hide away and refuse to break bread with non-vegans. In so doing, one would also miss opportunities to learn from and emulate the many independently positive qualities of people who happen not to be currently vegan.

Once seated at a table with people who are consuming their non-vegan food, what should the ethical vegan do? Some vegans will make a point of telling everyone that they should become vegan and that their food raises ethical issues. Others will conclude, as I have, that so long as people know that a meal companion is vegan, it is most productive for her to allow non-vegans to decide whether and when to ask questions about veganism. In a common space, vegans cannot realistically expect that other people will plan their own lunches or dinners differently just because a vegan happens to be present. In my own experience, making such demands can come across as self-righteous and does little to change people's hearts and minds.

Family and friends, however, may be different from co-workers. Like the gay person of forty years ago who might have "flaunted" his sexual orientation when home for the holidays, a vegan adult today deciding whether to spend time with her non-vegan relatives might conclude that it is legitimate and fair to ask that there be no animal flesh or secretions on the table. Taking this approach, one friend of mine had an interesting exchange with her father about Thanksgiving that went something like this:

Father: Why can't you come home for Thanksgiving, honey? We love you and miss seeing you then.

Daughter: I would be glad to visit you for Thanksgiving if only you would serve a delicious vegan meal for the holiday that everyone could enjoy. I would, in fact, be happy to cook the entire dinner so that you could relax in the hours before the meal. It would be delicious, and everyone could feel comfortable eating it.

Father: But we always have something for you to eat, sweetie. In fact, many of our side dishes are vegan, like the soup, the stuffing, the mashed potatoes, the sweet potato pie—

Daughter: Actually, the sweet potato pie you serve is not vegan. It contains dairy and eggs.

Father: Fine, but at least it's vegetarian. That's something, right? And we're accommodating you with a tofurkey and side dishes, so why can't you accommodate us? Turkey is a tradition for us, and you are asking us to put aside our tradition when we should all be able to sit down and eat the things that we are used to eating.

Daughter: I'm sorry, Dad, but I won't do that. I am grateful that you are willing to prepare some foods that I can eat, but my concern is not that I will go hungry at your house. It is that I will have to sit at a table with a slaughtered bird being sliced up for distribution. I understand that it is traditional, but I believe it is harmful and disturbing, like many other traditions.

Father: Please, sweetie, be a little flexible.

Daughter: Here's an analogy, Dad. Imagine that you are invited to a traditional dinner at which the main course is dog meat. When you arrive at the house, there is a dead, cooked dog laid out on a platter on the table, but there are also lots of side dishes that you can eat. What would you do?[201]

Father: I'd get the hell out of there! What kind of sicko eats a dog? Dogs are friendly and have personalities. They are not food; they're family. I love dogs!

Daughter: That is how I feel about dogs as well as birds and cows and other animals, including turkeys. They have personalities too and can be friendly as well. You haven't gotten to know many of them as individuals, but they deserve as much kindness and compassion as dogs do. When you have a dead bird sprawled out at the center of your holiday table, I find it as upsetting as you find the prospect of eating at a holiday feast centered on dog meat.

Father: That's different!

Daughter: Not really. Not to me.

A vegan may feel that her family exhibits indifference to her feelings and to her values when it chooses to place animal products on the table in her presence. Whether the vegan is able to avoid non-vegan family gatherings will depend on various factors, including her own personal style, her particular relationships and history with her family, and her subjective experience of what it is like to be in her family's company when it is consuming a non-vegan meal.

Few people fully embrace one or the other extreme approach to being gay or to being vegan in the world. As Kenji Yoshino said of gay people, one does not "come out" once and for all.[202] With each new person one meets, one faces a new choice of whether to "pass" as heterosexual by saying nothing, whether to be "out" but still "cover," or whether to "flaunt" one's sexual orientation.

Vegans make these choices as well, though the stakes may be far lower for the individual involved. In deciding how to proceed, the experience of gay liberation strongly suggests that visibility is a useful antidote to ignorance and fear. As people learn, from vegans who are "out and proud," that farming animals for their flesh, skins, hair, and secretions causes unspeakable and unnecessary suffering and slaughter, they may become more open to questioning the false proposition that meat, dairy, or eggs are necessary ingredients in a pleasurable and fulfilling human life.

AREN'T THE ANIMALS DEAD
ALREADY ANYWAY?

I became vegan gradually. I had always loved dogs, so it was easy for me to appreciate the ethical issues involved in eating mammals when I gave the matter some thought. Later, I read Jeffrey Masson's and Susan McCarthy's *When Elephants Weep* and learned about the rich emotional lives that not only mammals but birds too experience.[203] That was when I stopped eating chickens, turkeys, and ducks. Eventually I took the next steps, but that did not happen overnight.

About a decade ago, I was only halfway through my journey, when I visited a restaurant in another country with family and friends, and all of us ordered fish. Shortly after we had placed our orders, a server approached our table and gestured toward something that he was holding in his hand and that appeared to be moving. Much to my horror, I realized that the server was holding a live fish, and the fish was violently thrashing about, plainly suffocating. The server was proudly showing us how fresh our meal would be, given how closely after the fish's slaughter we would be eating it. I turned away, feeling guilty and disturbed, though I did nothing to spare that fish.

From the perspective of the animal killed, that meal was not any different from the thousands of meals containing animal products that I had previously eaten. Yet I have few specific memories of the other animals I consumed and a very distinct recollection of this one. Why the difference? The answer, I think, reflects a disparity between the sorts of experiences that engage our conscience and the sorts that leave us in a state of ethical slumber.

Concrete, Visible Victims Versus Abstract, Hidden Victims

We appear to be most conscious of the moral dimension of our harmful behavior when we directly observe the individual victim who suffers as a result of what we do. Why? The answer is not entirely clear, but psychological studies suggest that it has something to do with the difference between how we perceive concrete harms and how we perceive abstract ones.[204]

You can test your own intuitions with a pair of hypothetical examples. First imagine that a man named Smith kidnaps and gathers six people into a room, which he then locks. He promptly takes out a revolver containing six chambers. Smith has loaded a total of three bullets into the revolver. Smith picks up the gun, spins the chambers, and then points the weapon at the head of one prisoner and pulls the trigger. He next points the gun at a second prisoner's head and pulls the trigger. He points at the head of a third and pulls the trigger, and so on, until he has pulled the trigger six times and killed three of his prisoners.

Now imagine that a man named Doe also kidnaps and gathers six prisoners into a room, which he locks. Instead of a six-chamber gun containing three bullets, however, he takes out a fully-loaded three-chamber revolver. He then proceeds to approach three individuals, one by one, in different parts of the room, and to shoot each one of them in the head, until he has emptied the revolver and killed three of his prisoners.

In these two examples, it is clear that both Smith and Doe are committing murder and acting in a morally reprehensible fashion. Readers, however, may have a moral intuition that would distinguish between the two men and find that Doe, the second perpetrator (with one fully-loaded three-shooter), has acted more culpably than Smith, the first perpetrator (with a half-loaded six-shooter). For Smith, the identity of each of his three victims remained abstract at the time that he fired his weapon (except perhaps at the end, if he had already killed two people and had only one left to shoot). At no time, then, (except maybe at the end) did Smith know in advance of killing a particular person that he would in fact be killing that person. With respect to any one individual, he was simply taking a one-in-two risk, more or less.

Doe, by contrast, killed a particular, identified individual every time he fired. His harmful behavior was concrete in this way and accordingly may appear even more culpable than Smith's. Though both Smith and Doe deliberately killed three people, in other words, Doe—unlike Smith— acted concretely every time and thereby may seem somehow worse to us.

In addition to the concreteness of harming a particular, known individual, another dimension of experience that tends to heighten our sense of moral responsibility is our ability to see the suffering that our actions cause.[205] It is easier to drop a bomb on a city and thereby kill its inhabitants than it is to walk up to individual residents of a city and stab each one to death. This is true even though, in this comparison, both sets of victims are concrete and identifiable individuals.

The killer's proximity to the victims to be stabbed to death may effectively impress upon him the moral gravity of what he is doing. This could, in part, account for many people's reluctance to condemn the Allied bombing of Dresden and the atomic bombing of Hiroshima and Nagasaki during World War II.[206] Had the Allies instead kidnapped German and Japanese civilians, including men, women, and children, and burned them alive, one by one, such actions would more likely have occasioned condemnation and outrage, regardless of whether they served to hasten the end of the war against Hitler and Tojo (and thus might have been justifiable, under a pure utilitarian, cost/benefit analysis). When the victims of our conduct are both concrete and visible to us, we more readily appreciate the fact that what we do raises serious moral questions.

Those questions arise in our dealings with animals as well. Thinking back on my encounter with the suffocating fish, the appearance of the thrashing, suffering individual creature made the moral implications of my choice of dinner both concrete and visible. Here was the specific, individual fish who was going to die an agonizing death at my instruction, and I could see the suffering before my eyes. I could not easily entertain the illusion that my behavior was victimless or that it would cause no real distress.

Though I had made similar decisions to consume the products of animal suffering and death many times before, this occasion felt different to me. We seem hard-wired to be most conscious of the harm that we cause when we know at the time of our actions which particular, identifiable individual experiences that harm, and when we see the harm (or the beginning of that harm, as I did) occurring right before our very eyes.

These contrasts between concrete and abstract harms, and between visible and hidden harms, help explain why most of us do not feel guilty or regretful when we consume animal products. The suffering and death inflicted on the particular animals we eat as meat, poultry, fish, dairy, or eggs will have occurred somewhere else and before we came onto the scene. The harm that we inflict through consumption, by demanding the production of more animal products, falls on a group of animals whose members we cannot yet identify. Our victims remain abstract to us.

Furthermore, we usually see nothing of the suffering and slaughter that our choices occasion. The sights are concealed from our eyes and the sounds from our ears in well-hidden and soundproof slaughter facilities often given euphemistic names like "meat processing plants."[207] At the same time, developers of slaughter methods offer terms like "sedation" to describe the gassing of chickens prior to throat-cutting, because, in the words of someone whose family owns a premium chicken producer, "[m]ost of the time, people don't want to think about how the animal was killed."[208]

Though human society has always included some level of violence, we have increasingly outsourced extremely violent behavior, when possible, to a small number of people, to avoid precisely the sorts of guilt and trauma that many of us feel when we commit acts of violence against concrete, visible targets.[209] We delegate military violence to soldiers, death penalty violence to executioners, and violence against farmed animals to slaughterers. The people who do our "dirty work" pay a price, enduring a disproportionate share of psychological trauma to themselves.[210] And we tend not to hold ourselves accountable either for their suffering or for the suffering that they inflict. Although they do these jobs at our behest and on our behalf, we tend to think of ourselves as innocent of their conduct, offloading not only the violent activity itself but also the guilt for carrying it out.[211]

Why would this mechanism have evolved? Why would it be adaptive for us to feel little or nothing when committing violence through an intermediary, so long as the violence is far away and the victims abstract or indeterminate at the time of our own actions in ordering it done? I suspect that the answer lies in the fact that the human conscience evolved at a time when social groupings were relatively small, and people were therefore unlikely to be in a position to carry out much violence abstractly and from a distance. As long as your conscience deterred you from committing unnecessary violence with your own hands, your potential for causing tremendous suffering and death would be limited.

Human population growth, coupled with technological advances and global interconnectedness, have increased our violent potential manifold in a relatively short period of time. Again, that is true of violence to animals no less than of violence to our fellow humans. Many people who would shrink from the idea of killing a single gentle animal with their bare hands, if such violence were not necessary to their survival, comfortably support the killing of thousands of these animals, by consuming them in the form of animal-based food, clothing, and other consumer products. The technology of modern animal farming permits the anesthetizing of the human conscience.

Evolutionary biology can tell us why we think and feel the way we do about many things, but it is not, in itself, a branch of ethics. So the fact that concrete, visible harms may *feel* worse than abstract, distant harms does not mean that they *are* worse. To answer the ethical questions, it is not enough to take note of our moral intuitions. We need to interrogate them. In this context, we would want to ask ourselves whether we can draw a defensible ethical distinction between the consumers and the producers of animal products.

The Law of Supply and Demand

I will readily admit that there is an intuitive appeal to the idea that our consumption decisions cannot be immoral by virtue of others' actions that *preceded* those decisions. Suppose that a (very odd) hunter shoots and kills a duck, cooks that duck, and then leaves the resulting meat on a plate in a clearing in the woods. A few minutes later, a hiker comes upon the still-warm plate and decides to eat the duck. The hiker's decision to consume the duck could have played no role in causing the hunter to kill the duck in the first place. By the time the hiker happens upon the clearing and faces the decision of whether or not to consume the carcass, the duck is already dead.

Whatever the hiker might choose to do about the plate of duck meat, the animal will remain dead, and his death will have been the product of the hunter's actions, not the hiker's. Time and causation both move forward, and we cannot save the life of someone who has already died, no matter what we consume. Indeed, it might feel wasteful for the hiker to forgo eating the available carcass, now that someone has gone to the trouble of preparing it, however ethical or unethical the hunter's actions.

I think most would concede that the hiker faces an unusual decision. And that is just the point. The hypothetical situation is completely unrealistic and thus has little relevance for the actual decisions people face when deciding what to eat. If the hiker's choice to consume the carcass truly had no impact on another person's choice to kill an animal, it would be accurate to say that the hiker's actions do not in any way contribute to unnecessary animal suffering and death. In reality, however, the people who breed, "raise," and slaughter farmed animals do so because they feel confident, based on past experience, that people will come along and consume the products of that breeding, raising, and slaughtering. In behavioral terms, consumption "reinforces" or rewards production and thereby causes an increase in the frequency of the reinforced behavior.[212]

Slaughterers are not, in other words, killing animals arbitrarily or for the fun of it. They are instead producing products that consumers have demanded. In essence, buying and consuming products is how we communicate as consumers to producers, and the message is this: "Keep making your product, and I will keep buying it." The more popular a product is with consumers, the more of that product the producer will create for next time. This is a way of saying that demand drives supply.

When a turkey farmer breeds and slaughters a turkey for market, he is acting on the basis of his own and others' observed prior experiences. Previously, when he or another turkey farmer slaughtered turkeys, consumers paid good money for those dead turkeys. The farmer notices this phenomenon and accordingly concludes that people want to consume slaughtered turkeys, for which they will once again pay. Consuming one of the turkeys is therefore not an isolated act of eating; it is also an act of solicitation: it expresses a desire to have more of the consumed product produced, a desire that invites its fulfillment with the promise of a monetary reward.

Understood in this way, our consumption of animal products asks producers to create, harm, and kill more animals. The animal we consume may already be dead, but other animals who will be created and used for food in the future are not. By consuming the dead animal (or products, such as dairy and eggs, that necessarily involve the killing and hurting of animals) right now, we demand that more animals be killed tomorrow. By consuming animal products every day, several times a day, for long periods of time, we provide steady and consistent support and encouragement for the ongoing slaughter.

When you decide to become vegan, you withdraw your support from animal production and diminish the reinforcement that animal farmers and other direct animal exploiters receive for their work. If all consumers were to become vegan, producers would no longer be motivated to create animal products. The withdrawal of demand predictably diminishes supply. That is the most elemental principle of economics.[213]

In some other contexts, we seem intuitively to understand that when a person demands a type of product, he becomes morally implicated in the production of that type of product. The law reflects this intuition, as we can see by examining legislation governing animal-cruelty depictions and child pornography.

Case Study 1: Animal Torture Videos

In 1999, Congress passed a law that, with some limitations and exceptions, banned the possession, creation, and distribution of depictions of unlawful animal torture.[214] To simplify somewhat, this means that federal law made it a crime to have in your possession a video of animals being tortured. The U.S. Supreme Court ultimately invalidated the law, ruling that it violated the First Amendment right to free speech because it was written too broadly.[215] Nonetheless, the statute tells an important story about justifiable public outrage not only at individuals who directly torture animals in front of a camera, but also at consumers who seek out the recordings of such torture. As we shall see, the rationale for the cruelty-depiction law, if consistently applied, has implications for the question of what responsibility consumers bear for the suffering and death of the animals used to satisfy their demand for animal products.

Congress chose to pass the 1999 law in response to a disgusting phenomenon that had come to its attention: "crush videos." In a crush video, a woman tortures and slowly kills an animal by crushing him with her feet. Animals appearing in the crush videos include mice, guinea pigs, rats, squirrels, chickens, hamsters, cats, dogs, and monkeys, each of whom is typically taped or tied to the floor during the torture so that he cannot escape. According to people who have watched such videos, the woman in the recording talks like a sexual dominatrix to the animal, while the animal cries and screams in agony until he finally dies, reduced to a "bloody mass of fur."[216] Crush videos evidently appeal to people who have a sexual fetish for the torture and killing of animals.

The defendant in the case that came before the Supreme Court, Robert Stevens, was not actually involved in the crush video trade that had inspired the law. He had instead distributed videos showing dogs engaged in bloody fights with other dogs and viciously attacking other animals, both illegal activities in all fifty states and both involving great suffering as well as unnecessary and cruel deaths. Stevens was found guilty of violating the federal law by knowingly selling the depictions of animal cruelty.[217]

In defending their client against the federal charges, the lawyers for Mr. Stevens argued that the law could have fully addressed animal torture simply by prohibiting the torture itself, whether in the crush-video business or the dog-fighting arena. They said that the guilty parties are the ones who tortured the animal, not the people who created, distributed, or purchased the video recording of that cruelty. It was therefore unnecessary and inappropriate, the defense continued, to go after the people who made, sold, bought, or watched the videos.

This argument may sound familiar, because it rests on the same logic that people sometimes use to rationalize consuming animal products. Those who would feel moral reluctance to slaughter animals themselves might nonetheless consume animal products, believing that it is the person who carries out the mutilations, deprivations, and killings of the animals who is responsible for the suffering and death. The consumer, like the person who watches the torture video, comes in after the cruel deeds are done.

Defending the crush video law, the government's response recalls our earlier discussion as well: "possession of depictions of animal cruelty for profit provides an economic incentive for such conduct."[218] That is, when people spend their time, energy, and money subjecting animals to excruciating pain and death in front of a camera, it is primarily because other people have expressed their willingness to spend *their* money on the product created by the video-recorded agony, whether a crush video or a blood-sport video. Economic demand for the video (the product of the torture) motivates much of the torture in the first place. The trial judge found this argument persuasive.

To understand the role of demand in driving commercial conduct is to recognize that someone who purchases animal-torture videos is an accomplice and participant in torture, responsible for the animal cruelty of the torturer, who acts mainly to fulfill the consumer's desires. If an audience derives pleasure from watching torture and is willing to pay money to satisfy its desire, then in a market economy, someone will come along and give the audience what it wants. The same principle is true for consumers of animal products.

Maybe you are thinking: But didn't the Supreme Court say that the crush video law was unconstitutional? Doesn't that mean that it is inappropriate to hold someone responsible for other people's bad acts, even if his consumption habits drive demand for those kinds of bad acts? In a word, no. The majority opinion in *United States v. Stevens* did not say that market demand is generally innocent. The decision in the case turned on a free speech doctrine that says that a law whose wording could authorize the prosecution of much constitutionally protected free speech is an invalid law, even when prosecutors use it to pursue someone whose behavior *can* be validly punished and falls well outside the domain of what the First Amendment protects. Indeed, the majority opinion specifically reserved the possibility that a law specifically targeting the possession of crush videos would be constitutionally valid.

The Court in *Stevens* plainly accepted the idea of holding consumers accountable, because the case explicitly reaffirmed another line of decisions allowing states to punish people who demand a different product of cruelty against innocents: people in possession of child pornography.

Case Study 2: Child Pornography

Laws forbidding the possession of child pornography treat consumers of abuse products as accomplices in the abuse itself. If consumers of child pornography give any thought to moral responsibility, however, I suspect that most do not consider themselves culpable in the abuse of children appearing in the pornography. Some legal scholars have expressed agreement with this attitude, suggesting that it takes things a bit far to hold child-pornography consumers personally responsible for victimizing molested children.[219]

The pedophiles and the scholars alike seem to share the familiar intuition that people are not responsible for inflicting suffering when they merely consume the products of that suffering after the fact. And we should not feel morally superior to the scholars or even the pedophiles, because this is exactly how someone who might find the practices necessary to the farming and slaughter of animals sickening and offensive can nonetheless feel comfortable consuming animal products. We tend to feel that someone else, a slaughterhouse worker or a dairy farmer, is the one who caused the terror, the screaming and the bellowing, who cut throats and ended the lives of baby, adolescent, and adult animals. Consumers do not viscerally experience the connection between ordering a chicken dish at a restaurant and hanging a terrified seven-week-old rooster upside down by his feet and slitting his throat.

In the area of child pornography, however, our society has definitively rejected the idea that consumers can legitimately disavow responsibility for the misconduct that lies directly behind the products they consume.[220] We punish the possession of child pornography because market demand (as evidenced by possession) drives the misconduct itself. If there were no market for viewing child pornography, then people who sexually molest children for the camera would stop, or at least greatly curtail, that reprehensible behavior.

People who want to view child pornography, and who act on that desire by downloading or otherwise acquiring it, thus motivate the conduct that creates the product. Accordingly, we criminalize possession to deter (as well as to punish) the people whose demand for child pornography feeds the supply.

To be sure, it looks like there is an important distinction between possessing child pornography, which is illegal, and consuming animal slaughter products, including flesh, dairy, and eggs, which is legal. But slaughtering farmed animals is also legal, yet many people who routinely consume animal products would feel morally opposed to personally slaughtering an animal. And even though child pornography is illegal, some pedophiles who consume this material might be motivated by moral concerns to try to avoid molesting a child themselves. If we accept the logic of existing criminal laws against the possession of torture videos and the possession of child pornography, however, then we understand that consumers bear moral responsibility for the violent behavior that they demand.

Taking Responsibility for Harm

If we readily acknowledge the connection between supply and demand in the cases of crush videos and child pornography, why do we have such a difficult time seeing the same link in the context of animal products? Why do we find it easier to condemn people who purchase animal abuse videos or child pornography than to reflect critically on the food we eat and the clothing we wear? One possibility is that most of us regard crush videos, dog fighting, and child molestation for the camera as *deviant* conduct. As a result, we can stand back and evaluate the harm caused by a taste for viewing this sort of conduct. Most of us have no emotional investment in relieving those who consume crush videos or child pornography of responsibility for their behavior. We can therefore assess that accountability in a logical and clear-eyed way.

By contrast, we are invested in seeing the consumption of animal products as normal. Most of us consume animal products several times each day, and all of us live in a culture that thoroughly normalizes this behavior. Vegans, not people who eat flesh, dairy, and eggs, are the deviants on this question. So we can see the connection between demand for and supply of crush videos and child pornography, because most of us have nothing to do with these industries, but we may prefer to ignore the connection between supply and demand when it comes to animal products. We are inclined to rationalize what we do, and we experience what social psychologists call "cognitive dissonance" when we sense a conflict between our own regular, day-to-day behavior and our deeply-held values.

Does that difference in our own behavior explain why we want to hold viewers of crush videos and child pornography accountable while we simultaneously excuse our own consumption of animal products? Partly. It is no doubt true that it is easier to be objective when judging others' actions than when judging our own. I suspect, however, that there is more going on.

Another reason that many of us perceive people who consume crush videos as bearing greater responsibility for animal cruelty than meat-or-dairy consumers do is the relative immediacy of the victim in each of the two cases. The consumers in the two examples are similar to each other in that each one inflicts harm and death on an unknown future victim, someone who will be tortured and killed to satisfy the consumer's expressed demand. Yet the two consumers are different in one key respect: the person who buys a crush video can see the kind of harm that he is demanding in the video itself. Animal torture is not hidden in this product but is instead plainly visible to the consumer. The torture and slaughter behind dairy, flesh, and other animal products, by contrast, are well concealed. One can eat a chicken sandwich without ever seeing or even imagining the blood, sights, smells, and sounds that emerge from live chickens enduring the slaughter process.[221] Indeed, it is often difficult to look at a piece of flesh and see even a hint of the live animal that it once was.

The lack of immediacy may affect how people feel about the harm that occurs because they consume animal products, but does it relieve consumers of moral responsibility? To answer that question, let us reflect on how we experience differences between stabbing, shooting, and bombing victims to death. We know that it would be much more difficult for most people to take a knife and stab an innocent victim to death than it would be to shoot the same victim or to drop a bomb on him from a distance or to pay an assassin to carry out the killing.[222] The closer we are to violence, the more traumatic it generally is for us to see it or participate in it.[223] This fact of human nature explains why we must desensitize our armed forces before sending them into battle.[224] Desensitization, the systematic numbing of people's empathy for those outside our circle, is necessary to our ability to kill the "enemy."[225]

The difference between the experience of violence that we perpetrate up close and that which we carry out at a distance also explains why soldiers, but not officers who send the soldiers into battle, frequently experience post-traumatic stress disorder after returning from combat.[226] As I noted earlier in this chapter, we are hard-wired to be most disturbed by the violence that we experience or observe with our own senses.

But when we reflect on the matter, it appears that immediacy has no obvious moral significance. The vast majority of generations of human beings lived in small communities.[227] In evolutionary terms, as mentioned earlier, human beings have been living in conditions that allow us to kill from a distance for only the blink of an eye. So it is not surprising that our unreflecting moral impulses have yet to catch up with the social and technological developments that now permit us to carry out massive violence from a distance, sometimes never seeing, hearing, or smelling the reality of the harm that we inflict. There simply has not been enough time for our consciences to evolve in response.

The mismatch between the circumstances under which our moral instincts evolved and the world we inhabit helps explain why we can readily appreciate the moral responsibility of those who consume child- or animal abuse videos for the abuse: the consumer can see the abuse. By comparison, animal products, particularly eggs and dairy, look quite benign and innocuous, packaged in containers often illustrated with drawings of happy animals surrounded by their kin. It is therefore easy to avoid thinking of consuming such products as participation in the mutilation and slaughter of chickens, dairy cows, pigs, and other animals.

Does our failure to feel guilty for harming victims from a distance demonstrate that our violence against them is morally innocuous? No. Indeed, we recognize the moral irrelevance of distance in our criminal law. We do not classify shooting as better than stabbing, or bombing from a distance as better than shooting at close range. We treat murder as murder, no matter how close or far away the perpetrator is from her victim, and we consider the person who hires an assassin to be a murderer just as guilty in a killing as the man who carries out the deed directly.[228]

The ease with which we can hurt others, when their suffering remains distant and inaccessible to us, is a matter of grave concern rather than an authentic signal that distance mitigates moral responsibility. Our built-in difficulty processing the cruelty that we do not personally observe permits us to perpetrate atrocities from far away without feeling a thing, as though we have received a high dose of moral anesthesia. We might therefore want to be especially skeptical of our own ethical complacency when we cannot see what is happening to our victims.

Animal products will likely never come with pictures of what people do to the animals to turn their flesh, their milk, their eggs, and their skin and hair into food, clothing, and other consumer items. We would make a mistake in believing, however, as very young children do, that reality disappears when we close our eyes. Reflecting on the human tendency towards this error, Ralph Waldo Emerson observed: "You have just dined, and however scrupulously the slaughterhouse is concealed in the graceful distance of miles, there is complicity."[229]

Return now to my experience of ordering fish at the foreign restaurant. Prior to that day, I had chosen to avoid thinking about the fishes whom I ate as animals who had endured suffocation and bludgeoning for my culinary enjoyment. The fish who thrashed in the server's hand changed that for me, though. The connection between my behavior and the fish's suffering was neither abstract nor invisible to me anymore.

I could plainly see the fish's distress, and the victim of my decision to order the fish was dying right before my eyes. The harm that I inflicted was, in other words, both concrete and visually available. It was thus more difficult for me to ignore, though people's repeated exposure to socially accepted violence against fishes (through recreational fishing) likely blunts many consumers' emotional responses to even concrete and visually available evidence of that violence.[230]

I regret that I did not give up eating fish that day or even the next. I believed at the time that I would feel deprived if I stopped eating fishes, and that there would be little that I could eat, so I put the experience out of my mind. I did, however, give up eating fishes within the year, and my encounter with the poor animal that day in a foreign land helped wake me up.

Most of the fishes I had eaten before were slaughtered out of my sight, and I saw nothing of what they endured.[231] And most of the fishes I had consumed were not the same fishes who were killed in response to my demand as a consumer. Still, that day at the restaurant, I began to understand that I was as much a participant in the slaughter of those animals as the people who held the nets, the knives, and the clubs. Months later, when I finally chose to stop participating, my fears of feeling deprived if I did not consume "at least fish" proved utterly unfounded.

As consumers, we bear responsibility for the animal slaughter and suffering that we solicit. It is easy to feel that nothing we do can make a difference, but that feeling of impotence can become an excuse for refusing to change what we really can change. The truth is that our actions do not go unnoticed, by industry or by friends and family. By examining our consumption choices and by making different ones, we can withdraw our support from animal exploitation and slaughter. And because others notice what we do, our choices can influence people and further expand and strengthen the community of those who choose to stop participating in truly unnecessary violence against animals.

Just as we help protect children from sexual abuse by holding people responsible for consuming child pornography, so we can protect animals from human cruelty by acknowledging that when we eat a chicken, a turkey, or a cheese sandwich, we become an integral part of the violence that occurs at the farm and at the slaughterhouse, no matter how many miles separate us from those places.

ARE YOU AGAINST ABORTION?

When an acquaintance learns that I am an ethical vegan and that I believe that animals are entitled to live free of our violence, he will sometimes ask me about my views on abortion. His questions are natural and legitimate. After all, an abortion inflicts violence and death on the unborn, so if I am opposed to violence against nonhuman animals, then does it not follow that I must be opposed to violence against unborn humans as well?

Abortion is actually a very complicated and difficult issue for me. I have long supported a woman's right to terminate her pregnancy, but I am not unmoved by the arguments on the other side. I am inviting readers to become vegan because I believe that consuming animal products is unjustified, so I feel obliged to explain my view of abortion and why that view is consistent with ethical veganism. I hope that my own thought process will help shed light on some of the similarities and differences between consuming animals and undergoing an abortion. In this way, pro-choice and pro-life readers who share my opposition to unnecessary violence against the innocent—human and nonhuman alike—can see where and why we might differ somewhat on this (other) controversial issue.

Similiarities Between Abortion and Animal Consumption

My first reaction to questions about abortion is to acknowledge that consuming nonhuman animals and undergoing an abortion share several important features in common. First and foremost, both involve terminating the lives of innocents. Moreover, both consuming animal products and having an abortion closely resemble practices that involve no violence or death to anyone. In the case of consuming animal products, the act subjectively feels very much like consuming plant-based products. For this reason, a consumer can easily overlook the fact that eating a plate of chicken and drinking a glass of milk require animals to endure immense suffering and slaughter.

In the case of abortion too, the act may feel very much like other medical, gynecological procedures that a woman might undergo, including the removal of polyps, fibroids, or a malignant tumor. A woman can have an abortion and subjectively experience it simply as an invasive medical intervention with no ethical implications.

This common feature of consuming animal products and having an abortion allows us to engage in both without necessarily being aware of the moral dimension of our actions. I considered the importance of this "invisibility" factor in the last chapter. To summarize, a person who might shrink from hurting an animal whose suffering he can actually witness nonetheless participates in inflicting suffering and slaughter on animals he does not see, through his choices of food and clothing. A pregnant woman can likewise undergo an abortion without meeting the living fetus who will die because of her choice and without observing the death that results.

This invisibility makes both sorts of choices emotionally easier than they might otherwise be, and it helps explain why advocates for both nonhuman animals and unborn human babies have sometimes used videos and pictures to try to awaken viewers' conscience about these issues. Some animal rights activists try to expose the hidden cruelty of animal products by publicizing graphic footage of animals enduring routine violence and mutilation on farms and terrifying and grotesque (and equally routine) deaths at the slaughterhouse.[232] Anti-abortion activists likewise try to show people considering an abortion disturbing footage of what the procedure really looks like.[233]

Moreover, abortion opponents in some states have successfully campaigned for laws requiring medical providers to invite each patient to view an ultrasound picture of her own living fetus inside her womb prior to the procedure.[234] Some pro-choice scholars have criticized such laws on the ground that they impose an unwanted visual experience of the fetus as a woman's live offspring, which can cause distress to a woman who has decided to terminate her pregnancy.[235] That may be true, but it is not clear that people should have a legal right to turn away from seeing the consequences of their actions. A more sympathetic understanding of mandatory ultrasounds might note that they simply expose patients to the truth of what (or whom) they destroy when they choose to have an abortion.[236]

Now consider another fact about both animal consumption and abortion: most of us delegate the "dirty work" they involve to someone else. Most consumers of animal products do not slaughter cows, pigs, chickens, or fishes with their own hands. They do not personally separate dairy cows from their babies or throw male chicks into a meat grinder, fully conscious, shortly after the chicks hatch from layer hens' eggs. People who work in these industries do not have the luxury of closing their eyes to what consumers of animal products demand, but most consumers do enjoy that luxury.

By the same token, women who decide to have an abortion do not ordinarily perform the abortion themselves. They hire medical providers to do so. To be sure, the reasons for the delegation are obviously different in the two cases. Consumers delegate animal slaughter because it is an undesirable, dangerous, and disturbing job.[237] By contrast, patients delegate abortion at least in part because they lack the requisite expertise. Still, the delegation in both areas places physical and psychological distance between the consumer and the violence that he or she solicits. And defenders in both realms denounce as abusive and coercive efforts to use visual imagery to bridge the gap between actions and their consequences.[238]

There are still more similarities. Neither non-human animals nor human fetuses legally qualify as "persons," even though they may share important traits with those of us whose deaths and suffering do qualify for legal consideration and protection. As discussed in chapter 1, the farmed animals whom we consume, including cows, pigs, goats, sheep, chickens, turkeys, ducks, and fishes, are sentient. That is, they are capable of experiencing the world by suffering pain and fear, and by enjoying pleasure and comfort.

Some proportion of the fetuses whose lives we take in abortion are likewise almost certainly capable of feeling discomfort and pleasure. During the course of a pregnancy, the developing human baby at some stage becomes sentient. It would indeed seem fanciful to suggest that prior to the moment at which a baby emerges from the birth canal, he remains unable to experience sensations such as warmth, cold, pain, or pleasure.

Yet despite their sentience, neither of these groups of living beings enjoys the legal status of personhood. Our law treats corporations as persons for most purposes, but not birds, dogs, pigs, or human fetuses.

We can identify at least one more similarity: People consume both animal products and abortion services in circumstances falling short of what we might call life-and-death necessity. People who consume animal products or undergo abortions, in other words, are ordinarily not doing so to avoid death or serious threats to their health. And in both sorts of actions, people defend what they do on the basis of individual liberty and by reference to the lesser moral and legal status of the victim, whether a nonhuman animal or a developing human fetus.

Both issues accordingly pit a vulnerable being's interest in avoiding direct violence and death against another's interest in freely pursuing his or her own goals without outside interference. A pro-choice bumper sticker captures this sentiment: **"Against abortion? Then don't have one."** And those who feel strongly that they are entitled to consume animal products similarly maintain that while it is fine for vegans to limit their own dietary and other choices, we should not seek to impose our will on others. Both of these autonomy arguments are variants on the "let us all value and respect one another's choices" idea explored earlier, in chapter 5.

Do all of these similarities between animal consumption and abortion mean that we should hold the same position on the two issues? If so, we might wonder why people who are pro-life commonly oppose animal rights, while ethical vegans commonly support a woman's right to have an abortion.[239] One possible explanation is that society views both the pro-choice position and the animal rights position as falling along the liberal/left side of the political spectrum. Because people are inclined to adopt a group of political positions as a whole, rather than picking and choosing their political views "a la carte," it may be that those already on the left on one issue would tend unthinkingly to lean towards the left on the other, and vice versa.

I suspect, though, that there is more to the animal rights/fetal rights split than an unthinking adoption of politically aligned positions. For one thing, the pro-animal rights position is so unusual that it does not appear on any pre-packaged ensemble of political views. Progressives and conservatives alike choose in overwhelming numbers to consume animal products without carefully examining that choice. Whether in the *Wall Street Journal* or the *New York Times*, the *National Review* or the *Nation*, one will find complete acceptance for consuming and producing animal products, expressed through editorials and advertising alike.

Whether a person is pro-life or pro-choice therefore fails to dictate a position on animal rights. Conversely, someone who decides to become vegan despite the surrounding society's uncritical embrace of animal exploitation shows independence from the crowd, and we might expect such a person to give thoughtful consideration to both sides of the abortion issue as well.

The fact that people who favor animal rights also tend to be pro-choice cannot, then, be automatically attributed to a one-size-fits-all ideology. There must be some other reason that people do not usually treat abortion and animal exploitation as morally equivalent. What could that reason be?

Before we try to answer that question, we should acknowledge that people could be making a moral mistake in distinguishing between consuming animal products and having an abortion. Perhaps they are confused and ought to be either pro-life and vegan *or* pro-choice and non-vegan, if they wish to be morally consistent. If so, then as a vegan, I should not be pro-choice. Yet I am. I should either offer compelling distinctions between the two issues, or I should consider changing my views. Which shall it be?

Differences Between Abortion and Animal Consumption

Let us consider some differences between the two issues and determine whether any of the differences matter. People who are pro-life but oppose animal rights say that one moral difference is the beginning and end of the inquiry: a human embryo or fetus is *human*, and a nonhuman animal is not.[240] If one must be a member of the human species to have a right against violence, and if all humans hold this right in virtue of their humanity alone, then it makes perfect sense to oppose abortion and to simultaneously tolerate the consumption of animal products.

As we discussed earlier, however, our sense of why we should refrain from hurting or killing another human being has very little to do with anything uniquely human about our victim. Most of us have a strong moral intuition that we should not torture or kill someone who is able to experience pain and death, at least when doing so is not necessary. That is why many of us might view it as no better and perhaps even worse to inflict pain or death on an infant than on an adult, even though infants do not have the ability to use symbolic language or to deploy the other special talents that appear to distinguish humans from other animals.

Our intuitions confirm that what repels us from violence against the innocent victim is not the victim's linguistic ability but instead her sentience, her ability to have experiences in the world such as pain and pleasure. Because a baby can have such experiences, we take something precious away from the baby if we harm or kill her. Because a plant apparently cannot have such experiences, we appear to take nothing from the plant when we kill it.

So far, it may appear that we should oppose both the consumption of animal products and abortion, if we believe we should refrain from harming sentient beings. In the case of abortion, however, we are dealing with a human who is undergoing development from a single cell. Therefore, not every abortion kills a sentient being. A woman who terminates a pregnancy immediately after embryonic implantation, for example, almost certainly does not destroy a sentient organism. On the other hand, a woman who has an abortion near the end of her pregnancy is killing a sentient fetus.

Part of why many of us feel much less comfortable about late abortions than about early ones may be that the early human organism lacks the traits that we associate with human beings, most notably sentience. Pro-life doctors and pro-choice doctors differ somewhat in identifying the point of sentience, but not by much. The consensus seems to place the line somewhere between 20 weeks after conception, which is usually called 22 weeks gestation (because doctors typically measure gestation from the first day of the woman's last menstrual period), and 22 weeks after conception (24 weeks gestation).[241]

Therefore, I can favor animal rights for ethical reasons *and* favor a woman's right to have an abortion prior to fetal sentience, without any contradiction. A being who can have experiences has the moral entitlement not to be killed or subjected to pain and distress. One can be a human organism without being sentient, because one has not yet reached the developmental stage at which one can feel pain, pleasure, or anything else. And one can be a sentient nonhuman being, as cows, chickens, fishes, and other animals we consume are.

A human zygote or embryo is thus as different from a 30-week fetus, along the dimension of sentience, as it is from a newborn calf. Understanding this overlap in human and nonhuman sentience, we can view some but not all abortions as raising the kinds of moral questions that consumption of animal products raises. The moral question is one about sentience rather than one about species.

If we treat abortion in this way, the next question is whether we should oppose a woman's right to terminate her pregnancy after the fetus *is* sentient. A number of states have passed laws banning abortion beyond 20 weeks, with narrow exceptions to avoid the mother's death or serious impairment of her major bodily functions. [242] These bans rest quite explicitly on the theory that the fetus is capable of feeling pain by this point and therefore has the right not to be killed. [243] If we are committed to protecting sentient beings against human violence, then shouldn't we oppose abortion once a sentient human organism is living in the womb? Is the violence of abortion, when a fetus is sentient, the same as the violence of animal slaughter?

In one sense, the answer is yes. From the perspective of the victim, it may be no better to be killed at an abortion clinic than it is to be killed at a slaughterhouse. And just as I find the existence of slaughterhouses very upsetting, I find the fact of late-term abortions very upsetting as well. In his opinion for the U.S. Supreme Court upholding the federal Partial Birth Abortion Ban Act in *Gonzales v. Carhart*,[244] Justice Anthony Kennedy quotes from the testimony of a nurse, describing an "intact dilation and evacuation" abortion that she observed on a 26 ½ week fetus:

> [The doctor] went in with forceps and grabbed the baby's legs and pulled them down into the birth canal. Then he delivered the baby's body and the arms—everything but the head . . . .
> The baby's little fingers were clasping and unclasping, and his little

feet were kicking. Then the doctor stuck the scissors in the back of his head, and the baby's arms jerked out, like a startle reaction, like a flinch, like a baby does when he thinks he is going to fall.

The doctor opened up the scissors, stuck a high-powered suction tube into the opening, and sucked the baby's brains out. Now the baby went completely limp . . . .

He cut the umbilical cord and delivered the placenta. He threw the baby in a pan, along with the placenta and the instruments he had just used.[245]

If the question is whether the act described here represents violence directed at an innocent, sentient being, the answer would appear to be yes. This is the visceral reality of late-term abortion that most of us never observe directly and rarely hear about in such graphic detail. From the perspective of the sentient fetus, an abortion is an act of undeserved and extreme violence.

The Pregnant Woman's Unique Dilemma

One cannot accurately discuss the issue of abortion, however, without considering the perspective of the pregnant woman who carries the fetus inside her body, both before and after the fetus becomes sentient. The pregnant woman has a very different physical relationship with her pregnancy and with the consequences of what she does about it than the rest of us have with the people around us who may fall victim to violence. Let us consider how.

When we bear responsibility for someone else's death or suffering, it is almost always because we either acted in a manner that helped to bring it about, or we failed to intervene to keep it from happening. If we solicit violence against a human being or a nonhuman animal, our contribution to that being's suffering is through our actions. If instead, we see someone in trouble and do nothing to help, our contribution is through our omission or failure to act. Ordinarily, we hold people more accountable for their actions than we do for their omissions.

To make all of this more concrete, consider a hypothetical example. Cain hates Abel and wants to kill him, but Cain is a bit squeamish about weapons and blood, so he hires Delilah to carry out the killing. If Delilah stabs Abel to death for Cain, both Cain and Delilah are legally and morally responsible for the murder, because both acted culpably to bring it about.

Let us assume now that after Delilah stabs Abel, Bathsheba walks by and notices that Abel is bleeding to death, and no one else is around to help him. Bathsheba could tie her scarf around Abel's wounds, call an ambulance, and thereby save his life, but she decides instead to continue on her way to the neighborhood bookstore to purchase a copy of the book *Atlas Shrugged*. In this situation, Bathsheba bears some moral responsibility for Abel's death, because she could easily have averted it but chose not to. Nonetheless, virtually no law in this country would hold her accountable for the killing,[246] and I suspect that most readers would not consider her to be nearly as culpable as Cain or Delilah is.

Most of us would agree that failing to help an injured party is, in most situations, not as bad as affirmatively bringing about the injury in the first place. Furthermore, if it would have been extremely burdensome or risky to intervene to save someone, we might not even criticize the failure to intervene. If, for example, a different bystander, Deborah, would have had to donate a kidney to save Abel's life, very few people would fault Deborah (let us call her "Deborah 1") for failing to save Abel, even though her failure would have led to Abel's death.

If Deborah (let us now call her "Deborah 2") decided instead to undergo the surgery and donate her kidney to Abel, people would likely view her as an unusually generous Good Samaritan. A Good Samaritan is quite different from someone who refrains from actively killing. If an alternate version of Cain, named Refrain, felt tempted to murder Abel but decided not to, we would not praise Refrain in the way that we would praise Deborah 2, the kidney donor. Deborah 2 goes far above and beyond the call of duty, whereas Refrain merely *satisfies* a basic duty to refrain from killing.

When the person faced with the moral dilemma of whether to save a life is a woman carrying an unwanted pregnancy, the moral calculus becomes more complicated. If the woman goes to a clinic and has an abortion, then she is acting affirmatively to cause injury and death to the fetus. In this way, she is like (the original) Cain, who hired Delilah to kill Abel. If the pregnant woman decides instead *not* to have an abortion, however, then she immediately becomes like Deborah 2, who donated a kidney to save Abel.

Her decision to remain pregnant will result in her experiencing significant pain, discomfort, and risk to her own health in order to provide another person with what he needs to survive. For the pregnant woman who does not want to be pregnant, there is no third option through which she can decide not to inflict injury and death on the fetus *and* not to undergo the enormous burden of carrying a pregnancy to term, with all of the intimate cost and risk entailed. In the case of pregnancy, in other words, inaction is not an option.

We can appreciate the unique moral quandary of unwanted pregnancy by imagining a science-fiction alternative universe. Suppose that in this alternative universe a scientist has invented an incubator that can house a developing embryo and fetus until the end of the 24th week of pregnancy. After 24 weeks, however, the fetus will die unless transferred into a woman's uterus.

In this alternative universe, with a fetus living in such an incubator and approaching 24 weeks of age, the fetus's mother would become like other non-pregnant women and men who face moral choices about whether to act harmfully, do nothing, or intervene to help. Like Cain, she could act affirmatively and harmfully by smothering the fetus in the incubator. Like Deborah 1, she could fail to intervene to help another by refusing to transfer the fetus into her body (with the result that the fetus dies in the incubator). Or, like Deborah 2, she could act affirmatively to save another, by voluntarily undergoing a transfer of the fetus from the incubator to her uterus and carrying him for roughly the next 16 weeks, undergoing the burdens of pregnancy and childbirth.

By considering this alternate universe, we can see that the real world does not offer a pregnant woman the moral options usually available to everyone else. The rest of us can avoid actively participating in killing when we choose not to donate a kidney, bone marrow, or even blood, as many of us routinely choose not to do. A pregnant woman cannot similarly avoid actively participating in killing her fetus by remaining a bystander.

If the pregnant woman does not kill her fetus, then she will have to carry and gestate that fetus inside her body and then undergo either labor and delivery or major surgery at the end. She must therefore select between committing affirmative violence, on the one hand, and acting as a Good Samaritan, on the other. These are the only alternatives.

To be sure, the pregnant woman ordinarily bears some responsibility for the predicament in which she finds herself. Barring cases of sexual assault, the woman's voluntary decision to have sexual intercourse with a man played an essential role in bringing about the situation in which she must now choose between actively taking a life and actively enduring the physical burdens of pregnancy and childbirth. In that sense, the pregnant woman differs morally from a typical "bystander" who coincidentally happens upon a needy victim and either intervenes or fails to intervene.

Yet we cannot accurately say that simply by having sex, the pregnant woman takes on the obligation to carry a pregnancy to term. The reality is that having sex risks a pregnancy, but it does not invariably or even usually cause one. In any individual act of unprotected sexual intercourse, the odds of a pregnancy are quite low, on the order of 2-2.5%.[247] The odds are even lower among the many women who use contraception.[248]

Taking a relatively small risk of bringing about the dilemma of an unwanted pregnancy is thus quite different from voluntarily consenting to an intimately demanding and burdensome 40-week relationship with a developing fetus, followed by labor and delivery. Most risky behavior in which a risk comes to fruition, moreover, still leaves intact a three-part choice: give affirmative aid; be a bystander (even if a somewhat more culpable bystander); or cause affirmative harm. In stark contrast, the woman who becomes pregnant lacks any semblance of the second option—however culpable or blameless—and must choose between committing violence, on the one hand, and playing the very demanding role of Good Samaritan, on the other.

Once we understand this quandary that pregnant women alone face, we can see why abortion is such a divisive issue. One side views the woman who terminates a pregnancy as no different from an ordinary killer. Perhaps she is even worse, in fact, because the victim is her own child. This side focuses on the woman's affirmative act of violence in abortion and de-emphasizes the fact that her only alternative to that violence is to become a Good Samaritan, a major sacrifice of bodily integrity that we ordinarily do not demand of non-pregnant women or men, even when someone will die without the sacrifice. From the pro-life perspective, all that the pregnant woman must do is refrain from killing her fetus, just as the rest of us must refrain from actively killing other people. If the woman refuses to refrain, then she is as much a killer as Cain or Delilah is, in our earlier hypothetical example. The pro-life side, in other words, treats the woman who *remains* pregnant as a passive bystander to the fetus's continuing survival.

The pro-choice side, by contrast, views a woman who has an abortion as very much like a man who fails to donate a needed organ or bone marrow to save another's life. In this view, the pregnant woman is like Deborah 1, who decides not to help the dying Abel by donating a kidney. The pro-choice side focuses on the physiologically demanding and risky nature of pregnancy and birth and downplays the fact that abortion entails an affirmative act of violence, rather than a mere failure to come forward and provide life-saving assistance. The pro-choice side thereby treats having an abortion as the equivalent of being a bystander to the fetus's death. This perspective is the flip-side of the pro-life tendency to downplay the Good Samaritan demands and burdens that choosing to remain pregnant will place on a woman's body.

One reason that there is no simple solution to this impasse between pro-choice and pro-life visions is that the pregnant woman's circumstances do not neatly fit the moral categories by which we regularly and intuitively judge people's behavior. These categories provide for three morally distinct roles: the bad actors (Cain and Delilah), the bystanders (Bathsheba and Deborah 1), and the Good Samaritan (Deborah 2). Seeking the comfort of familiar categories, we are therefore inclined to pretend—in either one direction or the other—that these categories still apply and that having an abortion really is just an affirmative act of violence or that it really is just a failure to provide burdensome and risky life-saving assistance to someone in need. In truth, it is unavoidably both of these things at the same time.

We can choose to focus either on the direct violent action taken in having an abortion (the pro-life focus) or on the enormous physiological burdens involved in remaining pregnant (the pro-choice focus), but this selective focus does not alter the true complexity of the issue. As a consequence, although I am pro-choice, I acknowledge that someone could take a different position in the case of post-sentience abortions for reasons that are no less coherent and principled than my own.

The Ethical Vegan's Dilemma

The reader may perhaps be wondering whether I believe, as I do in the case of abortion, that the consumption of animal products might be as defensible, principled, and coherent as the consumption of only vegan products.

The answer is no. Despite the violence entailed in abortion, the person who has an abortion is not comparable to the person who consumes animal products, for a number of reasons. First, someone who faces the dilemma of whether or not to consume an animal product will not play the role of the Good Samaritan, either way. Ethical vegans are not Good Samaritans, any more than Refrain (who refrained from killing Abel, despite the temptation) is a Good Samaritan. Both vegans and Refrain are simply refraining from participating in violence. Neither is acting affirmatively to save anyone.

Understandably, organizations that urge people to become vegan will sometimes say that a vegan "saves" 95 (or up to 198) animals per year.[249] Such numbers are presumably based on the number of animals' deaths the vegan would have participated in causing if she had consumed animal products. It is exciting to imagine saving 95 (or up to 198) animals every year simply by eating different food and wearing different clothes.

Yet using the language of "saving" animals to describe vegans gives the misleading impression that if we consume animal products, we are simply bystanders who fail to rescue animals, comparable to Deborah 1 and other people who fail to donate blood, bone marrow, or a kidney that could save others' lives. And such language suggests as well that when I eat rice and beans with sweet potato fries and sautéed spinach and garlic instead of pulled pork or turkey dumplings, I am actively rescuing an animal.

Unlike the pregnant woman (and unlike the organ donor), however, I do not take on intimate discomfort, pain, and risk by being vegan. Indeed, as we have seen, I am likely to find that I am healthier, slimmer, and physically *more* comfortable because I became vegan. In addition, the vegan has plentiful alternatives to animal products for delicious, nutritious food and other creature comforts. Vegans do not suffer pain and risk in virtue of being vegan.

Consider, by contrast, some of the ways in which being pregnant does impose serious and ongoing burdens and sacrifices on the pregnant woman for the duration of her pregnancy. A vegan does not gain an enormous amount of weight or have difficulty breathing at times because she is vegan, but both of these conditions are a routine part of pregnancy.[250] Being vegan does not result in months-long trouble sleeping comfortably or an elevated risk of diabetes and hypertension, but being pregnant does. One does not lose calcium from one's bones by being vegan, but one does by being pregnant, because the placenta will draw minerals from the woman's body to meet the fetus's needs. Being pregnant, unlike being vegan, involves having one's body actively giving life support to another living being, a circumstance that, not surprisingly, carries significant health burdens and risks.

One can, of course, be a Good Samaritan for animals, just as one can be a Good Samaritan for humans. People who act affirmatively to rescue and save animals rightly belong in the category of Good Samaritans with respect to those animals. People who work at animal sanctuaries around the country contribute their time and energy to providing food, shelter, and safety to the tiny fraction of farmed animals who have been lucky enough to escape or to be rescued from farms and slaughterhouses before meeting their intended deaths there.[251]

Similarly, many people offer their homes to animals in need, including homeless dogs and cats who previously lived in shelters or on the street. When people provide shelter to homeless animals and thereby save their lives, they deserve praise for doing so. Simply becoming vegan, however, is not an act of Good Samaritanism toward animals. My former colleague, and the author of numerous excellent books and articles about animal rights, Gary Francione, has accurately described becoming vegan as just meeting the "moral baseline" regarding animals.[252] Refusing to participate actively in inflicting suffering and death on animals is, in other words, only the least we can do for them. Indeed, it is not really "doing" anything for them. It is simply abstaining from doing terrible things to them.

It is easy in our current world to become confused about the three moral categories (of doing harm, doing nothing, and helping, respectively) when it comes to animals. One reason for this confusion may be the fact that many of the people who act as Good Samaritans for some animals by giving shelter to dogs or cats who would otherwise have been killed, simultaneously hurt other animals by consuming such items as flesh, dairy, or eggs. If we think about this in terms of a different group of victims, this mix of activities is analogous to a person who rescues children from pedophiles by day, only to return home by night and proceed to purchase and consume child-pornography. We would correctly understand such a person to be living a contradiction. But we often miss the contradiction when it comes to animal victims.

In reality, then, we have the same three options available when it comes to animal suffering that we have in virtually all cases of human suffering: (1) we can be Good Samaritans and act affirmatively to save lives, by intervening and sheltering those destined for slaughter; (2) we can be ethical vegan bystanders and refrain from participating in causing the suffering, though we do nothing to intervene and rescue its victims; or (3) we can actively participate in the killing, by consuming the output of animal farming.

As consumers, then, we are different from the pregnant woman, who must choose between playing the physically demanding, painful, and risky role of Good Samaritan for her developing baby, on the one hand, and affirmatively bringing about that baby's death, on the other. That is why preventing a pregnant woman from committing violence against her fetus through abortion simultaneously and unavoidably compels her to endure pregnancy, labor, and delivery on the fetus's behalf. And it is why, while I support the right of every sentient animal to remain free of human exploitation and violence, I remain pro-choice on abortion, even in the gut-wrenching minority of cases that occur after the fetus is sentient.[253] Being vegan does not require pain and risk or a compromise of bodily integrity, while being pregnant does. Whether or not to permit post-sentience abortions therefore poses a difficult question. Whether to demand slaughter for products we do not need to live and thrive does not.

DON'T ANIMALS EAT OTHER ANIMALS?

One evening, I had occasion to enjoy dinner with friends, and one of the people at the table asked me about my progress on this book. Upon hearing that I was writing about ethical veganism, another guest offered me a great gift, though I did not realize it at the time. She expressed her strong opposition to animal rights and posed a series of questions to challenge the claim that it makes sense for us to refrain from hurting and slaughtering animals for food. I felt tired by the end of the evening, but one of her questions remained with me: Do you think that lions are immoral?

My initial inclination was to answer this question with a simple "No. I do not think that lions are immoral." But once I peered beneath the surface, I discovered that the question contained much more than first meets the eye. At least two separate arguments bring the question to life and allow us to explore its wisdom and implications.

The Two Lion Arguments

The first of what I will call the two "lion arguments" takes the form of what is known in logic as a "reductio ad absurdum," in which the person making the argument demonstrates that if we take the proposed idea to its logical conclusion, we will find that conclusion to be absurd. Because the conclusion is absurd, it follows that the proposed idea must also be absurd. For illustrative purposes, consider an example of a reductio ad absurdum argument, applied to the proposal that lying is always wrong:

1. You say that lying is always wrong.
2. This means that no matter what the circumstances are, lying is an immoral choice.
3. Suppose a child-molester is chasing a small child with a gun, and you know that he will molest and then kill the child if he finds her.
4. Suppose that you (but not the child-molester) see the child hide under a car near where you are standing.
5. Suppose the child-molester catches up to where you are and asks you "Is the child hiding nearby?"
6. According to your proposal that lying is always wrong, it would be wrong for you to say "no" or "she ran down that street" and thereby allow the child to escape being raped and murdered.
7. The right thing to do, if we accept your view, would be to tell the child-molesting murderer, "Yes, she is hiding nearby," which would foreseeably allow the predator to locate and harm the child.
8. The idea that it would be wrong to lie under these circumstances is self-evidently absurd.
9. Therefore, the proposition that "lying is always wrong" is absurd.

We can identify reductio ad absurdum reasoning in the first version of the lion argument. Here are the statements that would illustrate it:

1. You believe that humans act immorally when they consume other sentient animals.
2. Animals (like lions) consume other sentient animals.
3. It follows that you believe that animals, such as lions, act immorally when they consume one another.
4. The idea that lions are immoral is plainly ludicrous.
5. Therefore, the idea that humans act immorally when they consume other sentient animals is also ludicrous.

I will return shortly to lion argument number one, but first I want to examine a second sort of lion argument. This argument begins with the idea that morality consists of reciprocal obligations. If you show consideration for me, then it is right that I show consideration for you, but if you are aggressive and hostile toward me, than I am entitled to behave similarly toward you. The generous deserve generosity, while the miserly do not. Relationships are two-way streets.

A vision of reciprocity as the foundation of morality reveals the second lion argument. Consider some statements setting out that argument:

1. You believe that humans ought to extend our moral consideration beyond our own species to include other animals.
2. Humans have a moral rule that prohibits killing other humans, in the absence of a threat.
3. You therefore conclude that we ought likewise to refrain from killing other animals, in the absence of a threat.
4. Other animals, however, do not live by the rule prohibiting killing in the absence of a threat.
5. Other animals kill one another for their own purposes.
6. Other animals thus do not earn the right not to be killed.
7. We are therefore morally permitted to kill other animals for our own purposes.

Before responding directly to the reductio argument and the reciprocity argument, I shall consider the main difference between them. The reductio argument implicitly treats other animals' behavior as a model for our own. If animals legitimately kill for their dinner, it must be fine for us to kill for our dinner as well, it says. Under this approach, we can evaluate the morality of human behavior by observing how much it resembles the behavior of other animals. Animals naturally eat other animals, and we too are animals. It follows that we simply honor our nature when we eat other animals. We might describe this as an argument from "nature."

The reciprocity argument does not look to animals as role models. It assumes, instead, that moral rights and moral responsibilities go hand in hand. If animals do not forsake violence against others (including us), then we have no obligation to forsake violence against them. We might call this a "tit for tat" morality argument.[254]

Both of these arguments, from nature and "tit for tat," have considerable intuitive appeal. Nature often seems to hold clues to what we were meant to do and to be. To characterize someone's behavior as "unnatural" can thus be intended as an insult. If eating flesh, dairy, and eggs is what nature designed us to do, then it likewise feels dissonant to argue that we ought to stop eating these things. When we observe a lion chasing down a gazelle and consuming her body, such behavior may accordingly seem to provide powerful evidence confirming the natural wisdom and inevitability of our own choice to consume animal products.

The reciprocity argument is attractive as well. If another person shows himself to be unwilling to respect our rights, then we may strip him of many of his rights as well. This is why most of us feel justified in imprisoning murderers and rapists. Human dealings with one another strongly reflect a rule of reciprocity under which we deploy violence against those who would use violence against us, and we extend generosity and kindness to those who treat us well. We ordinarily operate under an unspoken understanding that each party in a stable and peaceful relationship will bring stability and peace to that relationship.

Let us now examine more closely how each of the two arguments works. The argument from nature holds that when behavior is commonly found in nature, unblemished by the peculiarities of culture, it would be foolish and wrongheaded to try to eradicate the behavior in humans. The expression "It's not nice to fool Mother Nature" nicely captures this sentiment. If humans and animals alike engage in particular conduct, then we might conclude that the conduct is legitimate.

Consider the following example. Mothers of mammalian species are fiercely protective over their young and become violent in the face of threats to their children.[255] Observing this behavior, we tend to view maternal loyalty as a virtue and its perceived absence as a profoundly disturbing moral lapse.[256]

When we say of an uncaring mother's behavior that "it is just not natural," we are doing more than simply making an observation of what "is." We are also evaluating what ought to be. Psychological studies have suggested, in fact, that we are hard-wired to prefer things that we perceive as "natural," even when there is nothing objectively superior about them.[257] Manufacturers of many processed foods capitalize on this feature of our psychology by labeling their products as "all natural."[258]

The "natural versus unnatural" dynamic will often make an appearance in political debates. For example, many opponents of gay rights claim that same-sex relationships are "unnatural."[259] In so doing, they rely on the view that if something is "unnatural" (which can mean that it is rarely found in nature—among humans or other animals), then it must also raise ethical questions.

Proponents of gay rights may respond to such claims by pointing out that human societies have, across cultures and eras, always included a sizeable and relatively consistent proportion of gay men and lesbians, constituting perhaps as much as ten percent of the population.[260] Proponents might note as well that homosexuality is commonly found among our non-human relatives, including the sexually prolific Bonobo (known also by the name of "pygmy chimpanzee").[261] These responses imply that homosexuality *is* natural, that it regularly appears in nature, regardless of cultural factors, and that it therefore cannot be objectionable, any more than being born with a sense of smell and a need for air can be "objectionable."

Advocates on both sides thus share an understanding of nature as a useful source of moral guidance. The reciprocity argument about animal violence against other animals reflects a significant strain in our thinking as well. From "an eye for an eye" to "you reap what you sow," we seem to manifest a strong inclination toward moral reciprocity. In deciding how to interact with another person or group of people, we feel justified in demanding that rights and duties flow in both directions, not just one. Legal systems in democratic societies, where popular attitudes toward justice are more likely to prevail, aim to create mutually beneficial arrangements that support an equitable give and take and that do not impose disproportionate burdens or confer disproportionate benefits on any one individual or group.

Given the power of each of the two arguments contained within the lion morality question, the "natural" argument and the reciprocity (or "tit for tat") argument, what can I offer in response? How can I propose opting out of something that is part of the natural "circle of life"? And how can we owe non-violence to animals when animals themselves practice violence and predation without a second thought? When people like me opt out of consuming animals and animal-derived products, aren't we going above and beyond the call of duty, given that animals offer no reciprocal promise of peace?

I shall begin by responding to the argument from nature.

The "Natural" Argument

Lions do kill and consume other animals. It does in fact appear to be part of their nature, in the sense that they are called "obligate carnivores," classified as such because they are thought to require animal flesh to live. There are anecdotal accounts of particular individual lions who were able to live without hunting or consuming the flesh of other creatures.[262] Such examples are exceptional, however, and when lions are observed in their natural habitat and examined anatomically, they seem well-designed to take down and digest other animals. This is true not only of obligate carnivores such as lions but also of members of other species that are classified as omnivores, including raccoons and bears.

In particular, the mammalian carnivores and omnivores share a number of physical attributes that make them well suited for killing and tearing apart their prey. They have a wide mouth opening, relative to head size; a simple jaw joint that operates as a stable hinge for effective slicing but which is ill-suited to side-to-side motion; and dagger-like teeth spaced apart to avoid trapping stringy debris. They also have sharp claws.[263]

The mammalian carnivores and omnivores additionally have huge stomachs that enable gorging, an important capacity in animals who tend to average only about one kill per week.[264] These animals also have a very low gastric pH (which means their stomachs are very acidic), enabling the breakdown of highly concentrated protein as well as the killing of dangerous bacteria that typically colonize decaying flesh.[265]

What does animal anatomy have to do with the morality of consuming animals and animal products? The first argument, which regards nature as a source of moral instruction, asserts that "natural" behavior is morally permissible behavior. Given what we observe about them, it is plainly natural for lions, tigers, and bears to kill and swallow the flesh of other animals. If we cannot condemn anyone for doing what comes naturally, then it would be inappropriate for us to accuse lions of immorality for consuming other animals. Thus, according to the reductio argument from lion behavior, because we and lions are both animals, it ought to follow that we cannot condemn the human consumption of animal products either.

The argument may seem persuasive. There are, however, at least two reasons to be skeptical. The first reason has to do with human morality, and the second has to do with human biology.

The fact that a behavior is commonly found in nature is ordinarily insufficient to demonstrate the moral rightness of the behavior. To take one example, forced sexual intercourse is very frequently found in nature.[266] What we call "rape" is common among males of various species who are not voluntarily selected by females, perhaps because of the males' otherwise poor genetic endowments. Through rape, an unwanted male is able to perpetuate his genetic lineage (including perhaps the inclination to engage in forced intercourse). A socio-biologist might interpret the history of rape by conquering human armies in warfare as an example of this phenomenon, through which men from an enemy nation force women who have no interest in coupling with them to extend the genetic reach of the invading enemy.[267]

Another instance of behavior found frequently in nature is infanticide, the killing of infants. Among a number of species, when a new male animal becomes the leader of a group of pregnant females, for example, it is common for him to kill the babies of the females as soon as they are born.[268] The evolutionary benefit of this behavior is clear. If the females are nursing another male's genetic offspring, the new male cannot impregnate them. Infanticide in such a case promptly terminates lactation and leads to fertility in the females. This, in turn, allows the male to mate with the females and expand his own genetic lineage.

A third common behavior among humans and our primate relatives is xenophobia. Literally the fear of foreigners, it describes a reaction of hostility to others within the same species that fall outside one's own group.[269] When one male chimpanzee encounters another with whom he is unfamiliar, a common reaction is extreme violence.[270] Likewise, racism, international conflicts, and inter-group hatreds have formed a persistent part of the human story.[271]

Perhaps a relic of a time in our evolutionary history during which strangers would generally pose an immediate threat, tribal loyalties and antipathy to outsiders may have become firmly ingrained in our DNA.[272] We can see disturbing echoes of such insider/outsider status allocation even among relatively young children.[273] This apparently naturally occurring behavior has recently led to school anti-bullying policies in response.[274]

The three examples, of naturally occurring rape, infanticide, and xenophobia, should help dispel the notion that acting in ways that come "naturally" automatically fulfills our moral obligations. In human societies, we evaluate our own behavior critically and negatively judge many instances of naturally occurring conduct. Indeed, if a particular behavior were sufficiently rare, it would suggest that people lack any drive to engage in it, and we would probably need no moral rules forbidding it. From this perspective, it is precisely because both virtue and vice come "naturally" to us that we must critically consider our activities and choose what to do (and what not to do) on the basis of moral reflection. We cannot, in other words, unreflectively do whatever we feel like doing and then rely on our inclination to act as necessarily vindicating what we have chosen to do.

But maybe there is some residual force to arguments from the natural. Yes, some things are natural *and* immoral, but perhaps the fact that particular behavior comes naturally counts at least *somewhat* in favor of its morality, even if other factors can outweigh the moral power of naturalness. After all, we do not judge lions to be acting immorally when they kill and devour their prey in part because lions *are* naturally carnivorous. On the assumption that our nature is relevant to figuring out what we ought to do, it is worth asking whether human beings are naturally and fundamentally a carnivorous species like lions or even an omnivorous species like bears.

Consider again the anatomy of the carnivore and the omnivore, including an enormous mouth opening, a jaw joint that operates as a hinge, dagger-like teeth, and sharp claws. Each of these traits enables the lion or bear to use her body to kill prey. Herbivorous animals, by contrast, have fleshy lips, a small mouth opening, a thick and muscular tongue, and a far less stable, mobile jaw joint that facilitates chewing, crushing, and grinding. Herbivores also generally lack sharp claws.[275] These qualities are well-adapted to the eating of plants, which provide nutrients when their cell walls are broken, a process that requires crushing food with side-to-side motion rather than simply swallowing it in large chunks the way that a carnivore or omnivore swallows flesh.

Herbivores have digestive systems in which the stomach is not nearly as spacious as the carnivore's or omnivore's, a feature that is suitable for the more regular eating of smaller portions permitted with a diet of plants (which stay in place and are therefore much easier to chase down), rather than the sporadic gorging of a predator on his prey.[276] The herbivore's stomach also has a higher pH (which means that it is less acidic) than the carnivore's or omnivore's, perhaps in part because plants ordinarily do not carry the dangerous bacteria associated with rotting flesh. The small intestines of herbivores are quite long and permit the time-consuming and complex breakdown of the carbohydrates present in plants.

In virtually every respect, the human anatomy resembles that of herbivorous animals (such as the gorilla and the elephant) more than that of carnivorous and omnivorous species.[277] Our mouths' openings are small; our teeth are not extremely sharp (even our "canines"); and our lips and tongues are muscular. Our jaws are not very stable (and would therefore be easy to dislocate in a battle with prey), but they are quite mobile and allow the side-to-side motion that facilitates the crushing and grinding of plants.

Our stomachs are only moderately acidic, a fact that becomes salient around Thanksgiving, when even slightly undercooked dinners of turkey flesh result in many cases of food poisoning from the illness-causing bacteria that easily survive in our stomachs.[278] Like herbivores and unlike carnivores and omnivores as well, we have long small intestines, enabling the digestion of complex carbohydrates, a process that begins in our mouths, where we, like the committed herbivores, have carbohydrate-digesting enzymes as well.[279]

Does any of this mean that people are incapable of eating and digesting animal products? Of course not. With weapons to kill animals, we do not need dagger teeth, and with fire to cook flesh, we can usually avoid the pitfalls of a stomach that is ill-equipped to kill the pathogens that populate raw flesh.

Despite our flexibility in accommodating animal-based foods, however, it nonetheless remains clear that we are anatomically well suited to plant-based eating. As we saw in chapter 3, animal-based foods are unnecessary for us, and they carry significant costs and risks. While it is beneficial to have complex plant carbohydrates slowly make their way through our very lengthy small intestines, the same cannot be said for having meat rotting in our intestines for extended periods of time.[280]

However much people may enjoy eating animal products, then, nature does not unambiguously commit us to, or reward us with good health for, consuming them. Our nature is quite different from that of lions, and our choices about what we eat are accordingly far more flexible and correspondingly susceptible to moral scrutiny. Where we have another choice—indeed a more healthful choice—for which our anatomy and physiology amply equip us, we cannot simply invoke nature to justify what we do. It is true that we could not reasonably accuse lions of acting immorally in consuming animals. But simply put, we are not lions.

The Reciprocity Argument

The second lion argument says that because animals do not refrain from killing other animals for food, it follows that we likewise have no obligation to refrain from killing animals for food: tit for tat. We are inclined to view it as fair and just to do unto others as they would do unto us, as a matter of reciprocity. Though saints may be kind even in the face of oppression and violence, we expect ordinary human beings to offer no better than they receive.

Let us assume that reciprocity is ordinarily a legitimate moral approach to our dealings with others. We can still identify at least two reasons to doubt the relevance of reciprocity to the human consumption of animal products. First, the principle of treating others as they treat us ordinarily requires that we examine how specific individuals or, at the very least, specific groups, treat us. The fact that some humans commit violent acts does not entitle us to write off the entire human race as violent and indulge the desire to inflict violence on whichever humans we choose. Instead, we must figure out *which* humans have been violent and confine our violence to them, even if we assume that violence is deserved and justified by reciprocity.

The specificity of reciprocal duties and obligations explains why we have criminal trials rather than simply punishing whichever person the police happen to arrest. We likewise reject the choice by some to commit violence against innocent members of a racial or ethnic group as a response to violent acts by other members of the same group. We understand that it is unfair to seek to harm an innocent individual and hold him responsible for misconduct by a guilty person to whom the innocent individual happens to be related in some way.

Once we appreciate the importance of targeting the "right" individuals for harmful treatment when we are responding to their violence toward others, it becomes clear that lions' predatory behavior does not really bear at all on our own consumption choices. Even if lions do not deserve better than they give (a proposition that I will dispute next), it would not follow that we can therefore slaughter, exploit, and consume chickens, turkeys, pigs, sheep, or cows. It makes no more sense to permit ourselves to eat animals because "animals eat other animals" than it would be to permit ourselves to murder humans because "humans murder other humans." In the case of animals, some animals eat other animals; others do not.

In the animal kingdom, we might better describe the "food chain" as a pyramid, in which the smallest number of "apex" species and individuals of those apex species (including lions) feed on other animals, and the greatest number of species feed directly on plants. This is the most efficient arrangement, because it takes far more plants to feed an animal who will then be eaten by another animal than it would take for the plants to feed the second animal directly.[281] Carnivorous living, in other words, does not use the earth's resources efficiently. This helps explain why humans' current, heavily animal-based food choices have had such a devastating impact on both the environment (i.e., air, water, and global climate) and the ability of many people outside this country to consume enough food to avoid starvation.[282]

We see that one cannot credibly defend on reciprocity grounds the consumption of flesh and secretions from primarily herbivorous cows, pigs, lambs, chickens, and turkeys, by saying that lions, tigers, and bears eat other animals. Nonviolent, herbivorous animals cannot *deserve* to be mutilated and slaughtered for consumption, because they are not among the animals to whose violence we could accurately refer in saying that "animals eat other animals." But does this perhaps mean that it is acceptable for us to consume carnivores and omnivores? Might it be ethical to consume wolves, bears, wildcats, and various of the fishes, because they *do* kill and eat other animals? In other words, is our error simply that we are slaughtering the wrong animals?

Moral Agents and Moral Patients

It will not surprise the reader to learn that I do not support our consuming carnivores and omnivores as a morally preferable alternative to consuming herbivores like cows and lambs. The premise for asserting that "if she is evil toward me, then I have the right to be evil toward her" is that the "she" in this equation is morally responsible for her behavior and may therefore deserve to be treated badly (especially by "me"). The non-human animals who hunt and fish for their food, however, are almost certainly innocent when they do so, and they also do not threaten *our* lives or well-being.

What do I mean when I say they are innocent? I mean that for an individual's actions to qualify as "immoral," she must be capable of understanding what she is doing in moral terms. This is why we do not hold a three-year-old human child morally responsible for her actions if she becomes angry at her brother and shoots him with a gun. It would be inappropriate for us to sentence her to prison, even though her behavior has brought about a tragedy.

Though we can train a three-year-old to avoid guns (or better yet, we can remove weapons from her reach), we cannot fully impress upon her the moral weight of the injunction against killing. Young children have a rudimentary understanding of right and wrong and are capable of empathy for others. They still, however, lack the brain circuitry involved in fully integrating the fact that not only will grownups become angry if you shoot your brother, but you will have done something wrong as well.[283]

In addition, children are not yet equipped with the ability to control their impulses very well.[284] This is why they will sometimes hit their siblings even though they know that their parents will punish them for doing so. Their moral understanding and impulse control are such that they are not "guilty" of acting immorally, even when their behavior would deserve moral condemnation if carried out by a competent adult.

We understand that young children can do horribly destructive things but nonetheless be "innocent" of their own misconduct in being unable to deploy the neural resources involved in bringing morality to bear on much of their behavior.[285] Moral philosophers refer to a young child as a "moral patient."[286] A moral patient is someone to whom moral agents owe moral obligations but who herself lacks corresponding moral obligations to others.

Another group of people resembles the category of babies or children in not currently qualifying as moral agents from whom we might fairly demand reciprocity. I refer here to the group of those people who do not yet exist but who will one day make up the population of future generations. Those in this group will never have the opportunity to do anything to us, whether beneficial or detrimental, that we might presently reward or punish in kind.

Do we nonetheless have ethical obligations to those people? In a 1983 essay titled "Duties Concerning Islands," Philosopher Mary Midgley raises this question by asking whether it would have been ethical for Robinson Crusoe to torch the island when he left it.[287] I suspect that most of us, like Midgley,[288] would say that we do owe duties to members of future generations, including an obligation to preserve the earth for them in a livable state.[289] Even with respect to people who have yet to come into existence as either moral agents *or* moral patients, then, our intuitions (as well as our religious traditions) tell us that we have ethical obligations to act and to refrain from acting in ways that can never be reciprocated.

Return now to beings who already exist in the world and carry out acts of aggression in the way that animals who kill other animals do: those humans who occupy the category of moral patients. Such people include not only children but also adults who suffer from brain damage or severe mental illness or intellectual disability.[290] Such people can invoke criminal defenses specifically designed for those whose mental impairments make it difficult or impossible for them to appreciate the wrongfulness of their actions.[291]

This observation about innocence returns us to our discussion of why lions and other animals who kill for their meals do not thereby become deserving of our violence against them. These animals do not appear able to internalize the idea that killing a living creature of another species who is not personally bonded to them might be unjustified.

This inability does not mean that carnivorous and omnivorous animals altogether lack the capacity for morality. Jonathan Balcombe, an expert in animal behavior, has documented some of the numerous examples of empathy, restraint, and what we might call emergent moral awareness in many species of nonhuman animals.[292] Other experts in the study of animal behavior have recorded similar observations.[293] One need only watch the video of "Christian the Lion" on YouTube to observe that an animal can experience gratitude, trust, loyalty, and other morality-related emotions.[294] Furthermore, predator animals are even capable of bonding with animals whom they would normally consider prey.[295]

What the lion and other nonhuman animals appear to lack, though, is the ability to engage in the sort of abstract moral reasoning that would lead to the conclusion that they should not cause suffering and pain to other living creatures who are strangers or members of prey species, when the lion or other animal feels hungry. When a polar bear who has been confined to a cage at a zoo kills a child who has slipped into the cage, we accordingly call the event a tragedy rather than concluding that the bear is immoral and deserves to be punished.[296]

The Necessity Argument

Notwithstanding the innocence of moral patients, it may be necessary on occasion to carry out acts of violence against some of them. If you found yourself face-to-face with a knife-wielding man threatening your life, you could kill him in self-defense, and your right to do so would not depend on whether the man is morally blameworthy for his conduct. He may be completely out of his mind, unable either to control his own actions or to appreciate their wrongfulness, but because it is necessary for you to kill him to protect your own life from his threat, few would cast judgment on your decision to kill him.

Just as we may defend ourselves against an innocent but psychotic human aggressor,[297] we may also defend ourselves against a nonhuman animal, however innocent, if she threatens our lives. If a man is walking down the street and a rabid dog comes running toward him, growling, with teeth bared and the tell-tale foam around her mouth, the man may use deadly force to protect himself against the dog, notwithstanding the fact that the dog is at the mercy of a disease that attacks her brain and compels her to act aggressively.[298] As a moral matter, then, in evaluating our choice to engage in violence, necessity in the face of a threat can be even more important than whether the target of our violence is guilty or innocent.

Necessity thus plays a crucial role in helping us determine whether and when to accept or reject the use of animals as a source of food. When we hunt an animal, it is virtually never the case that the animal poses a threat to our lives that we must confront with violent force. A hunt is, almost by definition, a pursuit of someone who is trying to escape from us rather than defensive action against someone moving aggressively against us.

In some cases, of course, the human or animal "at large" may pose a threat of harm to others. Police may use deadly force to stop a fleeing and violent human felon from escaping, if there is no less harmful way of stopping him.[299] This does not, however, describe hunting and fishing generally, and it certainly has no application at all in the case of the over-whelming majority of animals whom we consume, who are bred, used, and slaughtered to provide food. We are not killing them to protect our-selves from their imminent aggression against us.

Could one nonetheless argue need or necessity in a second sense? Maybe I do not have to kill the animal to avoid having the animal kill me, but what if I have to kill the animal to preserve my own life or health? In other words, couldn't we define necessary violence as extending to vio-lence that enables us to live and thrive, even if the targets of our violence are doing nothing to threaten our lives or health? If we needed to consume animal products to live a healthy life, then we might argue that this second form of "necessity" could justify our animal-product consumption.

It is useful to observe that this kind of "necessity" argument is not a slam-dunk, as a moral matter. We do not, after all, permit violence against other humans to satisfy our "need" for some part of the other humans' bodies to survive. Your neighbor may not forcibly remove your liver, even if he will die without a transplant and you are his only hope for survival. We draw a moral distinction between violence in self-defense to disable the source of a threat—which we permit, against humans and nonhumans alike—and violence in pursuit of life-saving resources, which we often prohibit.[300]

Let us put aside this caveat, however, and assume that killing and con-suming other animals when necessary to preserve our own lives is morally justifiable. We can readily sympathize, after all, with the starving inhabi-tants of a lifeboat who kill and cannibalize their human mate, even if we do not view this behavior as unambiguously justified.[301] It seems churlish, at best, for well-fed people to pass judgment on those who face the choice of committing violence, on the one hand, and suffering serious illness or starvation, on the other.

For people who live in the United States today, however, consuming animals and animal products as food or as clothing does not represent a response to any sort of necessity, including this second type in which one must have animal products to survive or to remain healthy. In fact, as we have already seen, consuming animal products, far from responding to a threat, *poses* grave threats to our well-being, both physical and envi-ronmental. As discussed in chapters 2 and 3, we can live healthy, happy lives filled with delicious and satisfying meals, without eating any animal products. We can, moreover, reduce our chances of becoming sick with cardiovascular disease, diabetes, and a variety of cancers by avoiding all animal products, particularly if we emphasize whole, unrefined, plant-based foods in our diets.

Beyond threatening our own health and longevity, the raising and slaughtering of animals generates planet-menacing amounts of air pollution, water pollution, and gases that contribute to global warming. In addition, the process of producing flesh and other animal products to meet consumer demand also contributes to the suffering of large numbers of people who will starve in developing parts of the globe. The colossal inefficiency of growing plants to feed animals who will be slaughtered to feed humans, rather than growing plants to feed humans directly, accounts for this sad reality.[302]

Land and water are limited resources, and using them inefficiently results in an inadequate global food supply and thus, ultimately, in human starvation. It is worth taking a moment to examine this often-overlooked feature of animal agriculture and the consumption habits that sustain it.[303]

We feed over 70 percent of the grain grown in the United States to livestock, and we use an even greater proportion of all arable land in the United States for livestock.[304] It can take about one hundred times as much water to produce one kilogram of meat as to produce the same amount of grain.[305] One acre of land used for vegetables, legumes, and/or grains produces between ten and fifteen *times* as much protein as the same acre dedicated to meat production.[306] Author Richard Oppenlander describes the problem in this way:

> Today . . . millions of acres of undeveloped third-world land are being used exclusively to produce feed for European livestock—and those livestock eventually end up in the United States . . . . 80 percent of the world's starving children live in countries where food surpluses are fed to animals that are then killed and eaten by more well-off individuals in developed countries. It is estimated that one-fourth of all grain produced by third-world countries is now given to livestock.[307]

In their own backyard, then, starving people can watch farmers grow animal feed to help satisfy distant consumers' demand for animal products. Our consumption of animal products thus contributes to human starvation in two ways: by using up the world's limited natural resources, such as arable land and water, and by diverting edible plant-based food away from places in which starving humans live, to support the consumption of animal-based food in places in which well-fed (or at least *abundantly* fed) humans live. Far from facing a threat that compels us to consume animal products, then, we face a threat that can be effectively addressed by choosing to become vegan.

We began this discussion by asking whether it might be morally appropriate to consume animals and animal products because animals consume one another. In exploring this question, we saw that it contains both an argument from nature and an argument about reciprocity. We examined these two arguments and observed that lions and other natural carnivores and omnivores are quite distinct from us in important ways.

Though they are sentient like us, committed carnivores and omnivores are unlike us in being anatomically designed to be predators and to consume dead animals. Unlike us as well, they do not appear capable of moral reflection about violence against strangers. They are accordingly innocent of the harm they inflict, whereas competent adult human beings are not similarly innocent. In the language of moral philosophers, animals are moral patients, while humans (albeit not all humans) are moral agents, accordingly responsible for our actions.

Significantly too, neither lions nor the species we routinely consume, including cows, pigs, chickens, turkeys, and fishes, choose to breed other animals for their own consumption, thereby inflicting massive environmental destruction and starvation in the process. Whether we hope to emulate the "natural" behavior of other animals or whether we aim to act toward other animals no better and no worse than their own actions warrant, a clear-eyed look at other animals' behavior cannot plausibly provide a justification for our choice to consume animal products.

DOESN'T GOD VALUE US MORE
THAN THE OTHER ANIMALS?

When the topic of veganism arises, people of faith sometimes express the worry that an embrace of animal rights might conflict with their religious commitments. Indeed, some wonder whether the whole idea of animal rights is inherently incompatible with a belief in God. In thinking about questions of religion, God, and animal rights, I find it useful to share my own religious background.

I grew up in an Orthodox Jewish home and attended a Yeshiva (which is a Jewish religious school) in New York City for twelve years. I discovered a tremendous number of intellectual and moral treasures in the religious community and the way of life represented by Judaism, the religion into which I was born. As I later learned, religions the world over offer similar treasures.

To be religious, for many, is not simply to have faith in a divine being or presence, but to believe as well that we humans have received a comprehensive moral code by virtue and in recognition of our unique status and place in the world. As a Jew and as a human being, I frequently heard the message that I can make choices and do what is right, while "animals" lack similar capacities. Because I held this unique ability, I held a correspondingly special place in the world. I mattered more than animals, and my life and death "counted" in ways that an animal's did not.

The notion that animals are inferior to us was part of my religious training, and it has played an important role in other religious traditions as well.[308] Animal rights and veganism might therefore seem to a religious person to be not only foreign but also potentially threatening to her moral values. By encouraging readers to consider veganism, I might appear to be a "fundamentalist atheist," attempting to mock or tear down what is sacred to religious people and offering my own substitute moral code in its place.[309]

I understand and empathize with this suspicion. In some ways, ethical veganism does resemble a religion. Participating in killing and exploiting other animals falls into a category we might call "sin," while living in a way that incorporates compassion and concern for the same animals might resemble an adherence to "commandments." Am I thus asking people to give up their religions for mine?

My answer is an unequivocal no. I do not ask that anyone give up her religion, and I do not offer ethical veganism as a substitute moral code. I am both more humble and more ambitious than that. I maintain that we can find in every religious tradition the embrace of vegan values, even as most religious traditions simultaneously include narratives and activities that may conflict with those values.

I suggest as well that being vegan will rarely require us to violate our religious commitments. An ethical vegan can be an observant Jew, Christian, Muslim, Buddhist, Hindu, or Jain, not to mention the many other religious possibilities, without facing a conflict or contradiction. Indeed, each of these religious groups includes ethical vegans among its numbers.[310]

Human Exceptionalism

We begin our exploration of religion and animal rights by considering the simple idea of human exceptionalism. Human exceptionalism holds that human beings are unique among the animals and that our uniqueness carries various moral implications. If being vegan meant believing that humans are equal to or exactly like other animals, then veganism would appear to clash with notions of human exceptionalism common to many religious traditions. We can usefully ask, then, whether a commitment to veganism and animal rights conflicts with human exceptionalism.

A common stereotype has animal rights activists believing that there are no important differences between humans and other animals, but I have never met any ethical vegan who feels this way. Of greatest relevance to our discussion, humans are plainly distinct in many respects from most of the animals whom people consume. Due to our particular capacity for symbolic communication, we humans can enact legislation, collect taxes, and act communally with deliberation and in a manner that appears to be unavailable to other species.

We are also capable of "progress" from one generation to the next, because we can record our discoveries, in writing and otherwise, and thereby leave behind us a legacy that saves us from having to "reinvent the wheel." In virtue of our apparently singular linguistic endowments, humans are capable of intentionally cooperating with millions and even billions of other humans in communal projects. No one could deny either these human abilities or the immense power that they vest in our species.

As Voltaire and others have said, however, "with great power comes great responsibility,"[311] and virtually all religions offer moral guidance for humans in an effort to harness our immense power for good rather than for evil. For Christians and Jews, the Ten Commandments direct people not to commit murder, while other religions likewise contain this prohibition.[312] Though humans are certainly capable of murder, a capacity the realization of which becomes a recurring theme throughout the Bible, religious rules require that we instead exercise restraint and allow others to live, even when we have the motive and the means to kill.

Over time, human power has grown exponentially. Humans today can inflict greater violence than we could have inflicted in prior centuries, by virtue of technological advances and the skills, of warfare and communal self-sacrifice, that we have inherited from our forebears. We are also, at the same time, capable of stunning positive achievements. We can not only destroy more than any other species on earth can destroy, but we can also build more, in a shorter period of time, and save more lives as well.

To be part of a religious tradition is therefore to understand not only how special humans are but also how important it is for us, out of all of the species, to appreciate the great possibilities that we hold in our hands. Religion thus demands not only a celebration of humanity but also a humility that comes from appreciating how much easier it is to destroy than to build, a humility that goes hand in hand with being in charge of our corner of the universe, as our unique abilities have led us to be. Ethical veganism shares this perspective, one that views humans as uniquely gifted, and accordingly asks that we exercise restraint in using our gifts, especially when it comes to how we act with respect to species less gifted in these ways than ourselves.

But what if your religion does not ask this of you? Judaism, Christianity, and Islam, for example, do not appear to prohibit the consumption of animal products across the board (though Judaism and Islam do prohibit eating pork and other particular animal products), and even the Eastern religions seem to accept the consumption of dairy products, a practice that inflicts significant amounts of suffering and death on cattle, as we discussed in chapter 4. Do these facts place ethical veganism on the other side of a serious divide with some of the major religions of the world? The perhaps surprising answer to this question is no.

Judaism and Animal Rights

I am most familiar with Judaism, so I will focus on the Jewish faith here. Other longstanding religious faiths, however, share in common some of the features of Judaism that raise difficult questions about how one can be a devoutly religious person while simultaneously living as an ethical vegan. Because there is the slaughter of other animals—as sacrifices and as food—throughout the Jewish Bible, the gap between Judaism and veganism may appear impossible to bridge.

By suggesting that Judaism does not rule out veganism, I therefore hope to inspire similar understandings of other religious traditions that might also seem hostile to the notion of animal rights. In this way, turning our attention to Judaism might help to shed light on whether or not veganism poses a threat to religious faith and practice more generally.

The rules of animal sacrifice detailed in Leviticus often emerge in debates over whether the Five Books of Moses could possibly be understood to tolerate veganism. After all, what could more dramatically reveal an antipathy to animal rights than the notion of killing animals and burning them for the Lord? It would seem that the animals subject to Temple sacrifices would necessarily be the property of humans—property for humans to consume or sacrifice to God. The loss, or sacrifice, appears not even to register as the loss of the animal's life but merely as the animal's owner's lost opportunity to use the animal.

Consider one of many Biblical passages to this effect:

> Speak unto the children of Israel, and say unto them: When any man of you bringeth an offering unto LORD, ye shall bring your offering of the cattle, even of the herd or of the flock. If his offering be a burnt-offering of the herd, he shall offer it a male without blemish; he shall bring it to the door of the tent of meeting, that he may be accepted before LORD. And he shall lay his hand upon the head of the burnt-offering; and it shall be accepted for him to make atonement for him. And he shall kill the bullock before LORD; and Aaron's sons, the priests, shall present the blood, and dash the blood round about against the altar that is at the door of the tent of meeting.[313]

The invisibility of the animal's interests and of the loss that he sustains in being killed is stark. In this narrative, the animal seems more like an inanimate object than a living, sentient being. Even before he is actually dead, his identity is presented as that of a "burnt-offering."

Beyond the detailed discussions of animal sacrifice in the Bible, a religious non-vegan could also invoke passages like this one from the Book of Genesis that expressly allows people to consume the flesh of animals:

> And God blessed Noah and his sons, and said unto them, Be fruitful, and multiply, and replenish the earth. And the fear of you and the dread of you shall be upon every beast of the earth, and upon every fowl of the air, upon all that moveth upon the earth, and upon all the fishes of the sea; into your hand are they delivered. Every moving thing that liveth shall be meat for you . . .[314]

In these verses, the chasm between the Biblical and the vegan approaches to animals, respectively, would appear impossible to traverse. God expressly invites Noah and his sons to view the animals listed in the passage as legitimate sources of sustenance. Vegans, in contrast, would reject the use and consumption of any animal who would experience "fear" and "dread" in the presence of human beings, precisely by virtue of the animal's capacity to be moved to experience that terror.

These and other Biblical passages seem to classify animals as live commodities for the taking and seem even to celebrate violence against animals. Might it then be blasphemous for religious Jews to criticize this view of animals? Might it appear to place their own consciences on a higher plane than God's word?

I do not think that it would, for two reasons, both of which ask that we look beyond the above passages and others like them to explore what else can be found in the Bible. To appreciate that one might be a religious Jew and a vegan, it is important to consider other strains of thought within the same holy books.

Violence and Compassion in the Bible

The first and perhaps most obvious lesson one gleans from reading the Five Books of Moses is that God appears to support and encourage violence against and exploitation of not only nonhuman animals but of other human beings as well. In the Book of Numbers, for example, God orders the Jewish people to make war on the people of Midian. After the war is over, Moses explains what the soldiers must do next:

> Now therefore kill every male among the little ones, and kill every woman that hath known man by lying with him. But all the women children, that have not known a man by lying with him, keep alive for yourselves.[315]

Stated differently, now that the war is over, the soldiers are ordered to murder most of the people they have taken captive, including women and male children, and spare only the female virgins, who will become the spoils of war.

In the above passage, God seems not only to condone but to command the murder of children and the sexual enslavement of women. Despite these passages in the Bible, however, I am aware of no Jewish authority or individual alive today who would defend the morality of murdering the children and enslaving the virgins captured from an enemy nation.

Beyond encouraging murder and rape, the Bible in places treats human slavery as an acceptable practice. In the Book of Leviticus, for example, we find the following verses:

> And as for thy bondmen, and thy bondmaids, whom thou mayest have: of the nations that are round about you, of them shall ye buy bondmen and bondmaids. Moreover of the children of the strangers that do sojourn among you, of them may ye buy, and of their families that are with you, which they have begotten in your land; and they may be your possession. And ye may make them an inheritance for your children after you, to hold for a possession: of them may ye take your bondmen for ever; but over your brethren the children of Israel ye shall not rule, one over another, with rigour.[316]

According to Biblical text, then, one of the legitimate stations to be occupied by human beings is that of slave, someone who can be the property of another human, subject to purchase, sale, and inheritance through the generations. Rather than asking the people of Israel to refrain from participating in this existing practice, God appears expressly to invite them to join in the slave trade and to treat the proceeds of such commerce as belonging to the master and to his family in perpetuity. One would be hard-pressed to locate here even a subtle intimation that human slavery ought to be eliminated.

I anticipate that the religious reader may be growing apprehensive at this point, wondering whether I am suggesting that one ought to be an atheist. Why else would I identify and quote from what are, at best, embarrassing passages from the Bible? I am not, however, taking issue with religion generally or with Judaism (or Christianity, which venerates the Five Books as the Old Testament) in particular. I cite these verses—and one could cite many similar ones—to demonstrate only that people of faith can be devout while simultaneously rejecting some of the values that appear to find direct expression in their holy books.

The Jewish religion can claim many observant adherents,[317] without any one of them having to view the murder of girls and boys, the rape of captive virgins, or the sale and inheritance of human slaves, as something other than a grotesque outrage against human life, freedom, and dignity.[318] Furthermore, one can account for the apparently uncritical appearance of such practices in the Bible by recognizing that humans, even those selected by God as intermediaries, are flawed products of their times. As such, the humans who translate holy ideas into books and oral traditions will foreseeably provide us with holy texts that in part reflect human prejudice rather than an unadulterated record of the Divine Will. Even the most religious person can accordingly engage in an exercise of judgment and discretion in reviewing and following the holy texts.

In his book, *The Dominion of Love*,[319] Norm Phelps identifies this unavoidable component of adhering to longstanding religious traditions. He suggests that the accepting inclusion of genocide, rape, and human slavery in the Bible gives us reason to turn a critical eye not only on these practices but also on the status of nonhuman animals in the Bible. As with our treatment of humans, we can more closely examine our relationship with nonhuman animals, without fear of showing insufficient deference to God. Phelps asks that:

> When we read in the Bible stories of God commanding or condoning the killing of animals, we should remember these tales of barbarities that God is accused of ordering against human beings. If we do not regard these as justifying the mass murder of men, women, and children and the rape of young girls, why should we regard the former as justifying the imprisonment, torture, and killing of animals? Why should Biblical verses that show divine approval of animal abuse set an everlasting precedent while passages showing divine approval of the murder of men, women, and children do not?[320]

To view holy books in context is thus to observe that they contain some residue of human frailty and confusion about how to incorporate infinite and divine perfection into our finite and limited experience of the world around us. When an infinite being converses with a finite one, some things will necessarily get lost in translation. We therefore do not challenge the greatness of God or the divine by acknowledging that some of the ideas which we find in the Bible and in other holy texts conflict with what we have come to know through the lessons of time and our own conscience: that we should not buy, sell, or use human slaves; that raping female captives is unjust; and that slaughtering helpless civilians in the aftermath of a battle is callous and inhumane. With the same conscience that permits this acknowledgment, we can reject animal slaughter and exploitation as well, while remaining true to the religions whose texts appear to condone these practices.

There is a second way in which we can usefully consider context in analyzing Biblical verses about animal sacrifice, slaughter, and exploitation as food sources. We can elsewhere find direct evidence of a Biblical attitude of kindness and concern for nonhuman animals. This evidence, of course, does not negate the passages that support the exploitation and killing of animals, any more than the Ten Commandments negate the passages that condone the rape and killing of enemy human captives. But it would be a gross misreading of the Bible to see it as simply endorsing barbarism.

The Bible does not unambiguously and unequivocally embrace the demotion of animals from living beings to commodities that we can use and slaughter to meet our spiritual and material needs. In the very same Bible, we find a competing vision of the animals with whom we share our world, a vision in far greater harmony with values of compassion toward the vulnerable among us, including animals.

Begin with Genesis. In keeping with the theme of animals-as-natural-resources explored above, Genesis contains a famous trio of verses that some have interpreted as God's authorization to dominate our fellow earthlings:

> And God said, Let us make man in our image, after our likeness: and let them have dominion over the fish of the sea, and over the fowl of the air, and over the cattle, and over all the earth, and over every creeping thing that creepeth upon the earth. So God created man in his own image, in the image of God created he him; male and female created he them. And God blessed them, and God said unto them, Be fruitful, and multiply, and replenish the earth, and subdue it: and have dominion over the fish of the sea, and over the fowl of the air, and over every living thing that moveth upon the earth.[321]

In these verses, God appears to draw an impermeable line between humans, the pinnacle of creation, and other, lesser, animals, placing humans in the position of rulers over all others.[322] Far less well-known, however, are the two verses that follow the trio above:

And God said, Behold, I have given you every herb bearing seed, which is upon the face of all the earth, and every tree, in the which is the fruit of a tree yielding seed; to you it shall be for meat. And to every beast of the earth, and to every fowl of the air, and to every thing that creepeth upon the earth, wherein there is life, I have given every green herb for meat: and it was so.[323]

These two verses provide an important context for understanding our relationship with animals, in at least two ways. First, God is here expressly directing humans to consume a vegan diet. This is striking, not only in its stark contrast with the animal slaughter that one finds elsewhere in the Bible, but also in its appearance in the verses that immediately follow those in which God grants humans dominion over other animals.

Consider the implication of this ordering: The exercise of dominion over other animals, as conveyed at the point when God first creates humans, does not endow people with the right to consume animals or their secretions. Indeed, the passage appears to anticipate that humans, blessed with dominion, will presume that they may now feast on the flesh of those over whom they have dominion. The verses that follow dominion thus serve swiftly to rebut that presumption.[324]

The second important lesson of the two verses is that although God blesses the humans first and gives them dominion over the others, he promptly turns to feeding and caring for the nonhuman animals as well. Here we see God's concern for nonhuman animals and his decision to give them food directly, rather than inviting a world in which humans feed other animals and then devour those animals as food, a world—in other words—of animal domestication, breeding, and animal farming. Notably, God feeds the animals a vegan diet as well.

We know, of course, that some nonhuman animals consume the flesh of other animals, a fact we closely examined for its moral implications in the last chapter. Yet most of the animal species, including those whom humans breed, exploit, and slaughter as food sources, are herbivorous. The two verses above suggest that in the most perfect and beautiful world, the world represented by life in the Garden of Eden, both humans and the animals over whom they exercise dominion would live in peace and satisfy their need for nourishment without slaughtering or forcibly feeding on other living beings.

Understood in context, God gives humans power over animals but teaches that humans can hold that power and live the good life for which they were designed, without consuming any of the other creatures.

This contextual information helps us see that adhering to a vegan diet is not antithetical to Biblical values and would seem instead to represent their most profound expression. Indeed, many observant Jews and Christians believe that in the future, when the world is redeemed, the vision of peace in the Garden of Eden will be fulfilled. The prophecy of Isaiah is instructive:

> And the wolf shall dwell with the lamb, And the leopard shall lie down with the kid; And the calf and the young lion and the fatling together; And a little child shall lead them . . . . They shall not hurt nor destroy in all My holy mountain.[325]

The first Chief Rabbi of pre-state Israel, Rav Abraham Isaac Hakohen Kook, approached the moral question of animal consumption in this way. Regarding the contrast we find between God's vegan dietary invitation when he first creates humans, and his subsequent authorization of animal consumption after the flood, Rav Kook argued that "[i]t is inconceivable that the Creator who had planned a world of harmony and a perfect way for man to live should, many thousands of years later, find that this plan was wrong."[326]

Rav Kook further theorized that God displayed his deep displeasure with humans slaughtering and consuming animals through the requirements of Jewish law, which contain numerous restrictions and prohibitions regarding the consumption of animal products. When it comes to plant-based foods, by contrast, Judaism imposes relatively few limits. An observant Jew may eat an apple, for example, without having to worry about whether the apple is of the correct type or about whether it was picked in a precisely prescribed manner.

The consumption of animal products, by contrast, comes with a multitude of dietary regulations and restrictions. Many animals (such as pigs) may not be consumed at all.[327] Those animals who are subject to consumption may not be consumed unless slaughtered in the required fashion.[328] And even when the permitted animal has been slaughtered in the approved manner, some parts of that animal (such as the blood,[329] the fat surrounding the animal's organs,[330] and the sciatic nerve[331]) may not be consumed.

And after meeting all of the above requirements, some animal products qualifying as Kosher may still not be consumed with other animal products that are themselves Kosher.[332] The separation of meat and dairy represents the primary example of this restriction, one to which I shall return below for other lessons that it contains. All of these animal-product-specific rules, Rav Kook believed, conveyed the degree to which God favored the consumption of plants.

Another Biblical scholar, Solomon Efraim Lunchitz, shared this understanding of the Jewish dietary rules:

> What was the necessity for the entire procedure of ritual slaughter? For the sake of self-discipline. It is far more appropriate for man not to eat meat; only if he has a strong desire for meat does the Torah permit it, and even this only after the trouble and inconvenience necessary to satisfy his desire. Perhaps because of the bother and annoyance of the whole procedure, he will be restrained from such a strong and uncontrollable desire for meat.[333]

Elsewhere in the extended Jewish Bible, going beyond the Five Books of Moses, we have indications that God may not have even been enamored of the animal sacrifices offered by his people. In the Book of Isaiah, for example, the prophet Isaiah tells his people that "[h]e that killeth an ox is as if he slew a man,"[334] an indication that animal offerings may not be pleasing to the Lord. One could infer from these words that the whole notion of animal sacrifices to God was, like the permission to consume animals, a concession to human desire rather than a true reflection of God's will.

In other parts of the Bible, there are specific injunctions against imposing unnecessary suffering upon animals. We will examine the significance of such injunctions shortly, but first consider five of the verses directly.

1. Exodus 23:12: "Six days thou shalt do thy work, but on the seventh day thou shalt rest; that thine ox and thine ass may have rest . . . ."[335]

2. Deuteronomy 22:6: "If a bird's nest chance to be before thee in the way, in any tree or on the ground, with young ones or eggs, and the

    dam sitting upon the young, or upon the eggs, thou shalt not take the dam with the young."[336]

3. Deuteronomy 25:4: "Thou shalt not muzzle the ox when he treadeth out the corn."[337]

4. Leviticus 22:27: "When a bullock, or a sheep, or a goat, is brought forth, then it shall be seven days under the dam; but from the eighth day and thenceforth it may be accepted for an offering made by fire unto the LORD."[338]

5. Leviticus 22:28: "And whether it be cow or ewe, ye shall not kill it and its young both in one day."[339]

These verses, to be sure, do not appear to promote a relationship between humans and animals that would inform any ethical vegan's vision of animal rights. On the contrary, each verse is part of an instruction on how to go about correctly exploiting, enslaving, and/or slaughtering animals. It is nonetheless noteworthy that these verses recognize, if in a minimal way, that humans do have moral obligations to animals. The verses directly acknowledge that animals are living beings who suffer exhaustion when they are forced to work without a break, endure hunger when they are made to thresh corn without the freedom to eat any of it as they go, and experience loss when their newborn babies are taken from them.

Acknowledgments of this sort fall within a current approach to animals widely known as "animal welfare" or "animal welfarism."[340] Animal welfarists who reject animal rights believe that humans are entitled to breed, exploit, slaughter, and consume nonhuman animals, provided we make some allowances to accommodate the feelings of these sentient beings and the suffering that they experience when their most basic needs go unmet. Just about all modern animal farmers pay lip service to animal welfare as an important part of animal exploitation,[341] an approach that fundamentally conflicts with the view that animals have rights and that humans are not entitled to use, kill, and consume animals as natural resources at all.

Given this conflict, why have I cited these Biblical verses as an argument for the consistency between the Bible and animal rights rather than as an argument against it?

The reason is that, as we have seen, even a devoutly religious person will find Biblical passages that offend his or her own deeply held moral commitments. One way to address the resulting dissonance is to observe that human prejudice and error will inevitably make their way into religious texts, even if the original speaker is divine. People of faith have implicitly (or explicitly) made this observation and therefore do not argue that the God they worship welcomes the mass murder of a conquered enemy's surviving children, or the rape of a defeated adversary's virgins, or the purchase, sale, use, and inheritance of human slaves, even though Biblical verses appear explicitly to endorse these practices.

If I include verses about animal welfare simply to exemplify human error in the Bible, however, then why do I bother citing them at all? Have I not already demonstrated human error by earlier quoting the verses permitting the murder, rape, and enslavement of humans? In what way do the verses about animal welfare advance the argument for animal rights?

I cite these verses for a different reason, even as I ask the reader to keep in mind that human error colors these as well as the verses discussed earlier. Despite their shortcomings and their failure to reject animal exploitation and slaughter altogether, a reflection of human prejudice, the nascent recognition in these verses of the respect that we owe to animals points the way to a more enlightened, divine path, one presaged in the vegan diet of the Garden of Eden.

In his work, Norm Phelps has suggested that incomplete restrictions within the Bible serve to invite readers over time to take such restrictions as clues to what divine justice truly demands rather than as an indication of what one may permissibly do without moral qualms.[342] People of faith can use the foundation of Phelps's life-affirming message to build a more compassionate and respectful world, consistent with Biblical values. Let me now offer one example of how we might find support for veganism in Biblical text. Consider the Jewish prohibition against the mixing of meat and dairy.

Jewish Dietary Laws

The prohibition against consuming meat and dairy together probably does not, at first glance, seem amenable to an animal-rights construction. It appears in fact to represent a view of food that says that a meal consists of either meat or dairy, though not of both. Without one or the other, one might infer, we do not have a meal.

This view of food and meals distorts reality, though it is sadly common among many Ashkenazic Jewish communities, including the one in which I grew up. Working from this prohibition against mixing the components of the two kinds of meals, meat and dairy, we arrive at the separate sets of dishes in the kitchens of most Kosher homes and restaurants.[343]

From where do observant Jews derive this prohibition against mixing meat and dairy? From a Rabbinic interpretation of a verse that appears three separate times in the Bible: "Thou shalt not seethe a kid in its mother's milk."[344] According to Jewish tradition, if a verse appears multiple times, then it should be interpreted to imply more than its literal meaning. Otherwise, the theory goes, the Bible would be redundant, which would appear to be inconsistent with divine authorship. Hence, one way in which religious Jews understand repetition in the Bible is that it provides clues to additional, important information.[345]

But what exactly do *this* verse and its repetition signify? Traditionally, the "seethe a kid" language is understood to prohibit the consumption of these two types of animal products—flesh and dairy—together, even if the milk is not from a goat but from a different mammal whose flesh is consumed (e.g., a cow or a sheep), and even if the flesh is not from the offspring of the specific mother whose milk is consumed but from a different and unrelated animal. The effort to broaden the prohibition reflects the traditional Jewish view that seemingly narrow restrictions that appear numerous times in Biblical text may and should be interpreted more expansively to better fulfill the essence of the original prohibition.

Stated differently, traditional Jews have rejected the literal interpretation of the "seethe a kid" phrase, concluding that the phrase's repetition signals a broader prohibition truer to the spirit of the language. Relying on this same canon of Biblical interpretation—one that looks for an underlying spirit and purpose in the text to amplify its meaning—we can arrive at a very different interpretation of the phrase in question.

The Hebrew word rendered as "seethe" means "cook" or "boil."[346] I would suggest that broadening the prohibition is a good idea, not primarily because the phrase is repeated three times, but because there seems to be more to the verse than meets the eye. Instead of reading the verse to require the separation of meat and dairy in our kitchens and at our meals, however, we might instead understand "do not cook a kid in his mother's milk" to mean that we must not consume baby animals at all. And ultimately, we can take the lesson that we may not consume any animals.

How might we interpret the verse as an admonition against eating baby animals? First, the Hebrew words that are translated to prohibit cooking a kid in his mother's milk might as readily mean "cooking a kid who is still drinking his mother's milk." The words "in his mother's milk," in other words, could be read to modify "kid" rather than to modify "cook." We would then understand "a kid in his mother's milk" as a nursing baby in the stage of life when he is still nourished on his mother's milk. Interestingly, the modern Hebrew word for a baby is Tinok or Tinoket, which literally means "one who is nursed."

A second, alternative reading of the prohibition leads to a similar outcome. In this reading, "in his mother's milk" modifies the word "cook," as in its conventional reading. Here, however, we recognize that any baby animal who is nursing will be filled with his mother's milk. If he is slaughtered and cooked as human food at this stage, it follows that he will necessarily be cooked in the milk that nourished him prior to slaughter. To avoid cooking a baby animal in his mother's milk, one must accordingly avoid killing and cooking a baby animal.

To understand the prohibition in one of these two ways is to find clear moral sense in it. To ban the slaughter of baby animals who are still in the process of nursing from their mothers is to express a level of compassion for the baby and for the relationship between the baby and his mother. For many people, there is something distinctively disturbing about the slaughter of babies, which may account in part for the special status that veal has had among those who have thought in ethical terms about the consumption of slaughtered animals.

If the prohibition were simply one regarding health or ritual purity, it would be odd for the verse to mention the relationship between the kid and his mother at all; that the verse does so strongly suggests that the moral concern is not simply about what we cook together but about *whom* we slaughter and consume. And killing babies, whether goats, lambs, chickens, or turkeys, deprives a mother of her baby and a baby of his mother. Anyone familiar with animal behavior will acknowledge that this deprivation is real and profound, and the earlier verses about mother birds and nursing animals acknowledge as much.

If one reads the verse in this way, some important implications follow. First, most farmed animals currently slaughtered and consumed would fall within the prohibition, as most of them are slaughtered before they

reach adulthood.[347] Chickens raised for meat are the most numerous of
the land animals consumed, and we slaughter them at about six or seven
weeks of age.[348] We slaughter turkeys when they are between twelve and
twenty-six weeks old,[349] pigs (whose flesh is, in any event, not Kosher),[350]
when they are between five and six months old,[351] "veal" calves at some
point between their birth and when they reach six months of age;[352] lambs
at between six weeks and a year old,[353] and the list goes on.[354]

The female animals exploited for their reproductive processes are
slaughtered later, once they are "spent," after undergoing several years of
painful reproduction and loss, as described in chapter 4. But their male
children are killed even earlier than most other farmed animals, as we have
also seen, because males do not produce eggs or milk. To prohibit the
slaughter of babies would therefore preclude the slaughter of most of the
animals from whom come the flesh and other animal products that people
currently consume.

Understanding the Biblical prohibition to apply to the consumption
of baby animals, one could, then, take the next and obvious step and not
consume animals at all, just as Adam and Eve were not invited to consume
them in the Garden of Eden, a model for nonviolence in the Biblical
world.

For those Orthodox Jews who might be uncomfortable with the idea
of departing from the traditional understanding of the text, a more conventional construction of Jewish laws that regulate dairy consumption
lends support to the vegan diet as "the new Kosher" approach to living.
Consider the prohibition against consuming the milk of a sick animal.[355]
Without even inquiring about the underlying purpose of such a prohibition, its straightforward application places virtually all products from the
modern dairy industry off-limits, according to Orthodox Rabbi Herschel
Schachter, among the greatest Jewish legal authorities in America. Rabbi
Schachter observes that because most modern dairy products come from
sick animals (suffering from mastitis and other illnesses), modern dairy
products are no longer Kosher, and the Rabbi has personally stopped consuming dairy for this reason.[356] In addition to my own vegan-friendly
reading of Biblical text, one may thus also rely on accepted doctrinal principles to conclude that the Bible is not only consistent with veganism but
may, in some instances, require it.

Throughout the Bible, we can observe apparently permissible, though regulated, practices that have since become unacceptable to people of faith. Religious people can approach a welfarist orientation toward slavery and the treatment of slaves in the Bible as fundamentally urging people to end the practice altogether. One can likewise approach the Bible's welfarist orientation toward animal exploitation, an orientation revealed in prohibitions regarding a "kid" and his mother's milk and the consumption of the milk of sick animals. By reading the Bible in this way, a person can remain steadfast in her faith while simultaneously embracing as the deep message of the Bible, which literally condones both human slavery and animal slaughter, a call for the abolition of both.

One can nurture religious faith and simultaneously recognize that human error inevitably distorts some of what are otherwise profoundly valuable moral lessons. A religious person need not accept the legitimacy of slavery or other atrocities against humans, even though the Bible seems to endorse them. She can instead find compassion and concern for slaves' well-being in the Bible and appreciate that true compassion must entail the end rather than the mere regulation of slavery.

The Bible says in one and the same verse to allow slaves and animals to rest on the Sabbath: "Six days do your work, but on the seventh day do not work, so that your ox and your donkey may rest and the slave born in your household . . . may be refreshed." It is not enough, of course, to allow one's slaves to rest on the Sabbath; they must be freed from bondage. And the same can be said of animal exploitation, torture, and slaughter. One can interpret the Bible's messages of compassion and concern for animals, then, not only to permit but to affirmatively support the abolition of animal exploitation, an abolition that begins with veganism.

10

BUT DON'T INDIGENOUS PEOPLES EAT ANIMALS?

As observed in earlier chapters, the politics of animal rights are complicated. They do not neatly correlate with other political commitments. Questions challenging animal rights can come from either side of the political spectrum. Liberals may wonder whether supporting animal rights logically entails an opposition to abortion. Religious conservatives may worry about the implications of animal rights for their faith.

For someone who considers himself liberal or progressive, ethical veganism may appear to pose a threat to the ways in which some of the least powerful and most oppressed groups of people in the world have lived. In particular, from the perspective of progressives, a commitment to animal rights might seem to pass negative judgment on indigenous peoples who have traditionally hunted and fished for their food. This judgment, in turn, could lead progressives to be wary of veganism on the ground that it further marginalizes people whose lives and cultures have already suffered tremendous violence and degradation at our hands.

The desire to protect indigenous peoples from harsh and oppressive judgments is laudable. We must not persecute those less powerful than ourselves, and the pursuit of animal rights should never provide a platform for such persecution. In championing rights for one group of oppressed individuals, we must remain mindful of other oppression and avoid implicating ourselves in that. For this reason, I am troubled by the sexism that some animal advocacy groups have deployed in their promotional campaigns.[357]

I join those who wish to resist insensitivity to the challenges that many groups face and to the varied circumstances in which people build their lives. In this chapter, I therefore address the question of indigenous peoples in several ways, each of which may help alleviate worries about unfairly judging the powerless.[358]

Traditions of Gratitude and Apology

In thinking about indigenous peoples and the exploitation of animals, it is useful to observe something that is often overlooked: indigenous people on the whole have consumed far less animal-based food and have used many fewer natural resources more generally than a typical modern American.[359] Many Native American tribes traditionally lived primarily on vegetables and grains, cultivating and harvesting foods like corn, beans, and squash, known as "the three sisters."[360] Though our Thanksgiving holiday has become a celebration of turkey slaughter and consumption, it began as a harvest feast, an event that had little to do with animal-derived food.[361]

The stereotype of the Indian surrounded by hides, furs, feathers, and the flesh of the buffalo he has killed does not provide an accurately representative picture of traditional Native Americans.[362] Some tribes consumed animals regularly, while others rarely did.[363] A common orientation among Native Americans toward the animals they ate, moreover, reflects an attitude far closer to a philosophy of animal rights and veganism than does the orientation of Western animal agriculture today.

Many of us have heard about a tradition among some Native Americans of expressing gratitude or regret toward an animal who was hunted and killed for human consumption.[364] People who hear of this practice sometimes view it as a sign that killing animals as a food source is morally acceptable, so long as we recognize and revere each life that we take.[365] But I would interpret traditional ceremonies of gratitude and apology as expressing a very different message, one of ambivalence and regret. Such ceremonies may tacitly acknowledge the harm and corresponding guilt associated with slaughtering another being.

To appreciate the complexity inherent in expressions of gratitude or apology to slaughtered animals, consider the roles that gratitude and apology more typically play in our lives. When we express gratitude toward someone, it is usually because the one to whom we give thanks has voluntarily parted with something valuable and has thereby enriched our lives. When we choose to share what is ours with another, we likewise experience joy as a direct consequence. The words "thank you," uttered sincerely, help share the positive feelings of the recipients of bounty, and thereby give pleasure to those who have chosen to share what is theirs.

When we apologize to someone we have harmed, we convey our feelings of regret for our actions, having confronted the injury that our actions have brought about. We say that we are sorry when we experience remorse for having made a decision to act at someone else's expense. One of the essential components of a true apology is that we intend, at the time of our apology, to refrain from behaving in a similar manner in the future. Had we the opportunity to do it over again, our apology signifies that we would exercise restraint and curb our impulses out of consideration for the needs of our victim, the one to whom we apologize, the one who did not agree or want to be hurt as a means of furthering our objectives. If one is truly sorry about what one has done, then one aims not to do it again.

By contrast to the typical expression of gratitude, thanking an animal for "giving" her life to provide us with food is dissonant and counterintuitive. The nonhuman animal wants to live rather than to "share" her flesh or bodily secretions with human beings. From the point of view of the animal, there is nothing voluntary about the conveyance of her life to the person who consumes her. To thank her therefore represents the expression of gratitude by an attacker to the victim of his violent crime.

Imagine how an armed robbery or assault victim might feel if her assailant thanked her after committing his offense. And imagine too the pointlessness of a murderer thanking his victim after taking her life. Expressions of gratitude to human victims would seem only to add insult to injury. They would make a mockery of what was in fact taken, without consent and against the victim's will.

Though apologizing to the victim of harm seems more reasonable than thanking him for his sacrifice, there is incongruence here as well. To apologize to an animal for killing him, while fully intending to continue killing animals in the future, does not provide what we ordinarily expect of an apology: a commitment to change. It says instead that although we acknowledge that we are doing something harmful and regrettable for which we feel remorse, we nonetheless have no plans of changing our behavior in the future.

Not only does an apology to the hunted animal fail to meet this ordinary criterion for a true apology—an intention to change one's behavior—but it also cannot effectively create the connection between perpetrator and victim that we ordinarily seek when we apologize. The victim is either already dead, in which case he is no longer even theoretically able to extend forgiveness, or, if the apology precedes the slaughter, the victim is in the peculiar position of being asked for advance forgiveness for an act of harm that the actor has yet to carry out.

Why, then, have some indigenous peoples thanked or apologized to the animals that they consumed? I would interpret a ritual of thanking or asking forgiveness of an animal to be consumed as a way of simultaneously denying and honoring a central truth about the consumption of animal products: it involves inflicting an undesired and undeserved harm and death on a living being who has no obligation or responsibility to suffer or die for us.

When we say "I am sorry" or "thank you" to the body of a slaughtered animal, we acknowledge that the animal's life belonged to him and not to us. In expressing regret or gratitude, we admit that by consuming the animal, we have taken what was his most valued possession and converted it to our own use. For this sort of an appropriation we might feel remorse, because we stole what was never offered to us by its rightful owner, or we might feel gratitude, because we have received a bounty to which we were not entitled. In these ways, some indigenous peoples may have traditionally given voice to the involuntary and undeserved transfer of one being's life to another's plate.

At the same time, however, the gratitude and remorse appear to deny the truth. Gratitude suggests a consensual conveyance, but the slaughtered animal does not consent to what she endures. Remorse, in turn, suggests a commitment to changing in the future, but these apologies to the animals co-exist with a commitment to continuing to slaughter and consume them. The denial inherent in thanking or apologizing to a victim in a line of victims may thus serve as a ritual to assuage the guilt that we experience when we do undeserved harm to others.

We behave as though our transaction with the animal is no different from our transactions with the humans in our lives, to whom we give thanks for consensual gifts and apologies for the undeserved infliction of harm. We pretend, in other words, that the animals are partners and participants in our decision to consume them, individuals who might voluntarily "give" us what we have taken or who might "forgive" us for the harm that we plan to continue to inflict.

What indigenous peoples have themselves said regarding the slaughter of nonhuman animals supports this interpretation. One eskimo hunter, for example, said:

> The greatest peril in life lies in the fact that human food consists entirely of souls. All the creatures that we have to kill and eat, all those that we have to strike down and destroy to make clothes for ourselves, have souls, like we have, souls that do not perish with the body, and which must therefore be propitiated lest they should avenge themselves on us for taking away their bodies.[366]

According to the zoologist James Serpell, this fear of the souls of slaughtered animals who may exact revenge is common in native cultures. Serpell explains:

> Although it varies in detail from place to place, the undercurrent of guilt and the need for some form of atonement for animal slaughter is common among hunting people. In certain African tribes, for example, hunters are obliged to undergo ceremonial acts of purification in order to remove the stain of murder from their consciences. In others, the hunter will beg the animal for forgiveness so that it doesn't bear a grudge. The Barasana Indians of Colombia regard the act of killing animals as spiritually dangerous, and believe that their flesh is poisonous unless ritually purified first . . . . Among the Moi of Indochina, expiatory offerings are made for any animal killed by hunters, because they believe that it has been taken by force from its spiritual guardian who may decide to seek revenge.[367]

A Non-Indigenous Analogue of Gratitude and Apology

Indigenous peoples who have observed these kinds of rituals may in many respects be quite different from most Americans. However, in thanking or apologizing to the animals they consume, their desire to deny the true nature of what is taken from animals—to pretend that the animal participates in her own exploitation—does not entirely distinguish them from us.

Throughout this country, we have animal-flesh- and secretion-serving restaurants with names such as "Happy Pig Café," "Dancing Pig Barbecue," "Happy Cow Diner," "Dancing Chicken," and "Gobbler's," each carrying a picture of a live animal having a splendid time.[368] The pervasiveness of this pretense that animals are in on the fun motivated a parody on the television show Saturday Night Live[369] that went like this:

[Open on exterior, Cluckin' Chicken fast food restaurant]
Jingle: Something's cookin' at the Cluckin' Chicken.
Clucky Chicken: [popping into the front of the screen] That's me!
    [flies up to a table filled with kids and their Dad]
Dad: Hey, Clucky—why's the Cluckin' Chicken so chick-a-licious?
Clucky Chicken: Everybody knows why. It's 'cause I'm flame-broiled!
    Yow-zee-yow-dow! But that's not all—I'm cooked fresh! First my
    head's cut off! [the cook chops Clucky's head off and sends it flying
    through the restaurant] Heads up! [Clucky's head appears before
    another chicken being gutted] Then I'm plucked and gutted—my
    intestines are pulled out. Trust me, you don't want 'em! Whee! Look
    at me! I'm gettin' quartered and split, breasts, wings, the whole nine
    yards! Chopitty, chop! Then the pieces of me get flame-broiled.
    Hear that sizzle? That's me! 550 degrees! Good thing I'm dead, or
    yow-wee! Then I'm seasoned just right, and ready to go! [takes a
    bite of a piece of chicken] Hey, I'm good! Finally, I'm served to
    you, so you can chew me, swallow me, and convert me into waste
    matter. [peers into the toilet] Ga-ga-ga-gooey!   [returns to the
    kids and their dad] Hey, kids, how's the meat?
Kids: [chewing ferociously] You taste great, Clucky!
Clucky Chicken: [head spinning around the restaurant] Holy fanoley!
    The oxygen's leaving my brain!
Dad: Any last words, Clucky?

Clucky Chicken: You betcha! [singing] If you want a place for the
greatest chicken, take it from my head, it's easy pickin', 'cause . . .

Jingle: Something's always cookin' at the Cluckin' Chicken!

Clucky Chicken: Being dead never tasted so go-nobbity good!

Clucky Chicken elicits laughter because the implicit conceit—ubiquitous among the names of fast-food restaurants—that chickens delight in
their experience of becoming someone else's meal—is so absurd.

The pretense that animals happily participate in their own slaughter
and consumption is evident as well in the inaccurate stereotypes that people tend to have of the animals who are farmed for their flesh and secretions. Many of us imagine that cows, turkeys, and chickens are stupid
and oblivious of what is happening to them or that pigs are gluttons who
eat when they are not hungry. To be called a "cow," a "chicken," a "turkey," a "goat," or a "pig" is an insult, because we have developed an image
of animals so dull-minded that they find being tortured and slaughtered
unobjectionable. It is far easier for us to consume flesh without guilt when
we indulge the fantasy that the animal who once lived was indifferent to
being slaughtered.

When some indigenous peoples, traditionally expressed gratitude or
apologized to an animal, they may have been offering an acknowledgement that the animal was a victim, that she valued her life and suffered
when it was taken from her, and that her slaughter left behind an imbal-
ance in the scales of justice that had to be righted. Our pictures of dancing
pigs and smiling cows and chickens without a care in the world, by contrast, fully embrace the lie of animal consent and indifference to their fate.
Our rituals, unlike some of indigenous peoples' thus consist exclusively in
denial. Theirs, by contrast, have tempered denial with truth.

The rituals of some indigenous hunters accordingly come closer to the
ethos of veganism than do the Western practices prevalent in the United
States. Understanding this fact raises a question, though. Given that many
Native Americans have long acknowledged implicitly that consuming animals calls for remorse, and given that so many Native Americans once
lived primarily on plant-based food, why didn't all Native Americans simply live as vegans?

One possibility is that they, like so many people in our own day and
age, were unaware that people can live and thrive without consuming

animal products. Another possibility is that as gatherer-hunters (a more accurate term than hunter-gatherers in terms of time dedicated to each endeavor[370]), some Native Americans may have worried that in the absence of animal flesh, they would have been unable to ingest sufficient calories for survival, a worry that modern Americans do not face.[371] Indigenous peoples in arctic areas, such as the Inuit, would certainly have had this concern, given the paucity of plant life available for sustenance, before global transportation of food became common.[372]

Many indigenous peoples have thus consumed animals out of necessity. When one faces the choice to eat animal flesh and secretions or starve, one understandably does what it takes to survive.

The choices made by some Native Americans and other indigenous peoples therefore offer no rationale for us to consume animal products today. Unlike people in those circumstances, we do not risk starvation when we avoid animal-derived foods. Indeed, as we have seen, we contribute to others' starvation when we choose to consume such foods.[373]

If we wish to learn from Native peoples, then, we can learn that many who killed animals did so with the recognition that they were taking something valuable from a living, sentient being. They demonstrated this recognition with rituals of gratitude or apology, rituals that simultaneously exposed and obscured the injustice inflicted against an innocent animal. Under conditions of necessity, we cannot ask for much more than that.

In today's developed world, however, we can best show reverence for indigenous traditions by acknowledging fully that animals yearn to be free of our violence, and that breeding and slaughtering sentient beings steals what was never ours to take. We can live as vegans and no longer feel compelled to nourish ourselves with the blood and tears of living creatures.

"The Noble Hunter"

In raising the question of indigenous peoples and their inclusion of animal-derived foods in their diets, one may be concerned about two separate matters. The first, addressed above, is the worry that a vegan approach to living may implicitly pass judgment on oppressed minorities who have suffered grave injustices at the hands of invading nations. Having decimated Native American populations and taken the land on which they once lived and thrived, it would seem to add insult to injury for descendants of European colonists to judge their ancestors' victims as wanting.

As it turns out, though, we have seen that the hunting rituals of some Native Americans and other indigenous peoples are quite resonant with our own practices, offering insights that therefore shed light on how we might think about our own behavior. In calling into question the consumption of animal flesh and secretions, ethical vegans say nothing that singles out indigenous peoples for condemnation. On the contrary, traditional cultures express a respect for animals and the losses that they endure, paving the way for veganism in circumstances that do not require slaughter.

Rather than defending oppressed individuals from unfair condemnation, a second approach takes the view that traditional indigenous peoples are morally superior to us. On this view, if we want to become better people, we should hunt for our food and otherwise follow indigenous traditions. The fact that Native Americans hunted, in other words, elevates hunting to a higher moral plane, worthy of emulation. From this perspective, to propose ethical veganism is to fail to honor the moral superiority of indigenous peoples.

This second approach seemingly elevates indigenous peoples by putting them on a moral pedestal. Consider, however, that historically, sexual subordination and oppression have thrived even as and in part because men characterized women as morally superior to men and thus best suited to "purer" pursuits in which they could aim to meet higher standards.[374] Such elevation of a group can thus prove as dangerous as their degradation as morally primitive or otherwise "un-evolved," and the two approaches can also function in concert.

To respect indigenous peoples is neither to demonize nor to romanticize them. It is instead to understand that they are people, just like others, and that what they do will include both the laudable and the reprehensible.

Rather than uncritically extolling a progressive version of the "noble savage," it is important to understand that indigenous populations are not angels or higher beings. They are simply other humans who have adapted in different ways to the conditions in which they have lived. Some of what they have done is thus praiseworthy and noble, and some of what they have done is not. They are, to state the obvious, human beings with the same human potential for good and evil that the rest of us have.

For most people, the fact that Native Americans or other indigenous groups have traditionally behaved in some way is not in and of itself a reason for everyone to behave in that way today, just as it is not a reason to avoid behaving in that way. For those who insist that all indigenous practices are, ipso facto, just and good, it is useful to remain cognizant of the human failings that afflict us all.

Readers may be surprised to learn, for instance, that some Native Americans owned African American slaves.[375] Just as Native Americans did not all opt out of animal slaughter, they also did not all opt out of the human slave trade[376] or the violent subjugation of women.[377] But to be very clear about it, Native-American participation in the institutions of slavery and sexual violence does not distinguish indigenous cultures from the European groups that persecuted them. Indeed, Europeans played a far more significant role in the slave trade, both numerically and philosophically, than did Native Americans. And an embrace of sexual subordination was part of British culture long before the Europeans even knew about the people native to North America.[378]

We are, in short, not that different from indigenous peoples. We and they have both been involved in exploiting and slaughtering non-human animals, an involvement that has made its way into our respective cultures and traditions. We and they have also participated in subjugating the human beings in our midst, subjugations that took forms that included slavery and sexual violence.

At the same time, indigenous peoples have—like us—created ways of coping with their own violence against animals through rituals of denial. Some indigenous hunters have given thanks to animals for gifts the animals never consented to bestow, and some have apologized for injuries that would be repeated many times over. We have consumed the flesh and secretions of animals in restaurants carrying the names and images of ecstatic, celebrating versions of those same animals painted on the entrance.

What distinguishes indigenous peoples from us, perhaps, is the fact that many of them traditionally used and exploited far fewer animals than we do today. The bulk of the diets of many tribes was plant-based, and their consumption of animals reflected actual or perceived necessity for survival rather than the quest for pleasure that it represents for most of us today.

Perhaps because the lives of Native Americans were not as thoroughly saturated with animal slaughter and exploitation as our own, their denial rituals likewise contained a grain of truth entirely absent from our own: to thank or to apologize to an animal is to demonstrate a partial acknowledgement of the animal's loss. With this grain of truth that distinguishes some Native Americans' rituals from our own, we can build on the sensitivity to what animals suffer and lose at our hands and choose to withdraw our support for that suffering and loss altogether.

We show no disrespect to indigenous peoples by becoming vegan. On the contrary, we honor their rituals of regard for the sacrifice of animals by living in a way that no longer demands such sacrifice of our fellow beings.

11

WHAT ABOUT "HUMANELY RAISED" ANIMAL PRODUCTS?

Some people who care about the issues discussed in this book have touted an alternative to veganism for improving the lives of domesticated animals.[379] This alternative attempts to restore various features of the traditional family farm, where animals were treated less like disposable production units than they are today on factory farms.

This approach typically takes one of two forms. One involves attempts to change some of the practices on factory farms and thereby modify the situations of the overwhelming majority of domesticated animals who spend the bulk of their short lives in concentrated animal feeding operations (CAFOs). Measures like California Proposition 2 exemplify this first way of attempting to mitigate the cruelty of factory farming, by requiring farms to phase in larger cages for pregnant sows, veal calves, and laying hens.[380]

A second form of intervention involves directly supporting specialty farming operations at which animals are able to enjoy the outdoors and interact with other members of their species in the time before they are slaughtered.

"Humane" Animal Farming Measures

At first glance, the "humane farming" approach may seem like it ought to be uncontroversial. At the moment, a large majority of human beings consume animal products. There accordingly persists a huge demand for the creation of animal products, and our market economy responds to this demand by producing an enormous supply, to the detriment of over one hundred billion animals on this planet every year.[381] Given this reality, who could disagree with the notion that it is better that the animals bred and slaughtered in the service of this demand experience less rather than more suffering on their way to slaughter, disassembly, and distribution to people's homes?

A gruesome thought experiment will help illustrate the appeal of "humane" farming initiatives. Imagine that you see a steer standing in a kill line at a slaughterhouse. Now imagine that a so-called "sticker" (a worker who "stand[s] in a river of blood, being drenched in blood, slitting the neck of a steer every ten seconds or so")[382] approaches you and says he is thinking about stabbing a steer in the eye before cutting his throat and wants to know what you think about that.

Do you say, "Sure; stab the steer in the eye. He'll be slaughtered soon anyway"? Probably not, because no matter how horribly an animal is already suffering, you would likely resist efforts to inflict even more suffering on him. Every additional injury is one more offense against the animal. For this reason, it would appear that supporting measures that may slightly mitigate some of the cruelty on conventional farms, or supporting family animal farms, does at least some good. But that conclusion may ultimately rest on false premises.

To see why "humane" initiatives may not be helpful, we need to ask what happens when laws regulate animal treatment by the food industry and when people purchase "humane" animal products. If there were a fixed number of animals who would be bred, raised, and slaughtered, then we might expect that regulating factory farms and shifting some demand from factory to family farms might give that fixed number of animals a somewhat less excruciating and less deprived existence than they would otherwise have experienced on an unregulated factory farm.

On the level of the individual animal, then, pig number 100,704 will be born and will be slaughtered, if demand and supply are fixed, and the

question is whether she undergoes 365 days per year of physical and emotional torture before slaughter or whether she perhaps experiences somewhat less torture instead. Of course, it is better that she suffer less rather
than more, all things being equal. So the argument for regulating factory
farms and purchasing animal products from "humane" farms seems sensible, if we imagine that demand for animal products is fixed.

In reality, however, it is not clear that supporting regulatory measures
will have any impact on the life of pig number 100,704. If this particular
pig is born on a conventional farm when the legislation is passed, it is
unlikely that the legislation will even apply to her treatment while she is
alive, because such laws have long phase-in periods.[383] On the other hand,
if the pig will be born years after the legislation passes, then it is crucial to
observe that whether she is born at all into what is (still) a life of grotesque
suffering and premature death will have at least as much (and probably far
more) to do with consumer demand for animal products as it does with
the particular regulations in place at the time.

If consumers continue to demand animal products, then conventional farms will continue to breed domesticated animals into existence
for slaughter. And even in the presence of rules that prohibit some of the
many inhumane practices on farms, farmers will routinely engage in noncompliance.[384] Why would there be so much noncompliance? Consider
what we are asking of an animal farmer when we demand that he place
"his" animals into larger enclosures or that he otherwise provide more
"humane" treatment of them. We are conveying the following message:

You are a property owner, and your property is the large number of
animals (literally "live stock") you are raising for slaughter. As you know,
these animals experience fear and pain, and we therefore ask you to refrain
from inflicting the enumerated sorts of injury. We do, however, permit
you to inflict other extreme forms of injury on them, as we understand
that it is necessary to do so as part of your business. We also permit you
to slaughter them when they are still very young and to do so in a manner
that will best preserve the post-mortem edibility of their flesh.

To a person whose job it is to bring large numbers of animals into
existence for purposes of using them and sending them to slaughter, this
message lacks coherence. Whatever suffering I inflict on these animals,
thinks the farmer, is in the service of economically creating my product,
whether it be meat, poultry, fish, dairy, eggs, leather, wool, or whatever

it happens to be. I am not a sadist, any more than the people buying my products are sadists, so I will not inflict pointless suffering. There is always a point—creating a quality product for an affordable price.

From the farmer's perspective: You, the regulator, are telling me not to inflict particular suffering that *you* deem pointless, but you are less knowledgeable than I am about what my business requires and far less invested in ensuring the most efficient production methods possible. Therefore, you make arbitrary choices between permissible and prohibited violence against animals. In fact, some of the regulations you hope to impose would actually worsen the lives of the very animals you seek to protect, all to satisfy consumers who want to think they can have their cake and eat it too.[385]

It is difficult to answer such accusations. The reality of breeding and keeping and killing billions of animals necessarily involves crowding, filth, fear, and tremendous suffering. So long as human beings demand animal products in the numbers that we do, it will therefore be "necessary" for those supplying our demand to do grotesquely inhumane things to sentient animals. Regulatory measures will accordingly be largely arbitrary—by requiring substitution of one cruelty for another—or unenforced, because true enforcement of meaningful regulations would carry costs that would frustrate consumers.[386]

You may be thinking that perhaps it still makes sense to support "humane" legislation, even if it is not especially effective because it is too modest or will yield noncompliance (or both). It may seem that at its worst, such legislation does nothing and can therefore be no worse than actually doing nothing. In fact, however, such regulation does do something detrimental. It contributes to a misleading picture of animal agriculture for consumers who might have considered veganism: it tells the public that regulations are in place to ensure that the animal products they consume are "ethically raised."

In addition to doing little to alter actual conditions on the ground at factory farms, then, the regulations can serve to reinforce demand for animal products by providing a public relations boost to the industry. Consumers troubled by what they view as outrageous cruelty toward animals may feel less troubled and thus less inclined to consider opting out. In this way, welfare-oriented regulations and the accompanying publicity can serve as an opiate, offering soothing narratives to quiet the conscience and keep the kill line moving.

The Temple Grandin Phenomenon

To understand this dynamic at work, consider the "Temple Grandin" phenomenon. Temple Grandin is a woman who has autism but who has, despite her challenges, succeeded in becoming a doctor of animal science and a professor at Colorado State University. She is also a consultant to the livestock industry and has designed about half of the slaughterhouses in which farmed cattle meet their deaths.[387] As a celebrated expert in animal behavior, Grandin has worked with the livestock industry to make it less expensive to slaughter animals, in part by reducing the amount of physical resistance animals offer as they approach their deaths.

In Grandin's view, her slaughterhouse innovations protect animals from suffering, and her view has received relatively uncritical acceptance and praise by American writers aware of her work.[388] A made-for-television film reflected and reinforced Grandin's image as a remarkable and humane woman who has a special gift—in virtue of her autism—for understanding the needs and feelings of animals, an ability that she uses to ensure that animals on farms live and die without undue pain.[389] Grandin has said that "animals could have more than just a low-stress life and a quick, painless death. I wish animals could have a *good* life, too, with something useful to do. I think we owe them that."[390] She describes the consumption of animals as a regrettable but somehow unavoidable feature of human existence.[391]

Why does Grandin believe that slaughtering animals as a food source is legitimate? So far as I have been able to ascertain, she does not explain this claim but simply assumes it to be true.[392] Even someone who assumes the legitimacy of using animals as a food source, however, eventually runs into the reality that farmed animals in this country *do not*, by any stretch of the imagination, experience the decent life or painless death that Grandin says is their due. She surely knows this, because she has visited the places where animals live and die.[393] Yet Grandin assists the industries from which people buy animal products in making the process more profitable and more palatable to consumers who share her stated view that animals are entitled to live free of human cruelty.

In an interview with Terry Gross aired on the NPR radio show Fresh Air,[394] Gross asks Grandin whether there is something peculiar or dissonant in her trying to design "humane" slaughterhouses, given that animals are at these places, after all, to be slaughtered. Is there not something contradictory about the juxtaposition of humaneness, on the one hand, and slaughter for food, on the other?

Grandin responds that one might as easily suggest that it is contradictory to provide morphine and other painkillers to hospital patients who are dying of a terminal illness. Since they are dying anyway, Grandin proposes, one might just as easily describe as pointless any effort to reduce their suffering, but she does not see it that way. She accordingly understands, by her own report, that even though animals will be slaughtered, it is still worthwhile to keep them as comfortable as one can while they are still alive.

Grandin's answer and her analogy to palliative care for terminal patients have a surface plausibility that dissipates upon closer inspection. If we could readily cure people dying of terminal illnesses in the hospital, then it would indeed be bizarre for us instead to give the people morphine and watch them die. Providing palliative care is a benefit to terminal patients only because we cannot save their lives. Similarly, if a nonhuman animal were dying of an illness and could not be cured, we would do him a kindness by providing painkillers or even a painless death as an alternative to his suffering.

A slaughterhouse, however, is very different from a hospital for terminally ill patients or a veterinary office where a beloved, suffering animal companion might be euthanized. A slaughterhouse is a place at which young and often baby animals have their throats cut. The animals there are not dying of an incurable illness. Someone is deliberately killing them.

To compare young animals on their way to slaughter to hospital patients dying of terminal illnesses is to deny the possibility of refraining from slaughtering animals at all. It is to offer a dangerous illusion in which a person who performs work to enhance the productivity and efficiency of animal farming—work for which she is well compensated by the livestock industry[395]—can successfully pose as a champion for animals.[396]

As the daughter of two Holocaust survivors, I recognize that Holocaust analogies are invariably fraught. Nonetheless, I found it illuminating to learn that in determining how to carry out the "Final Solution" against the Jews, Adolph Hitler inquired about what the most "humane" method of exterminating them would be.[397] Told that poison gas would be the most humane, he responded that poison gas it would be. He was evidently eager to make extermination of the Jewish people as "humane" as possible, a goal that seems incomprehensible but that we might best understand as an effort to reduce the psychological distress of those participating in implementing the process rather than as an effort to protect the actual interests of the victims of the Nazi death camps.[398]

As was true in the case of the gas chambers, the reality of animal slaughter is not humane at all. And how could it be? When the goal is to take the lives of millions or billions of innocents at minimal expense, the means cannot be compassionate in any sense of the term. Given this reality, attempts to eliminate one or another cruelty inflicted upon animals on intensive farms will tend to serve the industry, rather than the victims of the industry, by calming the public conscience that might otherwise lead consumers to withdraw their support.

Putting aside the real-world impact of "humane" legislation on consumers of animal products, it is also morally significant that when we support "reforms" in the industries that breed, mutilate, and slaughter animals, we implicitly endorse the legitimacy of breeding, mutilating, and slaughtering animals. That is, debates about whether a particular painful practice is or is not "necessary" to the industry and therefore acceptable take as their point of departure the underlying "necessity" and legitimacy of the industry itself. If one has to forcibly inseminate dairy cows and then take their babies from their side to slaughter, in order to allow for the economically viable production of dairy milk, cheese, butter, and ice cream, then those practices may continue, no matter how plainly cruel they are.

In other words, by advocating the elimination of some nonessential cruel practices, we implicitly lend legitimacy to the exploitation, injury, and slaughter of animals through practices that *are* deemed "essential." We are thereby accepting cruelty and slaughter by identifying as "gratuitous" only a small subset of individual examples of cruelty that does not measurably contribute to productivity. We essentially outlaw only "wasteful" torture and slaughter, an approach that further entrenches an understanding of sentient animals as commodities that should be profitably and economically exploited.

As Gary Francione has argued, animal welfare reforms serve to make animal agriculture more efficient and socially acceptable, and efficiency and social acceptance are both more likely to contribute to the expansion than to the abolition of animal agriculture.[399] Rather than support harm to animals by buying flesh and secretions from Wendy's rather than from Kentucky Fried Chicken—if the former but not the latter uses eggs from "cage-free" hens[400]—we can withdraw support from animal slaughter altogether by refusing to consume animal products from any supplier.

The Fallacy of "Humane" or Organic Farms

A second form of the "humane farming" alternative to veganism represents a smaller-scale phenomenon in which consumers consciously seek out animal products from vendors who claim to reject the factory-farming model of production. Such consumers might go out of their way to obtain animal products from farmers' markets or from one of the very few farms that truly run small operations at which animals receive treatment that approximates what their ancestors might have experienced prior to the advent of intensive animal agriculture. At such farms, animals may go outside, graze, and enjoy one another's company in the sunshine. They may fulfill their natural instincts and avoid having to live in a filthy, smelly, dark hell, waiting to die.

On a few farms, even slaughter may be somewhat less grotesque than the ordinary process, because animals may be killed one at a time, not on a kill line, and each one may be surrounded by the faces of familiar people, rather than those of frightening strangers, during the slaughter process.[401] If I buy a share in such a farm or otherwise support it by purchasing its animal products, have I not helped the animals? After all, I could have spent my money buying products from, and thus supporting the work of, factory farms, where animals spend every day of their lives suffering horrendous pain and deprivation. I have instead moved my money to what truly is a more "humane" operation, and with my demand have helped shift some of the supply from factory farms to gentler farms, right?

I feel ambivalent in answering this question. I certainly share the view that more suffering is worse than less suffering, and it does appear that a tiny minority of farms really may offer a setting in which animals spend less than their entire lives feeling terrified and helpless as they suffer constant injury and deprivation. There are several reasons, however, why I do not view such farms and the purchase of animal products from them as a constructive path for those who want to reduce their participation in hurting animals.

First, when we purchase animal products from such reduced-torture farms, we adopt the mindset of Temple Grandin when she says that slaughtering animals less cruelly is a kindness, comparable to offering morphine to terminal hospital patients. The mindset is one of resignation. It treats the suffering and slaughter of animals at human hands as inevitable. But why spend money to support reduced torture settings when we can become vegan and reject torture altogether?

If you had to choose between killing a zebra by stoning her to death and killing her by shooting her in the head, you would likely choose to shoot rather than to stone her. But the choice is a false one, because you do not need to kill the zebra at all. It is only compared to an even more horrifying alternative that shooting a zebra can take on the appearance of an ethical or compassionate choice.

By way of analogy, consider the question whether you would prefer to execute an *innocent* person by drawing and quartering or by guillotine. If these were truly the only two choices, the guillotine would obviously be preferable. Yet given the choice between one of these two methods of execution and no execution at all, the guillotine rightly appears far less merciful. Focusing on different methods of administering the death penalty to an innocent person, however, effectively distracts us from the fundamental injustice of executing an innocent person *at all*, no matter what the method is.

On every farm, even the most "humane," animals suffer unanesthetized mutilations, pain, the loss of beloved companions, and ultimately slaughter, at the point when support for their continued existence as living animals would cost the farmer more money, on net, than slaughter would. This is not primarily the farmer's fault—no one can earn a living by spending more than he earns—but it is useful to keep in mind when we are invited to imagine that a place that breeds and slaughters sentient beings is somehow a sanctuary for animals who can now live in peace.[402] Consuming animal products from any source supports the infliction of great suffering and slaughter on animals.

The Betrayal of Animals

A second reason not to consume the products of even the most "humane" of animal farms concerns betrayal and loss. A chicken or pig or cow who has enjoyed a relatively peaceful life may come to trust humans in general and the specific people who have fed and cared for her in particular. This animal does not know that she was brought into the world to be used and slaughtered. Her experience has perhaps taught her instead that the people around her are nurturing friends who seek what is best for her and will always ensure her comfort and safety from harm.

When an animal who has lived a relatively good life is brought to slaughter, whether at a mobile slaughter unit, by transportation to a slaughterhouse, or in a barn on the premises,[403] the journey represents a profound betrayal of the animal's trust. The people who had been acting as her nurturers have now become her killers. She goes willingly with the people she trusts, only to face a premature end to her life, because even on a "happy" farm, the animals are slaughtered long before they would otherwise have died of old age or illness.

I attended a lecture a few years ago at which the speaker, Victoria Moran, author of *Main Street Vegan*,[404] described her visit to a slaughterhouse years earlier,[405] when security at slaughterhouses was looser than it is today.[406] Moran was at first struck by the cold temperature (perhaps intended to prevent the onset of decomposition in the animals after they were killed) and the enormous quantity of blood on the floors. Despite the floor drains, she found herself standing in a pool of blood reaching up to her ankles. She felt overwhelmed by the sounds of the screaming animals and by the smells that enveloped her. She said she was unable to experience even empathy for the animals because she was emotionally flooded by the extremity of what she was witnessing, a freezing hell worthy of Dante.

In this state of numbness, Moran noticed a steer who looked different from the others. This steer appeared to be healthy, and Moran suspected that his life until that point had been on a family farm at which he had received relatively kind treatment. Here, in the slaughterhouse, however, the steer was terrified and was attempting without success to back out of the room. One of the people working at the slaughterhouse noticed the steer and acted as though the two had met before.

The worker looked directly at the animal and whistled to him, as one might whistle to a family dog. Upon hearing the whistle and seeing a friendly face, the steer ran toward the man, as Moran watched. She then saw the man swiftly slaughter the steer. Only moments after he had been trying to escape the kill floor, the steer was reduced to a huge slab of bloody muscle hanging on a hook, its head and skin removed. It was then that Moran wept for the steer who had innocently placed his trust in a man.

In a seemingly very different story that made the news a number of years ago, a woman encountered a friendly cat on the street and beckoned to her.[407] The cat approached the woman. After patting the cat, the woman picked her up and threw her into a dumpster. The cat's owner subsequently posted a video on the internet of what the woman had done to the cat, and the post went viral.[408] The reaction of the audience was swift and unforgiving.[409] People were outraged that someone would harm an innocent cat, and threatening rhetoric followed.[410]

One interesting analysis of these events pointed out the parallel between the cat who was thrown into the dumpster and the animals raised on "humane" farms.[411] In both situations, people have treated an animal with relative kindness up until the end, when they treat her life as expendable:

> For people who believe it's okay to kill or harm an animal as long as it was treated humanely prior to its death, Mary's [the woman who threw the cat in the dumpster] comment that "it's only a cat"—should resonate. After all, the cat had a good life . . . she had been treated well by her owners, probably from her earliest memory. That would explain her trusting nature toward Ms. Bale. Instead, though, a Facebook page with 30,000 members was recently removed due to death threats against her. Police are now guarding her home due to the anger that she has incited.
>
> Clearly, [the outrage is] really not about how the cat was treated prior to being put in a trash bin. It's not that Lola the kitty was able to roam free (her undoing, by the way), or chase bugs in the sunlight before this incident . . . . Mary petted the cat before tossing her into the trash. Yet, somehow this just doesn't make people feel better about it.
>
> Now consider the humanely reared animals that people are preferentially consuming. Perhaps the farmer is petting his calves and piggies every day, and they are allowed to frolic in green meadows, just like in children's books . . . does that really make us feel better when the time comes to lead these animals, literally, like lambs to the slaughter?[412]

One possible account of people's outrage might emphasize the fact that Mary Bale did not own the cat in question and therefore inflicted harm on the cat's rightful owners. I suspect, however, that the intensity of outrage reflected something other than the view that the cat's owners—and not a stranger—ought to have retained a monopoly on the privilege of throwing their cat into the trash. People's comments appeared to express horror on behalf of the cat herself, and the reaction would thus likely have been essentially the same if it had turned out that the cat belonged to Ms. Bale.[413]

The harm of such betrayal is salient for animals who have received "humane" treatment, because such animals may not know to anticipate, and therefore cannot prepare themselves for, the deliberate and lethal violence that every one of them will face after a relatively short life. They are treated in an exceedingly small minority of farms as though their lives and their relationships with other animals really do matter, as though they have inherent value as individual beings with preferences and fears. But then it turns out that they were mistaken in placing their trust in people. They misjudged the intentions of those around them as those of caregivers, when in fact their friends were actually their predators, more deadly even than the lion or the wolf, who kills only a small fraction of the prey she espies.

In Kazuo Ishiguro's novel *Never Let Me Go*, the narrator describes a world in which some human beings ("donors") are brought into existence through a cloning process for the purpose of supplying organs for other human beings in need of those organs.[414] Eventually, each of the donors will die, either on an operating table (for example, when a heart is removed for transplant) or due to complications that follow a less lethal donation. The narrator of the story is herself among the donors, though she has not yet begun her donations when the story begins and is still acting as a "carer" for another donor.

We learn from the narrator that she grew up in a special setting in which the children were treated with warmth and care, and were educated and given the opportunity to create art, initially ignorant of their status as resources to be mined by people within the community of donation recipients. Even as the children learned their ultimate fate, they heard a rumor that if two donors fell in love, they would receive an amnesty from having to provide donations, a freedom to pursue their romantic relationship.

It turns out that this more "humane" approach to raising and educating the donors had been controversial among those in charge of the donors. Some worried that it would give false hope in what was truly a hopeless situation and would cultivate an erroneous understanding by donors of their true place in the world. In reading the book, one has the sense of two independent harms committed against the people known as "donors."

One harm is the act of subjecting everyone in the group to involuntary surgeries and ultimately to death as a means of servicing the needs of others. A second harm is the betrayal involved in raising an individual to feel loved and valued and then slaughtering her as a resource in the end. The most "humane" farms commit this kind of betrayal.

A farmed animal may or may not understand that she has been betrayed by her owner. But even if she does not appreciate what has occurred, there is betrayal, all the same. The most trusting and guileless victim may not judge her killer or even know what is happening to her in the end.

What defines a betrayal is the cultivation of trust and affection, followed by a decision to treat the life of the trusting individual as a disposable commodity to be subordinated to the interests of others. An infant who sleeps calmly and happily in a nurse's arms is thus betrayed when the nurse decides to smother him in his sleep, even if he cannot understand or appreciate the treachery that befell him.

Killing an animal who has lived a comfortable, healthy, and pleasurable life takes away something that was of great value to the animal. When I watch footage from modern conventional farms, my reaction, in addition to sorrow and frustration, is to want to euthanize the animals to spare them the unending suffering and pain that they face. Slaughter is, of course, not euthanasia,[415] but death of a certain sort might seem a more humane alternative available to most of the animals living in a modern livestock factory.

In watching animals enjoying themselves, by contrast, on a farm at which they are nurtured and treated with kindness prior to slaughter, my reaction would be to want to allow the animals to live. If they are healthy and joyful, the last thing I would want is to ask someone to cut their throats and sell me parts of their bodies. Though slaughter harms every animal, it arguably takes the most from the animals who had, up until then, been enjoying their lives. I am not, of course, proposing that it is therefore merciful to treat animals with greater cruelty. I am saying that although treating them well is better than treating them badly, the slaughter of well-treated animals at the end imposes an even greater deprivation on those animals.

The Harm of Specialty Animal Products

Beyond the suffering and slaughter that animals endure because we purchase their parts and secretions, even if we do so from the most "humane"
operation, there is an independent cost to purchasing these sorts of animal products. Such purchases serve to reinforce for those around us the
notion that consuming animal products is somehow an important part of
living the good life, when it truly is not. Absorbing this false lesson, even
those people who prefer to patronize "humane" farms might purchase
the products of conventionally raised and slaughtered animals when the
"humane" alternative is unavailable. In the process, they might come to
see the "humane" animal products as an affirmatively charitable act toward
animals (akin to rescue) instead of participation in possibly-less-harm-
ful-but-still-horrible violence against animals.

Perhaps more importantly, the well-to-do people who can afford to
buy the parts and secretions of allegedly well-treated animals set a social
example of what is desirable food, and people who cannot afford such
luxury then view meat, dairy, and eggs from factory farms as the closest
approximation. Consuming specialty animal products—whatever the
reality of their allegedly "humane" origins—can accordingly generate
greater enthusiasm and perceived necessity for factory-farmed products, rather than shifting demand from one kind of violence against
animals toward another, possibly less extreme form of violence. Moreover, because it uses more land and more time per animal, the more
"humane" treatment of animals slated for slaughter will take an even
greater toll on the environment than "standard" animal farming[416] and
thus could not occur on a scale that would affordably satisfy existing
demand for animal products.[417]

"Humane" animal products may seem like a step in the right direction, but they carry significant drawbacks and may result in even more
suffering, rather than less. The actual lives of animals whose flesh and
secretions are labeled "cage free," "free-range," and "humanely raised" frequently bear little relation to the plain meaning of these phrases. Much
of the labeled food comes from factory farms with slight modifications
that may or may not reduce the amount of suffering that their inhabitants
endure. And even the few farms that treat animals with measurably less
abuse still carry out routine mutilations that would qualify as torture if

inflicted on companion animals; they still separate mothers and babies; and, significantly, they still slaughter each animal long before she would otherwise have died of old age.

There is, however, one ray of light in the quest for "humane" animal products. The quest is itself a sign of human progress toward an aversion to violence against animals, and it evidences a desire to improve the lot of the sentient beings who share our planet. Given the sadism of earlier eras, when people would regularly gather for public spectacles of animal and human torture, the fact that large numbers of people are motivated to try to spare nonhuman animals the suffering and pain of factory farming should be understood as a welcome evolution in human consciousness.[418]

But if the "humane" movement reflects a laudable attitudinal change, the concrete measures it offers are a disappointment. They leave in place tremendous and growing violence against animals, and they offer little in the way of improvement while falsely appeasing the commendable desire to do better by our fellow earthlings. We can best help farmed animals as consumers by consuming food, clothing, and other materials that do not rely on or emerge from an animal farm or a slaughterhouse. It is through this simple, joyous, and healthful choice that each of us can help close the slaughterhouse doors and look back on "humane slaughter" and "humane animal farming" as the contradictions in terms that they truly are.

12

IF WE ALL BECOME VEGAN, WON'T FARMED ANIMALS DISAPPEAR?

The argument I address in this chapter takes various forms, each of which amounts to a claim that the animals whom we farm have actually benefited from animal farming. If not for our consumption of domesticated animals, farmers would have no reason to bring the animals into existence, and there would eventually be no more of them. Therefore, the domesticated animals who do exist have consumers to thank for their lives, however brief and however painful.

The alternative to consuming farmed animals, in this view, is not "saving" or "sparing" their lives but is instead bringing about their extinction. Asserting that extinguishing domesticated species cannot represent a kindness to animals, those who take this view argue that the one way in which we can ensure perpetuation of domesticated species—by consuming animal products—is therefore, necessarily, the most generous thing we can do for the animals.

Why Domestic Animals Exist

One form of this argument emphasizes specialty domesticated breeds, including particular kinds of "heritage" pigs,[419] sheep,[420] turkeys,[421] and other animals. A former high school teacher of mine expressed ambivalence about consumption of specialty breeds, without which such breeds would cease to exist. He gave the example of a rare pig breed in which the pigs are very gentle and friendly and quite different in some respects from other types of domesticated pigs. He noted that it is only because some number of consumers enjoy eating the flesh of such pigs that a specialty farmer can afford the time and effort involved in breeding and caring for these impressive, intelligent, and charming animals.

In keeping with this sentiment, Peter Singer, the author of *Animal Liberation*, has asserted that if an animal has led a relatively decent life, then it is better for that animal to have existed than not to have existed, a conclusion that he believes supports the consumption of "humane" animal products.[422]

Although some commentators have articulated this claim exclusively to defend the consumption of specialty breeds, it works equally well as an argument for consuming the output of animal farming more generally.[423] Some contend that of all the species on earth, the domesticated breeds as a group, and domestic chickens in particular, represent the greatest evolutionary success story. Unlike so many other species of animals, who have become extinct or whose numbers have dwindled due to the scarcity of food and/or the proliferation of natural predators, domesticated and farmed animals have been fruitful and have spread their offspring throughout the globe, all because humans want to eat and wear them and their products.

There are at present, for example, approximately 19 billion domesticated chickens living,[424] three times the number of humans on the planet.[425] Within this framework, farmed animals dominate the globe numerically, precisely because people choose to consume their flesh and secretions. The consumption of animal-derived products may thus appear to be the farmed animals' lifeline.

The argument is an elegant one. It takes what might seem like a counterintuitive proposition—that eating the flesh and secretions of animals is good for animals—and invokes logic and human nature to make the paradoxical appear inescapably true. By contrast to claims that attempt to isolate the act of eating animal products from the slaughter and cruelty that precede it, this argument not only acknowledges but celebrates the important link between demand and supply. If we did not eat fried eggs with a side of bacon, fewer chickens and pigs would be slaughtered, but that is only because fewer chickens and pigs would be brought into existence in the first place.

Almost by definition, a bred domesticated animal exists because humans want to own and use that animal for some purpose. If humans no longer wanted to use, and thus no longer paid farmers to breed and slaughter, that kind of animal, the logical consequence would be the extinction of her breed.

As a point of contrast, if people chose to stop consuming a non-domesticated (a.k.a. "wild" or "free-living") breed, the animal could continue to live and reproduce, absent an extermination program.[426] Non-domesticated animals do not depend on humans for food and shelter in the way that domesticated animals do. The latter's dependency therefore means that someone must generally be motivated to breed and raise them as a prerequisite to their continued life on earth. And what stronger motive could there be for such breeding than the gustatory, sartorial, and financial?

Before criticizing this argument, I want to acknowledge the aspect of it with which I agree. I concur in the factual assertion that consumers' demand for the products of animal agriculture causally accounts for the proliferation of domesticated animals. Few, I suspect, would seriously dispute the central role of consumer demand in driving the astonishingly large population of domesticated animals relative to their non-domesticated cousins.

Therefore, if the members of a species necessarily benefitted from having large numbers of their species in existence, then consumers of animal products would indeed be conferring the benefit of existence on billions of domesticated animals every year. In disagreeing with the notion that consuming animal-derived products helps animals, I therefore dispute the underlying premise that bringing an individual into existence confers a benefit upon that individual.

The Hypothetical Case of Betty and Joan

To appreciate our common understanding that bringing someone into existence does not itself benefit the one who exists, consider the hypothetical case of a woman, Betty, who monitors her own fertility and knows that she has the greatest odds of becoming pregnant if she has sex with her husband today. She asks her friend Joan for advice about what to do, because she is unsure of the moral implications of her actions of either having sex or refraining from having sex today, assuming that she and her husband choose not to use contraception. What should Joan advise her to do?

Joan might want to have some additional information before giving Betty any advice on the question. Does Betty want to have a child? Does her husband want to have a child? Are the circumstances of Betty's life optimal for raising a child?

Imagine, however, that, without knowing anything about Betty, about her husband, or about her current situation, Joan insisted that Betty had a moral obligation to the potential person she might conceive to bring it into existence, and that if Betty decided not to have sex on her most fertile day of the month, Betty would thereby be wrongfully depriving the particular child she would have conceived of the benefit of that existence.

What would we think if Joan made this argument to Betty? We would likely find it unconvincing. Betty does not owe it to her potential child to bring it into existence. By virtue of its not yet existing, even on the most socially conservative view of when human life begins, we do not view the potential child, pre-conception, as currently having any entitlement to come into existence. In Joan's place, we could therefore comfortably counsel Betty to avoid having sex and becoming pregnant that day for any of a variety of reasons, including Betty's or her husband's preferences or the family's physical or financial health.

Most of us would probably reject the notion that, in making her decision, Betty has an obligation to take into account the loss of life to a potential person of having never been conceived. There is no loss, because a nonexistent individual does not have an affirmative interest in coming into existence.

Now assume that Betty comes to you instead of to Joan, and that Betty tells you she will go ahead and have sex with her husband today, because she wants to have the opportunity to donate a heart to someone suffering from heart failure. Confused, you ask Betty what she means by this, and Betty responds that she plans to conceive and bear a child with the aim of raising that child to the age of six and then donating the child's heart to someone who needs it. You tell Betty at this point that it would be a terrible thing for Betty to kill her six-year-old child to provide another person with a heart. Imagine that in response, Betty tries to reassure you that she will take good care of her child up until his or her sixth birthday.

Suppose now that Betty adds that she will not have a child *except* as a future heart donor. If you succeed in persuading her not to donate her child's heart at the age of six, she warns you, then she will simply refrain from having sex and becoming pregnant at all. She adds for good measure that you would then be depriving her child of having any life at all—a good six years of life—in your misguided effort to avoid depriving the child of life past the age of six. In the process, she observes, you would also be preventing her from saving the life of someone in need of a heart donation.

In making these points, will she have persuaded you that the right thing to do is for her to have sex, become pregnant, and use her six-year-old child as an organ donor? I suspect not. To avoid conceiving at all does no harm to the unconceived, but to kill a six-year-old child to harvest her heart does a grave harm to the child. As between the two options, there is no moral contest.

Now assume that Betty fails to heed your advice and goes on to conceive and bear a child, a daughter, planning as she does so to donate the child's heart at the age of six. Does the moral calculus change now? Does the fact that the child would not have existed in the absence of Betty's plan to donate her heart somehow redeem the plan? Certainly not.

Even if the child loves her short life and enjoys every minute of it, killing her remains grossly immoral. Indeed, for reasons discussed in the last chapter, killing someone who loves her life may inflict a greater harm than killing someone whose life consists of relentless misery.

Though the people who knew Betty's child might be grateful for even the short life that the child had, killing her would still represent an unjustified act of undeserved violence against *her*. To bring someone into the world does not confer a "benefit" on that living creature that provides moral "capital" on which those who brought her into the world may now draw to kill or otherwise harm her to serve another's ends. Ordinarily, in fact, we hold someone who brings another into existence to higher standards, obliging her to protect the other's interests, rather than extending a special license on the part of the "creators" to disregard the interests of their creations. That is why parents—no matter what motivated them to reproduce—acquire special responsibilities toward their children, not only to refrain from harming them but also to take affirmative steps to care for and protect them.

It follows that when an animal exists solely because our taste for animal-derived foods and consumer items motivated a farmer to breed the animal into existence, we have obligations of care toward that animal that we do not have with respect to a wild animal who is free and in whose creation we played no role. Domestication thus generates a debt that we owe—rather than an entitlement that we have earned the right to exploit—vis-à-vis domesticated animals.

When Large Numbers Do and Do Not Signal "Success"

Notwithstanding what I have said here, the intuition that chickens, cows, and pigs have in some way "succeeded" may remain intuitively appealing to some readers. While many animal species have become extinct or have neared extinction, including relatives of the domesticated breeds, the animals from whom we take our food and clothing have numerically flourished, haven't they?

First, it is useful to distinguish the concept of flourishing through large numbers from the related notion that an individual receives a benefit by having come into existence. It might be inaccurate to say that a parent "benefits" a child by conceiving him and bringing him into the world, but it could nonetheless be correct to say that existing members of a group benefit from the large number of others who belong to the same group.

An analogy to race and ethnicity may be instructive here. After the European Holocaust of World War II, some Jewish people felt obliged to have more children than they otherwise might have had, to "make up for" those who perished at the Nazis' hands.[427] It is obviously not possible to replace one person who has been murdered simply by creating another person, but there is a sense in which the Jewish people after the Holocaust felt injured not only by Hitler's murderous violence itself but also by the numerical consequences of that violence for Jews as a group: the Jewish population was far smaller than it had previously been. To the extent that Jews responded to this state of affairs by having many children and thereby increasing their number, this reaction would appear to confirm the view that members of a group experience as a benefit the expansion of the group's population.

I find this notion compelling, in part because my own family lost many of its members during the Holocaust. All four of my grandparents and six of my seven aunts and uncles were murdered, and I grew up with very few relatives as a result. Had there been more of "us," I would have felt personally enriched by "our" numerousness. For reasons I will now explain, however, this concept does not work as well when we try to extend it to domesticated animal species.

Animals who live on farms—places that are essentially breeding, holding, and slaughter facilities—do not derive satisfaction from the fact that they belong to a species with many exemplars. Their experience of having large numbers of conspecifics, in fact, is likely to be one of crowding, shared deprivation, and loss. Unlike human beings who decide to "grow" the number of people in their respective groups, animals do not have the opportunity to decide anything about their reproductive lives.

A dairy cow who gives birth does so because she has been forcibly impregnated on a "rape rack" to stimulate her production of milk for humans to consume. Repeat pregnancies and constant lactation cause painful conditions like mastitis[428] and the breakdown of the dairy cow's body, leading quite a few of them to become "downers"—animals who cannot even walk to their deaths—by the time they reach the slaughterhouse.[429]

Like other mammals, a dairy cow craves the company of her baby.[430] Yet the farmer takes this most treasured member of her species from her side, despite her bellows and cries. Just about every farmed animal mother eventually loses to the slaughterhouse every one of her babies and everyone else to whom she has bonded. Any awareness in farmed animals of their own great numbers is thus likely to come mainly from the grotesque crowding in farm facilities.[431]

A high rate of reproduction may be empowering to human beings who choose it as a means of building their own communities. Being forced to reproduce, however, is quite another matter, a fact that may help explain why Americans who are otherwise uncomfortable with abortion typically favor a rape exception to any proposed prohibition.[432] For domesticated animals, reproduction is a source of bottomless misery, both because the animals are forced into reproductive service and because everyone who matters to them, including each of their offspring, is removed from their side and destroyed.

It is therefore inaccurate to describe the numerical proliferation of domesticated animals as a benefit to those animals. Unlike human groups with large numbers of people, the astonishingly high numbers of sheep, pigs, chickens, and other animals who meet their deaths at the slaughterhouse do not translate into better lives for them. On the contrary, their lives and deaths become measurably worse as they are bred by the billions for our use.

Survival of the Least "Fit"

To see why the numerical expansion of farmed animals in existence today does not signify "success," it is useful to note the distinction between an individual living being and that individual's DNA. We can trace most of our individual characteristics in one way or another to our genetic endowment. Different environments and experiences, of course, lead to differing gene expression, but the codes on our chromosomes have an undeniably large impact on our lives.

Due to natural selection, DNA tends to be biased in favor of reproduction. Over time, DNA manages to survive best when it gives rise to traits and behavior that create more exemplars of the same DNA. Conversely, if an organism's DNA leads to characteristics or behaviors that reduce or altogether preclude reproduction, then there will be fewer or no exemplars of that DNA in the future.

DNA's bias toward its own replication has, within and among species, meant that when one species is numerically dominant relative to another species, it is ordinarily sensible to conclude that the dominant species' characteristics have made it particularly "fit" for the environment that it inhabits. If there are many times more green butterflies than white butterflies in a particular area, for example, it seems logical to infer that having a green hue has been beneficial for the butterflies in that area, while having a white hue has not.

Domesticated animals, and thus the DNA that gives rise to them, also have undergone evolution, but their evolution has altered them in a manner that differs significantly from the process by which natural selection ordinarily occurs. Take the example of turkeys. Ordinarily, turkeys living in the wild will benefit from genetic endowments and changes that make it easier for them to flee from predators, better able to find food for themselves, and more attractive to members of the opposite sex than their competitors. These traits not only enhance a wild turkey's odds of reproduction, but they simultaneously, and not coincidentally, enhance her quality of life as well, facilitating her ability to acquire the things she needs to avoid pain and an early death, either of which could cut short her opportunities for reproduction.

In the case of domesticated turkeys, however, the traits that will make one turkey more likely than others to reproduce do not coincide with the sorts of qualities that would make her life comfortable, pleasant, or long. The selected traits will instead have almost everything to do with pleasing the humans who raise, breed, slaughter, and eat turkeys. Such "desirable" traits include an extremely rapid growth rate, so that a turkey may be slaughtered earlier in her life and thereby provide savings on upkeep costs, a tendency to accumulate a large quantity of flesh, along with white skin and feathers.[433]

As a result, an overwhelming majority of the domesticated turkeys living in the United States and elsewhere are unable to fly and perch—natural behaviors that turkeys instinctually crave[434]—and their skeletons cannot easily support their enormous bodies, leading to difficulty walking, and an insatiable appetite that yields heart disease and strokes[435] as well as arthritis.[436] Because of domesticated turkeys' deliberately-bred physiology, moreover, they are physically unable to copulate with one another. Like many other domesticated species, they are bred through a process of forcible insemination, a process that—in the case of almost all domesticated turkeys—is the only available option for reproduction.

Domesticated turkeys are thus poorly equipped to perform some of the most basic functions of a bird—flying, walking, and mating. And though they exist in large numbers, they are permitted to live only a short time before slaughter, which they typically undergo when they are under six months old, even on "organic" farms.[437]

The egg-laying hen provides another illustration of "survival of the least fit" in the context of domestication. As discussed in chapter 4, the domesticated hen has evolved to produce so many eggs that she develops debilitating and excruciating physical conditions as a result.

Those animals who exist in large numbers because people have owned and bred them are quite differently situated from those who have multiplied through their own voluntary mating choices, even apart from the deliberately-bred characteristics that cause animals suffering and an early death. If given a choice, most human beings, I suspect, would refrain from procreating if they knew in advance that every one of their children would be taken away from them, mutilated, and killed before even reaching maturity.

We can understand the difference between being numerous and being "successful" when we consider that in some places like Barbados in the late seventeenth century, prior to the abolition of human slavery, the population of enslaved people outnumbered the population of free people.[438] Yet no one today would seriously argue that the slaves were therefore "benefiting" from slavery or that they were more "successful" than the group of people who owned them. We need to understand numbers in context.

There is one thing that does "succeed" when a species' numbers expand, and that is the DNA associated with the species in question. When there are almost twenty billion domesticated chickens living on this planet at any given time,[439] we can say that the DNA of the domesticated chicken has achieved a victory. Similarly, if there is a species of wild bird that no longer inhabits the earth, then the DNA of that species has undergone a catastrophic loss.

Species DNA, however, is not the same as the individual sentient beings who hold the DNA. We can therefore distinguish the success of DNA from the well-being of the individuals whose DNA has succeeded. This may seem like an obvious point, but much confusion results from a failure to differentiate between an individual and her DNA.

From her own perspective, an individual—whether she is human or nonhuman—has needs and wants and experiences that reflect a mix of joy and suffering in the life that she leads. It is this life, and the interactions that she has with others, that matter to the individual animal. From others' perspective, however—particularly others who may hope to use the beings in question as resources—it is DNA rather than the experiences of any given individual that matters most. Because our legal system treats animals as resources for our use and our enjoyment, it focuses primarily on their DNA rather than on their individuality. The Endangered Species Act[440] provides a good example of this focus.

On its face, the Endangered Species Act (ESA) may strike people as furthering animal rights, because it prohibits or limits the killing of animals who belong to endangered (or threatened) species.[441] Examined more closely, however, this federal law does not truly protect individual animals except incidentally, as exemplars of their DNA. An *individual* being is "endangered" or "threatened" whenever someone threatens that individual's life or health, while the DNA of a species is endangered or threatened only when its numbers dwindle to a point at which humans worry that there may soon be few exemplars of this animal species left in the world. Seeking exemplars of DNA, the ESA is indifferent to the particular experience of life or death that befalls any individual animal.

This orientation toward "conserving" species DNA leads people to accept the proposition that capturing and holding wild animals in cages—even animals who would ordinarily travel many miles every day—is somehow "beneficial" for the animals.[442] While individual animals captive at a zoo may pace around and develop stereotypies characteristic of severe mental illness,[443] their captivity may aid in ensuring the continued vitality of their DNA. Humans can then enjoy their existence, without necessarily worrying about the quality or length of their individual lives in captivity. The DNA orientation is therefore best suited to exploiting a species rather than to valuing and protecting the rights and interests of individual members of that species.

If we want a species to continue to exist because it benefits us in some way, then we might focus on the success of an animal's DNA and conclude that domesticated chickens have "succeeded" by virtue of our voracious appetite for their flesh and eggs. If, on the other hand, we wish to respect the living individual animal and her desire for comfort, safety, companionship, and life, then we will come to the very different conclusion that domesticated chickens have been singularly unsuccessful inhabitants of this earth.

In many cases, we as individuals and we as bearers of DNA have overlapping "objectives." We as individuals want to be comfortable, to form and nurture close relationships, to have enough food, to be safe, and to take care of our families. Our DNA is aimed at replicating itself, a "goal" that ordinarily corresponds with our individual pursuits of comfort, relationship, safety, and family.

Because you feel pain when you are injured, you will probably avoid whatever circumstances gave rise to that pain and you will thereby decrease your odds of meeting an untimely end and failing to replicate your DNA (i.e., reproduce). Because you feel pleasure in having sexual relationships, you are likely to pursue circumstances in which you are more likely to replicate your DNA. Avoiding pain and pursuing pleasure, in other words, increase your odds of passing your genes along. Thus, the pursuit of desirable individual experiences coincides well with maximizing genetic replication.

Human beings have, however, long ago figured out how to sever genetic proliferation from the pursuit of individual interest. The practice of birth control, for example, allows people to pursue the pleasure of sexual intercourse without thereby replicating their DNA. The very fact that people choose to use birth control highlights the difference between increasing individual well-being (which may entail the ability to limit one's own fertility), on the one hand, and increasing one's DNA footprint (by maximizing fertility), on the other.

The same could be said of vaccinations and medications that extend individuals' health and lives well beyond their fertility period. Such measures reduce the proportion of the population that is engaged in reproduction. But in these and many other realms, we may make choices that reflect our prioritizing of what is best for us as existing individuals over what is best for the proliferation of our DNA.

We have seen that through the domestication of animals, humans have very dramatically disrupted any overlap between what is best for an animal and what is best for the DNA of that animal. As we saw in our discussion of domesticated turkeys, human choices have given the survival advantage to DNA that codes for a bird whose skeleton can barely support her weight and who is physically incapable of copulating. Human choices have similarly given the survival advantage to DNA that codes for a hen who produces such a large quantity of unfertilized eggs that she will likely develop extreme osteoporosis when she is only a few years old.[444]

The selective breeding of sheep in the wool industry is another example of domestication leading to a disparity between what is best for an animal and what is best for her genes. Sheep, like egg-laying hens, are brought into existence to be farmed for the resources they can produce (i.e., wool). Domesticated sheep, unlike their ancestors, do not shed their fur naturally.[445] And ultimately, just like egg-laying hens, sheep used for wool production will be slaughtered and their flesh used to produce a meat product.

Human choices have thus given the survival advantage to DNA that codes for a sheep who cannot shed her own fur and who, moreover, has extra folds of skin, meant to ensure a higher yield of wool. These characteristics subject sheep to flystrike, or myiasis, where flies lay eggs amongst the extra folds of skin and fur. To prevent flystrike, wool producers practice mulesing, slicing off a live sheep's extra folds of skin around her bottom, generally without anesthesia and without any post-operative care.[446] And the shearing process itself causes injury and trauma to sheep, despite people's mistaken idea of shearing as comparable to a haircut.[447]

Even if we completely ignore the routine mutilations that farmed animals must endure, we see that human beings have deliberately multiplied DNA for traits that inflict pain and disabilities on the very animals created by that DNA (because the same traits make the animals' flesh and secretions more attractive to human consumers). It is therefore simply mistaken to assume that the genetic numerical "success" of farmed animals signifies well-being of any sort for these beings.

The Extinction of Domestication

A professor at a prominent law school once asked me what supporters of animal rights wish for the population of domesticated animals after the end of animal exploitation. What is our vision? Different people likely have distinct visions for the future, but some version of the following more or less approximates what I believe is a shared hope among ethical vegans for the future of nonhuman animals. It is that over time, increasing numbers of people will become vegan and withdraw support from the industries and individuals that breed and slaughter animals for human consumption.

As this happens, the numbers of domesticated animals in the world will steadily decline, as fewer businesses will be able to anticipate a profit from deliberately bringing large numbers of domesticated animals into existence for exploitation and slaughter. Understood in this way, the animal rights vision necessarily contemplates fewer, if any, domesticated chickens, turkeys, pigs, and other similar, human-dependent creatures living in our world in the distant future.

Seeking the extinction of animals whose rights we claim to defend might appear to be paradoxical. This appearance, however, confuses living individuals, whose rights to live and be free of exploitation deserve protection, with the DNA of those individuals, which may no longer find exemplars many generations from now. Furthermore, to resist animal rights to avoid the extinction of domesticated species would make little sense, even if we viewed extinction as an independent harm to individual members of a species.

Taking such a position ignores the impact of domestication on the lives of wild, undomesticated animals. In place of billions of farmed animals, many other wild animals of different varieties (including the wild relatives of domesticated breeds) could flourish. Instead, the U.S. Department of Agriculture Wildlife Services is tasked with performing "wildlife damage management."[448] This benign-sounding phrase refers to the extermination of large numbers of animals who might otherwise try to prey on some of the domesticated animals living on ranches and farms and slated for death inside of our slaughterhouses.[449] In other words, the government helps support the breeding of domesticated animals by exterminating wild animals living nearby.

Apart from this direct killing of other sentient animals, farming requires the clear-cutting of forests to provide land for animal agriculture, for the physical placement of the animals themselves and, perhaps more importantly from a numerical and spatial standpoint, for the cultivation of crops intended as livestock feed for billions of animals.[450] This destruction of forests results in the deaths of the animals who lived in those forests, thereby also reducing the population of their progeny—animals who would have been able to inhabit the forests.[451]

Despite claims by some ranchers and their allies that grass-fed cows use land that would otherwise be unsuitable for any purpose,[452] the reality is otherwise. Land left fallow for a period of time will eventually return to fertility.[453] And when farmers instead use such land for ranching, it becomes unproductive within a few years.[454]

Quite apart from its inefficiency, the use of land to feed and support livestock destined for slaughter eliminates areas that would otherwise have supported large populations of non-domesticated animals. The consumption of domesticated breeds accordingly contributes enormously to the deaths of non-domesticated animals and the extinction of wild breeds.

To imagine that consuming animal products assists in the "conservation" of valued species is therefore most charitably characterized as misguided. And this is true even when we put aside the fact that multiplying species DNA through selective breeding for slaughter does not represent "success" for individual sentient beings.

More importantly, to bring an animal into existence for the purpose of using her flesh and bodily secretions is to do violence to that animal. The violence is most obvious in the everyday lives of these individuals and the painful mutilations and deprivations that they experience prior to their terrifying loss of life to slaughter. Moreover, there is tremendous violence in their selective breeding, because it replaces animals well suited to thrive in the world with animals whose very bodies betray them to serve human appetites.

To bring closer to home the philosophical question whether existence is a gift we bestow on the animals we consume,[455] imagine the following hypothetical scenario.[456] An alien being from another planet arrives on earth and approaches you. The extraterrestrial is able to communicate in your language and has the same moral capacities that you have.

He tells you that he wants to bring human slaves to his home galaxy but that he has no intention of utilizing any of the "wild" humans currently living on our planet. The plan is instead to give you a swab with which to lightly scrape your cheek. The alien being will then take the swab back to his galaxy and create trillions of clones of you to people the thousands of planets in the galaxy.

Creating these clones will ensure that there will be many trillions of human beings not only on Earth but elsewhere in the universe where no humans currently exist. Cloning will further ensure that the human species does not become extinct when it otherwise would (for example, when our sun burns out or prior to that). The alien being adds that he will genetically modify your clones' DNA over time to create a better fit between the extraterrestrials' needs and the humans' characteristics.

Finally, because these humans will all originate as clones of you, you will have the satisfaction of knowing that you have left an individually identifiable and potentially infinite genetic legacy that extends well beyond your own planet to many others. Hearing that, what would you be inclined to do?

From my perspective, the prospect of such cloning would be horrifying, not only despite but *because of* the fact that individuals so much like me would be its victims. Far from delighting in my "proliferation" across the universe, I would take as a grave injustice every moment of suffering compelled by enslavement to the alien beings. The more numerous these humans were, the more outraged I would feel. If given the choice, I would not swab my cheek.

I would much prefer that my particular genetic makeup never reappear than that it appear in trillions of individuals held in servitude. And if the alien being gave me no choice and took my DNA by force to create trillions of human clones, I would view this initial act of bringing humans into existence for the purpose of enslaving them as an injustice that would certainly do nothing to validate the further outrage of actually enslaving them afterwards. In other words, the alien being would have behaved immorally and not charitably in creating people to serve as slaves, and the alien beings' obligation—once the people existed—would be to meet their needs (if "domesticated" people could not take care of their own needs on distant planets) and to refrain from carrying out the enslavement plan. If the plan were nonetheless carried out, moreover, it would be absurd to suggest that the human slaves had achieved great success by virtue of their numbers and that they owed the alien beings a debt of gratitude.

The question whether it is better to exist as a farmed animal than not to exist at all is both unanswerable and beside the point. It is unanswerable because there is not a category of individuals who all share the quality of having never existed to whose experience we may profitably compare the category of individuals who have existed under various conditions.[457] Comparing an animal's existence to her nonexistence is thus only sensible from the perspective of others who prefer to inhabit a world where that animal exists than to inhabit a world where she does not. This is why a couple might decide to bring a child into the world, because they favorably compare a world with a child of theirs in it to a world without one. As we saw earlier, however, it would be incoherent to assert that they have committed a moral offense against their countless non-existent children by deciding not to procreate or to have only a limited number of children.

Even if one believed existence to represent a gift to the being who exists, it would remain true that bringing a living being into existence would not entitle us to inflict harm on that being, regardless of why we brought him into the world. Only a deranged or monstrous person, like the hypothetical "Betty" from earlier in the chapter, would bring a child into the world for the sole purpose of using him as an organ donor later in life.

Perhaps she would not have had any children in the absence of this objective: her child is a "purpose-bred" child, like the "donor" children in *Never Let Me Go*. Notwithstanding that fact, we would properly condemn Betty if she ultimately utilized the child as an organ donor, and the fact that she was the one who brought the child into the world would increase rather than diminish our sense of outrage. Even if Betty's daughter was glad that she was born and grateful for the short life she was able to live, we understand Betty to have behaved reprehensibly if she acts on her plan. Conversely, had she instead never conceived the child in the first place, we would understand her to have behaved innocently with the respect to her nonexistent daughter.

We accordingly cannot rely on the benefits we confer on farmed animals to justify their breeding and slaughter. We harm them first by selecting for traits that are detrimental to their health and longevity. We harm them next by inflicting pain on them and then slaughtering them for our consumption.

To those billions of animals who already live in the world due to our prior consumption of animal products, we have greater obligations than we do to other animals. They are dependent, and we ought to care for them and allow them to live out their lives in peace. The domesticated animals owe us no gratitude or payment for their lives, and we have no corresponding right to take those lives and to dispose of them for our own purposes.

13

THERE ARE NO PERFECT VEGANS, SO WHY BOTHER?

I was quite disappointed the day I learned that even the most conscientious vegans cannot completely avoid relying on resources that have utilized some animal products somewhere along the line. This is the unfortunate truth, though, and it means that if we defined vegan as living 100 percent free of all animal-derived ingredients, then just about no one could plausibly claim to be vegan. The mass production of animal flesh and secretions in our non-vegan world yields enormous quantities of slaughterhouse byproducts that are then cheaply distributed and used as ingredients in items as wide-ranging as roads, automobile tires, prescription medications, manure fertilizer, and plywood inside the walls of most homes.[458]

Such products do not in fact *require* the inclusion of animal ingredients. Because enormous numbers of animals are slaughtered and processed for direct consumption, however, the resulting byproducts are inexpensive and available, so they are used. So long as humans demand huge quantities of animal-derived products that necessarily involve slaughter—products like meat, poultry, fish, dairy, eggs, leather, and wool—the resulting animal byproducts will predictably make their way, in some form, into virtually everything. If one drives a car or cycles on the roads or eats vegetables, fruits, legumes, or grains, one will invariably rely on the use of some animal-derived ingredient somewhere in the process.

In addition to consuming ubiquitous slaughterhouse products, there is another way in which vegans and non-vegans both participate in supporting violence against animals. Contemporary farming methods for cultivating crops kill animals who live among those crops. Combines used for harvesting, for example, kill mice and other small vertebrates, as does other industrial farming machinery.[459] When we consume corn or wheat from a farmer, we therefore support a process that causes the deaths of many sentient beings. Being vegan thus does not entirely eliminate one's participation in violence against animals.

Given this current reality, some skeptics have posed the question whether there is any point to trying to live as a vegan.[460] Perhaps, they argue, there is no real distinction between buying an ear of corn from a farmer who fertilizes her fields with manure and harvests her crops with a combine, and buying a pint of dairy ice cream or cheese from a farmer or a store.[461] Are all choices equally doomed to support animal slaughter?

Sometimes people might ask these questions of vegans because they imagine ethical vegans to be self-righteous, judgmental kill-joys who think themselves morally superior to the wicked animal-users around them. Many of us have encountered the stereotype of the holier-than-thou, angry vegan, to whom it may be tempting to say: "You're part of the problem too because you use some animal products, so get off your vegan pedestal!"

I think only a small minority of ethical vegans actually behave in this judgmental manner, but those who do so predictably inspire accusations of hypocrisy. When people judge us, we are likely to feel inclined to judge them right back. It may be no accident that many sex scandals involve people who had previously and publicly condemned others for the kinds of acts in which they too were indulging.

When a judgmental person is also a hypocrite, it becomes easy for his audience to dismiss his moral claims because he appears to lack standing to make them. This is most unfortunate when the judgmental person happens to care about a just cause, because we can lose sight of the cause and see only its unappealing proponent.

For anyone who shakes a finger and calls people names as a strategy for motivating vegan transformations, the impossibility of completely avoiding harm to animals in our world can serve as a useful reminder. None of us is beyond reproach, so in this sense, we all—vegans and non-vegans alike—live in glass houses. Luckily, most ethical vegans do not live the way they do as part of a quest for moral superiority or as a platform for passing judgment on other people. Veganism is instead, for most, a journey away from violence against the weak and vulnerable sentient beings who share our world. And like any other life-long journey, it is an ongoing process rather than a destination point.

I was not born into veganism, nor were the other ethical vegans who have become my close friends over the years. Each of us found out information of which we had previously been unaware. (The essential role of slaughter in dairy production is a prime example.) Each of us also learned to notice things about animals that we did not previously see and to better appreciate animals' simultaneously pervasive and invisible role in almost every facet of our lives.[462] In response to what we learned, each of us, in our own time, absorbed the information, cognitively and emotionally, and began our respective journeys.

If any of us was inclined to become self-righteous and judgmental, then we would have to direct that judgment against our own former selves. A far more productive and attractive approach is to allow our self-awareness to make us humble, empathic, and understanding of others, and of ourselves in the process. In an important sense, many of us did not experience ourselves as either making or even as fully *having* a choice when it came to the consumption of animal flesh and secretions.

Under the circumstances, not only is judgment alienating and off-putting; it also ignores the feeling of autonomy that one requires to opt out of a mainstream practice widely perceived as inevitable. The people who inspired each of us to become vegan did so by awakening our autonomy, and that is in turn the only fair and effective way for us to pay it forward.

So what is the answer? If pure, 100 percent independence from all animal-harm-derived ingredients is not possible in our present world, is there any point to striving for imperfect veganism? Assume that you are no longer confronting a self-righteous person who needs to be taken down a peg, but are instead having a dialogue with a kind friend who has invited you to become vegan. If we cannot fully escape from animal-derived ingredients, you ask the friend, then shouldn't we give up and just do whatever we feel like doing? That way, we will not be futilely spinning our wheels to no apparent end.

We can best understand this question as two related inquiries. The first asks whether there is any point in trying to opt out of animal exploitation, given that even vegans cannot entirely avoid animal products in today's world. The second asks whether the ways in which *vegans* rely on animal products are really any different from the ways in which non-vegans do. If the answer to either of these questions is no, then there would seem to be no good reason to consider veganism an ethically preferable way to live.

Why Imperfection Is Not an Argument

The first question of whether even to bother poses a general objection to moral action, not just to veganism or animal rights. It is really a question about whether one ought to pursue a goal when one cannot fully accomplish that goal, given present realities. Understood in this way, we see that to answer the question "no" is to surrender to moral despair. Under this approach, because we know that we cannot live in absolute congruity with our values, we do not bother to make efforts to do what we can to make the world a better place for ourselves and for those around us.

We could similarly ask "should we even bother?" every time we do (or avoid doing) anything to enrich (or, respectively, to worsen) someone else's life. Many of us give money to charitable organizations or volunteer our time to help alleviate suffering in the world. Many carpool or carry a reusable shopping bag instead of using the paper or plastic offered at the market, to reduce the amount of pollution we generate. We strive to be kinder or more patient with our loved ones and with strangers.

In each of these cases, it might occur to us that we will almost certainly fall short of perfection. We could be giving more of our money or our time to charity; we could be purchasing fewer items or taking fewer car trips than we do; we could be kinder than we are, and so forth. Does this realization negate the value of what we have either done or refrained from doing? It does not. The fact that we could do even more (or even less, depending on the activity at issue) is not a good reason to do nothing.

There is a part of the Mishnah (a portion of the Jewish oral tradition), known as "Pirkei Avot" in Hebrew (translated as "Chapters of Our Fathers" or "Ethics of Our Fathers" in English),[463] which contains some moral teachings central to Judaism and no doubt shared by other religious traditions. Chapter 2, verse 21, speaks to the question posed here: "You are not required to complete the task, yet you are not free to withdraw from it."[464] Recognizing the limits of our capabilities does not supply a basis for giving up.

As a parent, I know that I sometimes become impatient or annoyed when it would be better for my children if I remained patient and serene instead. This knowledge inspires me to substitute warmth and patience for irritation when I become conscious of the urge to express anger toward my children. Does this mean that I am gentle and sweet every time I interact with them? No.

I still act impatiently with them from time to time. I do so less frequently, however, than I did before I made the conscious decision to cultivate patience. I could do better, without question, and this fact too inspires me to work in that direction, even though I know I will fall short of perfection.

One alternative would be for me instead to surrender myself to irritation and annoyance at my children, because I will never achieve perfection. This alternative does not appeal to me, and would certainly not appeal to my children. It would seem to guarantee an outcome that is not only imperfect but affirmatively bad.

For me, becoming vegan was like consciously deciding to cultivate patience with my children. It has been an ongoing process in which mindlessly inherited habits have given way to consciously chosen ones, and life is as easy as it was before but far more consistent with my vision of the world that I want to inhabit. Even though I cannot completely eliminate all animal products from my life right now, I can eliminate most. And as I continue on my vegan journey, I find ways to eliminate some that I previously thought were unavoidable. I know that I cannot be perfect, but that does not stop me from doing what I can.

Why Choosing Animal Consumption Matters

The second question about imperfect veganism does zero in on veganism rather than the general problem of moral imperfection. It asks whether the ways in which vegans presently rely on animal-derived products are categorically different from the ways in which non-vegans rely on animal-derived products. This question is important, because it determines whether veganism in particular—as opposed to imperfectly executed ethical choices more generally—has anything to recommend it as an alternative to non-vegan consumption choices.

Even if it makes sense to try to better ourselves, notwithstanding our inability to achieve perfect success, some might ask whether the choice to live as vegans truly *is* a way of bettering ourselves and the lives of animals. If vegans are simply carrying out *different* harms against animals than non-vegans carry out, then the choice to become vegan might seem no more sensible than the choice to consume more dairy products in place of cow flesh or to consume more egg products in place of chickens—a choice to embrace what attorneys sometimes call "a distinction without a difference."

To answer this question, it is useful to consider why it is that even conscientious vegans cannot avoid animal products altogether at the present time. It is not because animal products are inherently necessary to our survival—we have already seen that they are not. And it is also not because there are pleasures central to human joy and inherently tied to animal products—we have seen that this too is not the case.

We can nourish ourselves with health-promoting and delicious plant-based food, and we can clothe ourselves in warm, comfortable clothing without the hair, skin, or fibers of sentient beings. The reason that vegans cannot avoid animal products is that animal byproducts are routinely and unnecessarily used to make almost everything.

Consider an analogy from American history. There was a time when cotton in the United States was cultivated almost exclusively through slave labor.[465] One can, of course, grow cotton without slavery. Apart from some cotton sold by Quaker abolitionists,[466] however, almost anything that contained cotton in the United States during the slavery era would inevitably have been the fruit of that odious institution. Purchasers of those products would therefore have been participants in the institution without necessarily having had any direct awareness of their participation.[467]

By contrast to cotton with respect to human slavery, there are products that are inherently and unavoidably the "fruit" of animal suffering and slaughter. One buys beef, chicken, dairy, or eggs intending to buy the flesh or secretions of previously living animals. Cotton is not inherently a slave-labor product, but these animal products are fundamentally animal products, and the overwhelming majority of slaughter and cruelty that occurs right now occurs as a response to consumer demand for animal products as such.[468] People in the business of animal agriculture bring animals into existence for the sole purpose of using and slaughtering those animals, for one reason: Consumers unequivocally demand this activity by purchasing such things as meat, poultry, fish, dairy, eggs, leather, and wool.

If no one chose to consume these items, it would no longer make economic sense to breed and slaughter billions of animals. It would be inefficient, in other words, to grow plants and then convert the plants into animal flesh (by feeding the plants to farmed animals) simply to make raw materials for roads, tires, or plywood, all of which can be made with plant-based and synthetic materials. Animals are not a necessary part of these items, but animal products are used because they come out of the slaughterhouse and would otherwise become slaughterhouse garbage.

The same is true for fertilizer. One need not use animal manure to grow plants.[469] There are currently a number of veganic farms,[470] farms that use only vegan materials to cultivate their fruits and vegetables. Although such farms make up a small minority, there would certainly be many more if it were no longer profitable to breed animals for food and clothing.

Given the availability of alternatives, we would not house and feed millions of cows every year just so that their excrement, blood, and bones could be used as fertilizer.[471] Reducing and eventually eliminating the demand for the products that come *only* from animals will thus simultaneously reduce the demand for the fungible byproducts that are part of so many consumer items as a side-effect of animal-farming and slaughter.

Reducing Incidental Deaths

We confront a somewhat different problem in examining the lethal impact of industrial machinery on small animals living in the fields. The problem is distinct because farmers are not intentionally killing these animals. Unlike the cow who is bred and slaughtered for human consumption, a mouse who dies under a combine is, in the language of warfare, a "collateral" casualty of the farming process. The goal, in other words, is to harvest the crop, and the death of field mice and other small animals is an unintended consequence.

Why does this distinction matter? If we kill animals, what difference does it make whether we do so intentionally or not? One difference is that, as a general matter, we do not attach the same level of moral blame to actions with unintentionally violent consequences as we do to actions whose violent consequences are intended. We classify as "murder" the intentional killing of a human being,[472] while accidentally causing another's death qualifies as either a lesser offense such as involuntary manslaughter[473] or as no crime at all.[474]

Perhaps more to the point in discussions of violence resulting from consumption and production, we currently produce and utilize a large number of products and technologies that foreseeably and consistently cause the deaths of some number of human beings. Doctors prescribe medications, even for non-life-threatening conditions, that will foreseeably cause the deaths of some number of patients who take them, and the same is true for other medical treatments.[475] Car manufacturers produce vehicles that will predictably bring about the maiming and killing of large numbers of human pedestrians and drivers.[476] Purveyors of alcoholic drinks know in advance that the alcohol they distribute will result in some number of alcohol-related deaths.[477]

In none of these cases, however, do we hold these actors legally accountable for the deaths that they foreseeably but unintentionally cause in their otherwise reasonable and lawful activities. We understand an actor's intentions to be central to evaluating the morality of what he does.

Turn now to the person who consumes grains that were harvested with the use of a combine. The combine probably killed some number of animals during the harvesting process, just as cars kill human beings (and nonhuman animals). In both of these cases, however, the killing is unintended. Were the same grain to be harvested without killing a single animal, consumers would not complain that they were receiving an inferior product. The violence of the harvesting process is therefore incidental to the product.

To say that violence is unintended is not to suggest that it is unimportant. No one who supports animal rights is unmoved by the plight of field mice and other innocent, sentient beings who lose their lives to plant-based agriculture. I personally find very disturbing the prospect of contributing to the deaths of animals, even if no one—not I and not the people driving the combine—intended for those animals to die.

For this reason, it is useful to remember that the process of raising livestock for people's consumption has its own unintended animal (and human) victims. As discussed in chapter 8, most of the plant-based-food cultivated in the United States and elsewhere goes to "fatten up" animals who will be used and slaughtered. This means that consuming vegan food will serve not only to reduce the intentional slaughter of sentient domesticated animals, but also to reduce the unintentional killing of small animals in the fields as well.[478]

The inefficiency of consuming farmed animal products thus greatly multiplies the unintended violence involved in crop cultivation, because it takes more crops to feed tens of billions of farmed animals than it does to feed a far smaller number of human beings directly. For this reason, it is not that surprising that vegan living has a lower "lethality footprint" than omnivorous or ovo-lacto-vegetarian living, even if we consider more than just the intended violence involved in raising and killing farmed animals for our consumption.[479]

The move to veganism can reduce the incidental deaths of animals in another way as well. As in the current use of slaughterhouse byproducts for tires, easily eliminated with a reduction in demand for slaughterhouse products, a demand for non-violent products has great potential to yield substitute methods of harvesting plants as well. Though a farmer does not intentionally kill animals in the fields, many of the deaths could be avoided with the farmer's choice of different harvesting methods.

It is plainly unrealistic, though, to expect a farmer to make a priority of selecting equipment that spares the lives of mice when the same farmer is growing corn or soy to feed farmed animals headed for slaughter. But as more consumers become vegan, the increasing demand for non-violent products could support the development and proliferation of harvesting machinery that spares the small animals in its path.

Each time a person decides to become vegan, that decision accordingly yields a reduction in the demand for animal products and a corresponding reduction in the demand for the activities that are an inherent part of these products—holding animals captive, using them, and then killing them (or killing them first and then using their slaughtered remains). It also reduces the number of unintended animal deaths, both by much more efficiently utilizing farmland and by introducing a concern for sparing the lives of animals more generally into the market. A refusal to consume meat, poultry, fish, dairy, eggs, leather, and wool therefore effectively reduces violence against animals, even if one still buys vegetables from non-veganic and combine-using farms (the overwhelming majority of existing vegetable farms), drives a car on the public roads, and lives in houses in which animal ingredients were used in constructing the walls.

Becoming vegan also has a multiplier effect. We are an extremely social species, which is part of what makes opting out of consuming animals intimidating to many people. By joyfully embracing veganism—the imperfect sort which is possible in our current world—every individual can inspire others to consider making the same choice.

Before I encountered my first vegan, I had never even considered becoming one. And all of the vegans I know have had similar experiences. Before encountering or reading about the experiences of a real-life vegan, most of us lack the motivation to step outside of our comfort zones. We need to be inspired by others before changing the way we live, and each new vegan inspires others to help build our world into a place where animals live in peace and free of human cruelty and violence, while humans eat healthfully and happily.

The Trouble with Sugar

Once we decide to become vegan, there are still veganism-related ethical choices to make. Will we eat products that contain refined sugar? Unless otherwise specified, cane sugar may be refined with bone char—the charred remains of bones from slaughterhouses.[480]

The sugar may not literally *contain* bones, but it results from the use of an animal product. Will we drink the particular beers or wines that were filtered or fined using animal products? Again, there may be no animal ingredients floating around *in* the alcohol, but such ingredients might have been used in the production process.

And what about honey? Are bees and other insects entitled to the same vegan ethical consideration as mammals, birds, and fish are? If so, how do we deal with the fact that bees are bred, "managed," moved from place to place, and exploited not only to make honey but also to pollinate food crops?[481] Cultivation of nuts, vegetables, apples, cantaloupes, cranberries, pumpkins, and sunflowers currently rely on bee pollination,[482] and wild honeybees are not sufficiently numerous to support contemporary agriculture levels.[483]

Different vegans deal with these various problems differently. Begin with bone-char-refined sugar. We do not need refined sugar to live, and there are, in any event, plenty of vegan sweeteners, including unrefined, raw cane sugar—also called "evaporated cane juice"—and refined sugars that specify that bone char was not used.[484] Therefore, avoiding bone-char-refined sugar is quite easy. If one enjoys processed foods containing sugar, the task is somewhat more challenging, but vegan products—including those containing sugar—are increasingly labeled as such, which makes things easier, even in the junk-food aisle.

At the same time, though, one might plausibly argue that the purchase of bone-char-refined sugar has no impact on the breeding and slaughter of animals, because without a market for meat, dairy, and eggs, it would no longer make economic sense to breed, feed, water, and slaughter a domesticated animal for bone char, given alternative methods of refining sugar. As with animal byproducts in roads, car tires, and plywood, they are there because they come out of the slaughterhouse and would otherwise become garbage.

The same set of arguments could apply to wine and beer: it is easy to find vegan versions of these products because animal products are not essential to fining or to filtering,[485] but the consumption of non-vegan beer and wine may play no significant role in motivating the breeding, exploitation, and slaughter of animals. I know committed vegans who take differing approaches to these questions. I personally like to avoid such products, because they are easily replaced, but I do not consider their inclusion or exclusion an essential feature of veganism.

The Trouble with Bees

The issue of bees is a more difficult one, I think. Avoiding honey is easy, and now there is even a product that has the same taste, fragrance, and consistency as honey, called "Just-Like-Honey," for those who feel that they cannot live the good life without it. It is also true that bees may be capable of subjective experiences and seem to find invasions of their hives aversive, which may be why beekeepers need to wear protective gear when they remove honey from a hive.[486]

Bees make honey to feed bees, not humans, so I am uncomfortable participating in what I view as a gratuitous appropriation of their food. I also cannot see much reason to insist on consuming honey, and I suspect that describing myself as a vegan who feels compelled to eat honey would needlessly complicate the process of communicating about veganism with people who currently feel similarly compelled to eat cheese.

At the same time, the agricultural role of exploited honeybees (as opposed to wild or "feral" honeybees) is not primarily in producing honey but, as I mentioned earlier, in cultivating crops. Among feral bees, the cultivation process is voluntary, and our eating the fruits or vegetables that result does no harm to the bees. But due to the scale on which crop cultivation occurs, most of the commercially exploited bees "participating" are moved around, sold, and manipulated in the process.[487]

In fact, human manipulation and exploitation of bees might be one of the reasons for "colony collapse syndrome" or "colony collapse disorder" among bees, a condition in which a bee colony disappears.[488] Commercial bee-keeping operations also regularly spray irritants at the bees and kill the queen.[489] How can vegans be comfortable consuming fruits, vegetables, and other plant-based foods that have been cultivated with exploited bees?

This question is more difficult, because it no longer involves a product like honey, which is unnecessary and easily replaced. If vegans refrained from eating plant-based foods because of bees, then there would be little left for vegans to eat. Stated differently, eating fruits, vegetables, beans, and grains is necessary to survive. If one must choose between participating in bee exploitation and eating nothing, then it is understandable that one will choose the former over the latter.

Gary Francione has described analogous scenarios—in which people consume animal products when their lives or health depends on it—as "excused" rather than "justified," because even if we need something, we are not ordinarily entitled to take it from another being by force.[490] To say that behavior is "excused" is to suggest that it is not "justified" or benign but to simultaneously take into account the circumstances and pressures that might reduce or eliminate the actor's moral culpability in connection with the behavior. Whether we believe the consumption of commercial-bee-pollinated plants to be justified or excused, asking a person to die or become sick out of an ethical commitment is something quite different from asking a person to make healthful and beneficial changes for ethical reasons. Being vegan is about the latter, not the former.

In response to the argument that vegans eat plants (even though they are cultivated by "managed" bee colonies) because they have to eat, one might ask why this differs from eating meat or dairy. In other words, if all eating involves the infliction of harm and exploitation on animals, what difference does it make whether we eat an apple that was cultivated by directly exploiting bees or whether we eat an ice cream sundae that was produced by directly exploiting cows? This is an important question that goes to the heart of veganism. If all food choices were equally harmful, then there would be no good reason to prefer veganism to other alternatives.

If we consider the options, however, it turns out that all food choices are not equivalent. If virtually all food—including plant-based food—at the present time involves the exploitation of animals, that exploitation is reduced dramatically when we consume plant-based food rather than animal-based food. This is because of the staggering inefficiency of cultivating crops only to feed them to animals whom we will then slaughter and use for food.

Consider that one needs far more bees to grow enough alfalfa to feed a cow who will be impregnated and lactate and who will then be slaughtered for her flesh, than one would need to cultivate plants for people to eat directly.

By consuming only plant-based food, one therefore substantially reduces one's support for bee exploitation. We do far less harm to bees when the food we eat is plant-based than when it is animal-based. And if everyone were to become vegan, it might even become possible to cultivate crops successfully with the assistance of only feral bees.

Of course, veganism is not primarily about sparing bees. Refraining from participating in cruelty to vertebrates is independently important, quite apart from its role in reducing our "bee harm" footprint. We can be far more confident that vertebrates suffer as we do, when they are injured, when they are separated from their families, and when they are killed—as all of them are killed within every kind of animal agriculture—than we can be about insects.[491]

We know that mammals (such as pigs, cows, sheep, and goats), birds (such as chickens, turkeys, ducks, and geese), and fishes (such as trouts, tunas, salmons, and goldfish) respond to pain in much the same physiological and chemical way that humans do.[492] They, like we, produce endogenous pain-killing substances for which they have receptors,[493] and they exhibit anxiety as well, demonstrating that they have processed pain cognitively as well as physiologically;[494] they are, in other words, sentient.

Insects, by contrast, are different enough from us to yield questions about whether they are capable of suffering.[495] In response to injuries, insects behave in contradictory ways that suggest that they may or may not suffer. For example, an insect might eat *while* being devoured by another insect.[496] Still, we do not know for sure, and there is evidence of sentience in insects as well.[497]

When asked where he draws the line between sentient and non-sentient creatures, animal behaviorist Jonathan Balcombe has said that wherever he may draw it, he is sure to do so in pencil rather than in pen.[498] When there is a ready alternative to harming insects, I would err on the side of selecting that alternative, whether it be a non-honey sweetener or a non-lethal method of removing insects from one's home. Even if I am not sure that insects suffer, I have enough reason to think they might to make sparing them the best course.

When it comes to animals who are unquestionably sentient, however, the insect issue represents little more than a distraction. The fact that completely sparing insect life may be impossible provides no reason at all to consume the products of the slaughterhouse, where animal suffering is so great and so relentless as to traumatize even the humans who work there and witness it.[499]

The Three Imperfections

To summarize, there are three primary sorts of imperfection that might trouble us when we consider becoming vegan: the ubiquitous presence of slaughterhouse byproducts everywhere we look; the unintended deaths of small animals in most forms of crop cultivation; and the direct exploitation of honeybees that currently accompanies the production of plant-based crops. The first sort of imperfection provides no argument against veganism, because by choosing no longer to demand the products that necessarily harm animals—meat, poultry, fish, dairy, eggs, leather, and wool—we remove the basis for bringing farmed animals into existence.

No one will breed, feed, and slaughter a cow simply as a means of creating adhesives, if there are not customers already demanding the cow's slaughtered flesh and her baby calves' nursing fluid.

A second sort of imperfection—the incidental deaths of small animals in plant agriculture—is significant but differs in important ways from direct and intentional harm to farmed animals. For one thing, we have long treated intentional killing as worse than accidental killing. For another, many fewer animals die in crop cultivation for plants that feed humans directly than for crops that go to livestock who will then be slaughtered for human consumption. And finally, growing the vegan community holds great promise for motivating farmers, through consumer demand, to use cultivation methods that spare the lives of field mice and others.

A third sort of imperfection—the involvement of honeybees in crop cultivation—also does nothing to undermine the case for veganism. First, we reduce and eventually may eliminate the need for commercially exploited honeybees when we consume plants directly and thereby avoid having to cultivate enough plant-based food to support tens of billions of farmed animals for our consumption. Second, consuming animal products promotes violence against animals whom we know to be sentient, causing those animals to suffer physical and emotional distress and anxiety, while consuming plants cultivated by manipulated honeybees promotes (quantitatively less) injury to insects whose sentience is contested. Because we must eat something, the choice between animal-based and plant-based products is accordingly straightforward, notwithstanding the imperfections that accompany any choice of food.

Every vegan is different and will respond differently to the day-to-day choices to be made in a world saturated with violence against animals. Some days, I dream of moving to an island of veganism, where I would never have to see another animal corpse or hormonal secretion on a table at which I am eating. On such an island, there would be no honey, and the roads would be made of plant-based and synthetic materials.

But then I remind myself that only seven years ago, I would not have been admitted to this island, and if all vegans had lived there, I might never have had the opportunity and the privilege to become vegan myself. Living away from the vegan island means that I face dilemmas I would rather not face. When I take a prescription medicine, it will have been tested on animals and likely manufactured with animal-derived binders. I find this disturbing and wish it were different.

At the same time, however, I am very grateful that I am able to opt out of the greatest driver of violence against animals, by consuming plant-based foods. I would never claim to be perfect, but because I have become vegan, my life is vastly more peaceful than it was just seven years ago.

Conclusion

I have written most of this book with an audience of non-vegans in mind. As a consequence, I have responded to the questions posed by each chapter with my own story and experience as well as with information and reasoning that might help address the questions. Some of my readers, however, may be vegans already and may have read this book in an effort to help determine what they want to say (or not to say) when such questions come their way.

Why Do People Ask Vegans So Many Questions?

For a new vegan, the questions from friends, family, and even complete strangers can sometimes seem disrespectful or dismissive and may give rise to one big, unspoken question in response: Why are non-vegans asking me challenging moral, philosophical, and nutritional questions about veganism? Why are they putting me on the defensive for living in a manner that reflects my values? In this conclusion, I hope to address the concern that underlies these questions from vegans, both new and seasoned. I will propose that we can best understand the questions as a very positive development that bodes well for the future of animal rights and veganism.

When I became vegan a little under seven years ago, I immediately started encountering questions from different quarters about why I had made this choice. When I ordered food at a restaurant, people noticed that I was avoiding not only the beef and the chicken but the fish, dairy, and eggs as well. My new veganism was obvious even before I explicitly said anything about it.

The first question I would often hear was whether I had become vegan for health or for ethical reasons. Once I answered "for ethical reasons," more questions would follow: Why did I think it was okay to eat plants? Didn't I crave steak or bacon? What did I think of animals eating one another? What's the problem with dairy and eggs? And didn't I admire Native Americans for thanking the animals they consumed?

My initial reaction to these sorts of questions was to feel defensive. Why did I have to justify my decision not to consume animal products when the person posing the questions could sit back comfortably and feel no obligation even to consider, much less answer, the question "Why do you choose to eat animal products?" On one occasion, when my then-three-year-old daughter took the initiative and asked the mom of her friend "Why do you eat meat and eggs?," her friend's mom looked puzzled and then smiled and replied, "I guess because I'm not a vegan."

At the time, I had to bite my tongue to avoid saying, "That's actually not an answer; it simply restates the question in declarative form: "Why aren't you a vegan?" "Because I'm not a vegan." I would not cross-examine a friend in this way, but I was nonetheless struck by the fact that an intelligent and insightful adult had no response to a toddler's straightforward inquiry. This experience demonstrated to me just how infrequently this question is posed at all in polite conversation.

Like many new vegans, I found the sudden, frequent questions about my choice surprising and sometimes frustrating. "What if I don't have an answer?" I worried. If this is my one shot at convincing a friend to become vegan, will I feel like a failure if I am unable to do so? Is it fair for me to have to be constantly prepared for cross-examination?

In time, though, I have come to see the challenging inquiries as more of a gift than a burden. When a person asks me a question about veganism, it means that he has noticed that I am doing something different, and he is curious about how and why I came to depart from the customs around me. Because we tend to have many things in common with the people with whom we share our meals, the one thing that immediately distinguishes vegans—what we consider ordering from the menu—naturally stands out to our neighbors and invites discussion.

"Stereotype Threat"

One reason that a vegan might bristle upon hearing one of the questions discussed in this book is that she worries that she must now not only answer the question but simultaneously dispel whatever negative stereotypes her companions might have about vegans. As Claude Steele discusses in his fascinating and important book, *Whistling Vivaldi*,[500] the fear of confirming group stereotypes (a fear that Steele calls "stereotype threat") can distract us from being fully attentive and thus most effective in performing the thought processes required of us. If I am distracted by thoughts like "I don't want this person to see me as 'the angry vegan' or 'the self-righteous vegan' or the 'self-denying, ascetic vegan' or 'the misanthropic vegan,'" then it will be difficult for me to give my full attention to responding authentically and thoroughly to the question that he has posed.

When vegans experience such stereotype threat, it is useful to remember that many people know almost nothing about vegans, and they ask us questions because they hope to learn something new. Though there are negative stereotypes about vegans, we have probably already begun to dispel those stereotypes simply by being the diverse, friendly, and open sorts of people that we are and that those around us have understood us to be before they even learned that we were vegan.

From the non-vegan's perspective, it may be disorienting to find out that he is dining with a vegan. Like learning that one's dinner companion, someone who is by all appearances "just like us," hails from an unfamiliar and perhaps maligned culture, finding out that one's neighbor is vegan may inspire questions meant to uncover what the other culture is all about. It is a sort of "Everything You Wanted to Know About Vegans But Were Afraid To Ask" moment. Questions provide the opportunity to share and connect with people. In this light, it is possible to reappraise what might have felt like a hostile cross-examination and understand it instead as an invitation to connect, one that enables us to become closer with a friend by sharing a minority perspective with him.

It is true that vegans rarely ask their non-vegan friends, "Why do you eat animal products?" From the perspective of the non-vegan, however, a vegan's simple act of ordering an animal-ingredient-free meal can trigger the same sorts of feelings as a direct question. As soon as the vegan makes her veganism apparent by ordering exclusively plant-based food, the non-vegan becomes aware of the fact that ordering the steak or the macaroni and cheese or the omelet represents a decision to consume animal products.

What previously felt like an unimportant choice driven exclusively by taste has now become something different, something with moral overtones, and this transformation can be unwelcome and discomfiting. A non-vegan may feel as defensive when a vegan orders food as the vegan feels when the non-vegan asks "why?" This may explain the common follow-up query about whether the choice is motivated by health or ethical concerns. An ethically motivated choice implicitly calls into question the ethics of making a different choice.

To identify one's conduct as ethically motivated, in other words, can trigger the listener's suspicion that he is being judged, a suspicion that can generate a defensiveness of its own. The concern about being judged could also help explain the question discussed in chapter 5, "Mind If I Order the Cheeseburger?" In asking this question, the speaker may be attempting to gauge whether a decision to order the sort of food that he routinely orders at restaurants will offend or anger the person with whom he is dining.

This attempt is understandable, given the connection between veganism and ethics. It is unlikely, by contrast, that one's dinner companion would say the following: "I noticed that you just ordered the lentil soup. Would you be offended if I ordered the gazpacho rather than the lentil soup?" To ask whether the vegan would object to an order of animal-based food is to acknowledge that selecting a vegan option is quite different from preferring lentils over gazpacho or Indian food over Chinese food or chocolate over vanilla. This difference helps account for the "Do You Mind?" question that many vegans find so difficult to answer authentically.

A Valuable Opportunity

Notwithstanding the potential for defensiveness, many of the non-vegan's questions come from a place of open-minded curiosity. We can best communicate productively with one another if we are able to focus on the curiosity and put the suspicion and defensiveness to one side. A person who has had little opportunity or occasion to think systematically about animal rights and veganism may be quite interested in hearing what the vegan has to say about the role of animal protein in human health or about the relationship between dairy, calcium, and osteoporosis.

Most of us—vegan and non-vegan alike—have heard that it is "important" or beneficial to drink milk or to eat fish, and when we meet someone who avoids these foods, we naturally wonder why and how they do that.

The question gives vegans the chance to share valuable information about nutrition.

Along with questions about health, people who are used to eating animal products are probably thinking that being vegan would "deprive" a person of one of the great pleasures of life: joyful eating. In a world that treats meat, dairy, and eggs as the three-part foundation of culinary ecstasy, many non-vegans have no idea that millions of people find the flavors and varieties of plant-based cuisine truly wondrous. "There's no way this is vegan!" is a common, incredulous response when a non-vegan tries one of the countless delights that come out of a vegan kitchen. A question about "blandness" or "cravings" thus provides an opportunity to address the understandable but mistaken worry that vegan food is less flavorful, indulgent, or satisfying than its animal-based counterpart.

Some questions are particular to ethics, of course, and those may seem inherently hostile. They need not be, however. The same curiosity that leads people to wonder where a vegan gets her protein and calcium will also give rise to questions about how the vegan reconciles her veganism with other values that she shares with her surrounding society.

Other values may include religion and the hierarchy of creation. They can also include views about other forms of legally permissible killing, such as abortion and the consumption of plant life. And they will likely include some notion of what appears to be "natural" behavior when a lion downs a gazelle or a fox slays a rabbit. In addition, with increased multicultural awareness and sensitivity comes another important, shared value: respect for indigenous cultures whose members have robust, longstanding traditions and rituals that surround hunting and otherwise participating in the killing and consumption of animals.

Vegans can therefore expect and welcome questions on the topics of God's elevation of humanity, abortion, the natural behavior of other animals, and the hunting practices of Native Americans. All of these queries give the vegan a wonderful opportunity to explain that her ethical worldview is largely like that of the people around her and, specifically, like that of the person with whom she is talking at the moment. She can reassure her companion that she has not rejected all that her society holds dear. She can continue to be religious (or secular), pro-choice (or pro-life), a lover of nature with no ill will towards lions or tigers, and a culturally sensitive individual who respects indigenous peoples' ways of living in the world.

Rather than simply making arguments to justify her position, then, a vegan encountering these questions can offer a coherent narrative that leaves in place the ideas and priorities that are common to the surrounding society and that give value to all our lives.

Other questions represent intuitive responses to veganism that are based on misinformation about its alternatives. "Aren't the Animals Dead Already Anyway?" exposes the character of a market in which the consumer has very little direct contact with the process of production and can therefore feel like his behavior has no impact on what must happen to animals to meet consumer demand. Eating a hamburger, a slice of cow cheese pizza, or a fried egg does not "feel" like participation in violence, because it appears to happen after the fact.

As Timothy Pachirat argues in his riveting éxpose of a contemporary slaughterhouse, *Every Twelve Seconds,* the continuing vitality of the slaughterhouse depends on its literal, linguistic, and emotional concealment from the population whose demand it serves. It is this concealment that allows a package of beef (or of any other animal product) to seem no more violent than a handful of raspberries. When someone questions us, we have the chance to bring that concealment to light and expose what our audience already understands from other contexts about the connection between demand and supply.

The same psychological concealment permits people to think that there exist "humanely raised" and "humanely slaughtered" animals and animal products. In this case, the use of the word "humane" manages to obscure the cries and bellows of animals experiencing slaughter. In an entertaining video clip,[501] Dr. Jeffrey Masson responds to the claim of Alice Waters that every animal she serves in her restaurants, which includes lamb, has had a good life. He says, "Wait a minute, Alice. F*!?ing liar. . . . How can you talk about a good life for a personality that's lived for a few weeks?"[502] It becomes far easier to question and ultimately to reject faulty ethical assumptions after one has begun a dialogue with a trusted friend who has already stopped believing in them.

The question why someone would choose to be a vegan rather than a vegetarian also cries out for much-needed but largely-unknown information. For many of us, the "middle" position has an automatic appeal. We prefer not to be "extreme" in any direction, so we are inclined to opt for moderation. This impulse is often a wise one, as it brings to mind the

"Goldilocks" principle: the idea that we ought to favor things that are "just right" rather than "too hot," "too cold," "too hard," or "too soft."

A problem arises, however, when one of the two extremes occupies almost all of the spectrum along which human behavior is organized. For a Goldilocks analogy, imagine a house in which the first bowl of porridge is three hundred sixty degrees (Fahrenheit), the second bowl of porridge is two hundred sixty degrees, and the third is one hundred sixty degrees.[503] Here the "coldest" bowl of cereal is "just right." In this example, the "go for the middle" approach would result in Goldilocks badly burning her tongue.

For people who are unfamiliar with the process of producing dairy, then, consuming these products while rejecting flesh might seem "just right"—the sweet spot between a perceived extremism in either direction. It is plain, even if well concealed, that to create flesh food, someone must have slaughtered a sentient being. Dairy and eggs, on the other hand, seem like peaceful and innocuous products.

When a non-vegan asks a vegan why she chose to go beyond ovo-lacto vegetarianism, the question provides an opportune moment for the vegan to acknowledge that dairy and eggs *do* seem distinct from flesh, and the decision to be vegetarian appears correspondingly attractive. Most vegans were vegetarians first, and there is a reason for that, grounded in what appears to be a self-evident distinction between foods that come out of an animal, on the one hand, and foods that *were* the animal, on the other.

Despite the sensible appearance, however, an ethical vegan can explain why this intuitively attractive distinction between the different animal products is in reality a distinction without a difference. She can explain that purchasing and consuming dairy and eggs, whether from a factory farm or a small family farm, requires and supports the mutilation and slaughter of cows and chickens, just as the consumption of cow flesh and chicken flesh does. Indeed, the consumption of dairy supports the additional cruelty of taking baby calves from their bellowing mothers each time the latter give birth.

To understand these facts is to realize that ovo-lacto vegetarianism draws an imaginary line between harming and killing cows and chickens through one business and harming and killing cows and chickens through another business. Having come to this realization, the non-vegan can understand why it might not be accurate to characterize vegetarianism as the "moderate" or "just right" ethical choice.

Consider another analogy, this one involving women's rights. Think about progress in the fight against sexual violence. Just a few decades ago, many people who cared deeply about the women in their lives believed strongly in prohibiting and punishing rape. Yet their definition of rape excluded nonconsensual sexual relations between married couples.[504]

They were taking what they might have characterized as the "moderate" position then: prohibit the bad kind of rape, by people who have no business having sex with the woman whom they have forced, and permit the acceptable kind of rape, by husbands of their lawfully wedded wives. We now understand that rape is never justified, not because the wrong men are raping the wrong women, but because every person has an absolute right to refuse an unwanted sexual intrusion.

To object to the consumption of flesh and simultaneously condone or accept the consumption of dairy and eggs, as some theorists have done,[505] is no less arbitrary than to object to a man raping a stranger and simultaneously to accept his raping his wife. If the problem is violence and violation, then the solution is peace and respect rather than violence and violation of a different sort or against different victims.

The remaining questions offer two opposing scenarios: first, if vegans were to succeed, there would ultimately be no more domesticated animals, and wouldn't that be undesirable from the animals' perspective?; and second, because no one person can be the "perfect vegan," the questioner wonders whether the whole enterprise of veganism is pointless and bound to fail.

In some ways, these questions are in tension with each other. One hardly needs to worry about domesticated animals becoming extinct, if becoming vegan cannot make a dent in their exploitation and slaughter. And if domesticated animals were to become extinct, then it would be far easier for every human on the planet to aspire to be the "perfect" vegan. Avoiding slaughterhouse byproducts that currently make their way into everything from a car's tires to the seats on public transportation would no longer pose a challenge if the world were to become vegan.

Notwithstanding any inconsistency between the premises of these two questions, I have attempted to address both by explaining and examining the underlying assumptions behind them.

To the question about whether we would be "harming" domesticated breeds by no longer bringing them into existence, I have pointed out that it is individual animals who experience pain and death, joy and comfort, not DNA. But it is DNA that becomes extinct. Domesticated animals have been bred to be easy for us to use in various ways, but the traits that they have—however pleasing to us—are not the traits that best suit them to live happily in this world. Once they are here, I believe it is our obligation to care for them and to stop hurting them, but we are under no obligation to bring more of them into the world, especially when their births result in great pain for themselves and those who become attached to them, as well as for those wild animals who threaten to compete with humans as their predators.

To "protect" dependent livestock has involved killing and sometimes causing the extinction of animals whose habitats must become farms to grow animal feed and to grow animals. I want us to avoid confusing the survival and thriving of an individual, for whom life can go "better" or "worse" from that individual's own perspective, with the survival and thriving of a species, whose numerical growth can reflect its misery, in the case of domesticated animals who are born and raised in trauma and slaughtered before even reaching maturity.

In the case of "why bother?" I have suggested that no one person can achieve perfection in any sphere of life, but that this is no reason to give up. At the core of veganism is a life-affirming invitation to people to live and play an active role in the world around them, to remain fully engaged while simultaneously choosing compassion over predation by refusing to participate in the most direct and pervasive forms of violence against animals.

Every person who accepts this invitation has an impact on those around him or her and inspires people to think about things that were previously ignored or taken for granted. By doing this, people reduce the demand for animal suffering and slaughter that are inherent in the farming of "livestock." This in turn creates a "virtuous circle," altering the market to make veganism increasingly simple for everyone. If everyone in the past had doubted the power of each individual's choice to become conscious and take the peaceful and compassionate path, then the abolitionist, humanitarian, and civil rights movements might have never gained any traction.

As vegans know, I cannot answer every single question that comes our way in the form of "Why are you vegan, given . . . .?" What I can do, and what every ethical vegan can also do, is to tell our stories and explain that we too were in the non-vegan's shoes not that long ago but that we learned something that changed our lives immeasurably for the better. The reason that we believe in people's capacities to make significant changes in their lives is that we have done so in our own lives, and we are neither "better" nor "stronger willed" nor more "righteous" than anyone else.

We have found that the values to which we subscribed long before becoming vegan, a morality of compassion toward all living, feeling beings, is best enacted when we remove as much violence as we can from our kitchens, from our wardrobes, and from our lives. Each of us continues to learn more and to try to adjust our behavior accordingly, over time. And I hope that by sharing my own thoughts and answers to the most common questions that I have heard about veganism, I will help support other vegans and future vegans in their respective journeys toward greater peace on earth.

Acknowledgments

I gratefully acknowledge the enormously helpful comments, feedback, and editing suggestions I received from Michael C. Dorf, Taimie Bryant, Jonathan Balcombe, Harold Brown, David Cassuto, Melanie Joy, Jeffrey Masson, Alan Scheller-Wolf, Steven H. Shiffrin, Ronald K. L. Collins, and Luis Chiesa. I am indebted as well to my Cornell Law School library liason, Matthew M. Morrison, and to the research assistants who supported the development of this book with painstaking hard work and careful research and editing suggestions: Sarah Hack, Antonio Haynes, Danny Fischler, Meghan Bowman, Ian Brekke, Temidayo Aganga-Williams, J.R. Rothstein, Judah Druck, Divya Rao, Aaron Frazier, Lucas McNamara, Melissa Cabrera, Robert Jerry, and L. Sheldon Clark. Last but not least, I thank my editor, Wendy Lee of Lantern Books, for her expert editorial feedback, Nancy Rosenfeld, for finding a happy home at Lantern for this book, Kara Davis of Lantern Books and Eric Charles Lindstrom for helping in the creation and development of the cover for the book.

Endnotes

1 Tiffany Hsu, *More Vegans, Vegetarians Fuel Meatless Market. Soy Burger Anyone?*, L.A. TIMES (Mar. 20, 2012, 9:53 AM), http://www.latimes.com/business/money/la-fi-mo-meatless-vegans-vegetarians-20120320,0,3945988.story.

2 *See* T. COLIN CAMPBELL & THOMAS M. CAMPBELL II, THE CHINA STUDY 119 (2006).

3 FOOD AND AGRICULTURE ORGANIZATION OF THE UNITED NATIONS, LIVESTOCK'S LONG SHADOW: ENVIRONMENTAL ISSUES AND OPTIONS 267 (2006).

4 Robert Goodland & Jeff Anhang, *Livestock and Climate Change: What if the Key Actors in Climate Change are Cows, Pigs, and Chickens?*, WORLD WATCH, Nov./Dec. 2009, at 10, 15-19.

5 EDGAR G. HERTWICH ET AL., UNITED NATIONS ENVIRONMENT PROGRAMME, ASSESSING THE ENVIRONMENTAL IMPACTS OF CONSUMPTION AND PRODUCTION: PRIORITY PRODUCTS AND MATERIALS: A REPORT OF THE WORKING GROUP ON THE ENVIRONMENTAL IMPACTS OF PRODUCTS AND MATERIALS TO THE INTERNATIONAL PANEL FOR SUSTAINABLE RESOURCE MANAGEMENT (2010) 12, 72, 78-82, *available at* http://www.unep.org/resourcepanel/Publications/PriorityProducts/tabid/56053/Default.aspx.

6 Though people conventionally refer to nonhuman animals with the words "it," "that," or "which," this book generally avoids these terms in favor of the words "him," "her," "who," or "whom," to better reflect the reality that nonhuman animals are conscious beings who experience the world, rather than inanimate objects or things that are merely acted upon.

7 *See e.g.*, THE ENCYCLOPEDIA OF APPLIED ANIMAL BEHAVIOUR AND WELFARE 639 (Daniel S. Mills et al., eds., 2010); JOHN WEBSTER, UNDERSTANDING THE DAIRY COW 114 (2d ed., 1993).

8 *See* HUMANE SOCIETY OF THE U.S., AN HSUS REPORT: THE WELFARE OF ANIMALS IN THE VEAL INDUSTRY (2012), *available at* http://www.humanesociety.org/assets/pdfs/farm/hsus-the-welfare-of-animals-in-the-veal-industry.pdf.

9 *See id.* at 3; *Dairy Cows Fact Sheet*, ANIMALS AUSTRALIA, http://www.animalsaustralia.org/documents/factsheets/DairyCowsFactSheet.pdf (last visited Oct. 3, 2012).

10 *See The Dairy Industry*, PETA.ORG, http://www.peta.org/issues/animals-used-for-food/dairy-industry.aspx (last visited Oct. 9, 2012).

11 *See* Jennifer Welsh, *Hens Feel for Their Chicks' Discomfort*, LIVE SCI. (Mar. 9, 2011), http://www.livescience.com/13135-hens-show-empathy-chicks.html.

12 *See* PEACEABLE KINGDOM: THE JOURNEY HOME (Tribe of Heart 2009), *clip available at* http://www.peaceablekingdomfilm.org/pk_videos_english.htm.

13 *See* Marion Rumpf & Barbara Tzschentke, *Perinatal Acoustic Communication in Birds: Why Do Birds Vocalize in the Egg?*, 3 OPEN ORNITHOLOGY J. 141 (2010), http://www.benthamscience.com/open/tooenij/articles/V003/SI0124TOOENIJ/141TOOENIJ.pdf.

14 *See* HUMANE SOCIETY OF THE U.S., AN HSUS REPORT: THE WELFARE OF ANIMALS IN THE EGG INDUSTRY 1 (2009), *available at* http://www.humanesociety.org/assets/pdfs/farm/welfare_egg.pdf.

15 *See, e.g.*, *Hens from the Egg Industry*, ANIMALPLACE.ORG, http://animalplace.org/animal-care.html (last visited Oct. 9, 2012).

16 *See* ERIK MARCUS, VEGAN: THE NEW ETHICS OF EATING 102–03 (2d ed.. 2000).

17 *See* HSUS REPORT (ANIMALS IN THE EGG INDUSTRY), *supra* note 14, at 1; Vegetarian Society, *Fact Sheets: Cattle*, VEGSOC.ORG, http://www.vegsoc.org/page.aspx?pid=556 (last updated Feb. 2010).

18 *See, e.g.*, *The Emotional World of Farm Animals* (EarthViews Productions, KQED-TV, San Francisco television broadcast Oct. 2004), *available at* http://video.google.com/videoplay?docid=-8312987796490958256#.

19 *See* MARC BEKOFF, THE EMOTIONAL LIVES OF ANIMALS: A LEADING SCIENTIST EXPLORES ANIMAL JOY, SORROW, AND EMPATHY—AND WHY THEY MATTER 1 (2007).

20 *See* ELIZABETH MARSHALL THOMAS, THE HIDDEN LIFE OF DOGS xvii (1996).

21 *See* GARY FRANCIONE, INTRODUCTION TO ANIMAL RIGHTS: YOUR CHILD OR THE DOG? 2 (2000).

22 *See* Marc Bekoff, *Animal Passions and Beastly Virtues: Cognitive Ethology as the Unifying Science for Understanding the Subjective, Emotional, Empathic, and Moral Lives of Animals*, 41 ZYGON 71, 75 (2006); VICTORIA BRAITHWAITE, DO FISH FEEL PAIN? (2010).

23 CLARE PALMER, ANIMAL ETHICS IN CONTEXT 9 (2010).

24 *See* Michael J. Murray & Glenn Ross, *Neo-cartesianism and the Problem of Animal Suffering* 23 FAITH & PHIL. 169, 178 (2006); R.G. Frey, *Rights, Interests, Desires and Beliefs*, 16 AM. PHIL. Q. 233, 237 (1979).

25 *See* IMMANUEL KANT, THE METAPHYSICS OF MORALS 33 (Mary Gregor ed., 1996).

26 *See* ANDREW LINZEY, WHY ANIMAL SUFFERING MATTERS: PHILOSOPHY, THEOLOGY, AND PRACTICAL ETHICS 30 (2009).

27 *See, e.g.*, Eric Moskowitz, *YouTube Dog Clip Sparks Outrage*, BOSTON GLOBE, Mar. 1, 2009, at B.3, *available at* http://www.boston.com/news/local/massachusetts/articles/2009/03/01/youtube_dog_clip_sparks_outrage/.

28 JEREMY BENTHAM, INTRODUCTION TO THE PRINCIPLES OF MORALS AND LEGISLATION 311 (2d ed. 1823).

29 *See, e.g.*, MARTHA C. NUSSBAUM, FRONTIERS OF JUSTICE: DISABILITY, NATIONALITY, SPECIES MEMBERSHIP 387 (2006).

30 HUMPHREY PRIMATT, A DISSERTATION ON THE DUTY OF MERCY AND SIN OF CRUELTY TO BRUTE ANIMALS 7–8 (1776).

31 *Id.* at 13–14.

32 Jonathan Leake, *The Secret Life of Moody Cows*, SUNDAY TIMES, Feb. 27, 2005, at 13.

33 JOHN WEBSTER, ANIMAL WELFARE: LIMPING TOWARDS EDEN: A PRACTICAL

APPROACH TO REDRESSING THE PROBLEM OF OUR DOMINION OVER THE ANIMALS 50 (2005).

34 PETER SINGER, PRACTICAL ETHICS 133 (1993); BENTHAM, *supra* note 28, at 311.

35 Epicurus, *Letter to Menoeceus, in* GREEK AND ROMAN PHILOSOPHY AFTER ARISTO-TLE: READINGS IN THE HISTORY OF PHILOSOPHY 50 (Jason L. Saunders ed., 1994).

36 *See* Kennedy v. Louisiana, 554 U.S. 407 (2008); Coker v. Georgia, 433 U.S. 584 (1977).

37 *See* JULIAN FRANKLIN, ANIMAL RIGHTS AND MORAL PHILOSOPHY 10 (2005).

38 *See, e.g.,* Jaime Solano et al., *A Note on Behavioral Responses to Brief Cow-calf Separation and Reunion in Cattle (Bos indicus),* 2 J. VET. BEHAV.: CLINICAL APPLICATIONS & RES. 10, 11 (2007).

39 MELANIE JOY, WHY WE LOVE DOGS, EAT PIGS, AND WEAR COWS: AN INTRO-DUCTION TO CARNISM 61 (2010); Frances C. Flower & Daniel M. Weary, *Effects of Early Separation on the Dairy Cow and Calf: 2. Separation at 1 Day and 2 Weeks After Birth,* 70 APPLIED ANIMAL BEHAV. SCI. 275 (2001).

40 *See* Anne L. Engh et al., *Behavioural and hormonal responses to predation in female chacma baboons (Papio hamadryas ursinus),* 273 PROC. ROYAL SOC'Y B:BIOL. SCI. 707, 710–11 (2006).

41 Humane Methods of Livestock Slaughter Act, 7 U.S.C. §§ 1901–1907 (2006); *see also* Treatment of Live Poultry Before Slaughter, 70 Fed. Reg. 56624 (Sept. 28, 2005).

42 *See, e.g.,* TIMOTHY PACHIRAT, EVERY TWELVE SECONDS: INDUSTRIALIZED SLAUGH-TER AND THE POLITICS OF SIGHT 144–45 (2011); FRANCIONE, *supra* note 21, at 12.

43 *See, e.g., The Girl Who Can't Feel Pain,* ABCNEWS.COM (Dec. 9, 2005), http://abcnews.go.com/GMA/OnCall/story?id=1386322.

44 *See e.g., Exodus* 20:13 (King James); QURAN 17:33 (Saheeh International Transla-tion); WILLIAM BLACKSTONE, *Of Homicide, in* COMMENTARIES ON THE LAWS OF ENGLAND: BOOK THE FOURTH 177 (12th ed. 1795).

45 Dec. 21, 2009, at D2, *available at* http://www.nytimes.com/2009/12/22/sci-ence/22angi.html.

46 *See* ROD PREECE, SINS OF THE FLESH: A HISTORY OF ETHICAL VEGETARIAN THOUGHT 293 (2008).

47 *See* NATIONAL INSTITUTES OF HEALTH, UNDERSTANDING THE IMMUNE SYSTEM: HOW IT WORKS 2 (2007), *available at* http://www.niaid.nih.gov/topics/immuneSystem/Documents/theimmunesystem.pdf.

48 *Id.* at 2–3, 42.

49 *See* Mark Bittman, *A Food Manifesto for the Future,* N.Y. TIMES: OPINIONATOR, (Feb. 1, 2011, 10:28 PM), http://opinionator.blogs.nytimes.com/2011/02/01/a-food-manifesto-for-the-future/; Leo Horrigan et al., *How Sustainable Agriculture Can Address the Environmental and Human Health Harms of Industrial Agriculture,* 110 ENV'T HEALTH PERSP. 445 (2002).

50 *See* HERTWICH ET AL., UNITED NATIONS ENVIRONMENT PROGRAMME, ASSESS-ING THE ENVIRONMENT IMPACTS OF CONSUMPTION AND PRODUCTION: PRIORITY PROD-UCTS AND MATERIALS 82 (2010), *available at* http://www.unep.org/resourcepanel/Portals/24102/PDFs/PriorityProductsAndMaterials_Report.pdf.

51 *See* JONATHAN BALCOMBE, SECOND NATURE: THE INNER LIVES OF ANIMALS 16 (2010).

52 *See* BALCOMBE, *supra* note 51, at 137; BEKOFF, *supra* note 19, at 13; BRAITHWAITE, *supra* note 22, at 11; LESLEY J. ROGERS, MINDS OF THEIR OWN: THINKING AND AWARENESS IN ANIMALS 20–21 (1997); *Can You Ask a Pig if His Glass is Half Full?*, SCIENCEDAILY.COM, July 28, 2010, *available at* http://www.sciencedaily.com/releases/2010/07/100727201515.htm.

53 *See* Charles Stahler, *How Often Do Americans Eat Vegetarian Meals? And How Many Adults in the U.S. Are Vegan?*, 30 VEGETARIAN J., no. 4, 2011 at 10, *available at* http://www.vrg.org/journal/vj2011issue4/VJIssue42011.pdf; Charles Stahler, *How Many Vegetarians Are There?*, 28 VEGETARIAN J., no. 4, 2009 at 12, *available at* www.vrg.org/journal/vj2009issue4/Issue%204%202009.pdf.

54 *See, e.g.*, Vegan-TV, *Interview: A Lifelong Vegan*, YOUTUBE (July 29, 2007), http://www.youtube.com/watch?v=teJSFIYczhQ.

55 *See* DANIEL GILBERT, STUMBLING ON HAPPINESS 92, 232 (2006).

56 *See id.* at 99.

57 Colleen Patrick-Goudreau, *Life After Cheese, Vegetarian Food for Thought: Inspiring a Joyful, Sustainable, Compassionate Diet* (Feb. 26, 2007) (downloaded using iTunes), *available at* http://feeds.feedburner.com/VegetarianFoodForThought.

58 *Cf.* Milton R. Mills, *The Comparative Anatomy of Eating*, VEGSOURCE (Nov. 21, 2009), http://www.vegsource.com/news/2009/11/the-comparative-anatomy-of-eating.html.

59 *See* Tara Parker-Pope, *Tasty Vegan Food? Cupcakes Show It Can Be Done*, N.Y. TIMES: WELL (Sept. 6, 2010, 5:10 PM), http://well.blogs.nytimes.com/2010/09/06/tasty-vegan-food-cupcakes-show-it-can-be-done/.

60 John Pomfret, *Diplomacy in the Operating Room: U.S., Chinese Scientists Cooperate to Unravel Esophageal Cancer*, WASH. POST, June 7, 1998, at A17, *available at* http://www.cicams.ac.cn/epi/woshingtonpost.htm.http://www.cicams.ac.cn/epi/woshingtonpost.htm.

61 *See* CAMPBELL & CAMPBELL, *supra* note 2, at 102, 139-40; Caroline Wilbert, *Vegan Diet Good for Type 2 Diabetes: Vegan Diet Beats ADA-Recommended Diet in Lowering Heart Disease Risk*, WEBMD, (Oct. 1, 2008), http://diabetes.webmd.com/news/20081001/vegan-diet-good-type-2-diabetes.

62 *See, e.g.*, Alexander Stephens, Vice President of the Confederacy, Cornerstone Address at Savannah, Ga., (Mar. 21, 1861); WILLIAM JOHN GRAYSON, THE HIRELING AND THE SLAVE viii (2d ed. 1855).

63 CTR. FOR NUTRITION POL'Y & PROMOTION, U.S. DEP'T OF AGRIC., THE FOOD GUIDE PYRAMID 1–2 (1992, rev. 1996), *available at* http://www.cnpp.usda.gov/Publications/MyPyramid/OriginalFoodGuidePyramids/FGP/FGPPamphlet.pdf.

64 JOEL FUHRMAN, EAT TO LIVE: THE REVOLUTIONARY FORMULA FOR FAST AND SUSTAINED WEIGHT LOSS 138 (2005).

65 *Id.*

66 *Id.* at 137–39.

67 *See id.* at 166, 118-119.

68 *Id.* at 166.

69 *Id.*

70 Mary Pilon, *Sculpted by Weights and a Strict Vegan Diet*, N.Y. TIMES, Jan. 4, 2012, at B10, *available at* http://www.nytimes.com/2012/01/05/sports/vegans-muscle-their-way-into-bodybuilding.html.

71 *Id.*

72 *Id.*; *see also* www.veganbodybuilding.com/forum.

73 *See* Pilon, *supra* note 70; *see also* One Man, One Day, 4,300 Vegan Calories, N.Y. Times, Jan. 5, 2012, *available at* http://www.nytimes.com/imagepages/2012/01/05/sports/05vegan-graphic.html?ref=sports.

74 *See* Pilon, *supra* note 70.

75 *See* Stephen Honig, *Osteoporosis: New Treatments and Updates*, Bulletin of the NYU Hosp. for Joint Diseases 68, 166, (2010); National Osteoporosis Foundation, *Prevalence Report*, NOF.org, http://www.nof.org/advocacy/resources/prevalencereport (last visited Oct. 11, 2012).

76 *See* Paul Lips, *Epidemiology and Predictors of Fractures Associated With Osteoporosis*, Am. J. Med., Aug. 18, 1997, at 3S, 3S–4S.

77 *See, e.g.*, California Milk Processor Board, *About the Brand*, got milk?, gotmilk. com (follow "About" hyperlink) (last visited Oct. 11, 2012).

78 Fuhrman, *supra* note 64, at 88.

79 *See* Campbell & Campbell, *supra* note 7, at 204–05; Anteneh Roba, Letter to the Editor, *Dairy: A Re-Evaluation*, 97 J. Nat'l Med. Ass'n 843 (2005). *See generally* S. Maggi et al., *Incidence of Hip Fractures in the Elderly: A Cross-National Analysis*, 1 Osteoporosis Int'l 232, 238 (1991).

80 *Id.* at 86; Ji-Fan Hu et al., *Dietary Intakes and Urinary Excretion of Calcium and Acids: A Cross-Sectional Study of Women in China*, 58 Am. J. Clin. Nutr. 398, 401 (1993); Linda K. Massey, *Does Excess Dietary Protein Adversely Affect Bone? Symposium Overview*, 128 J. Nutr. 1048 (June 1998).

81 Fuhrman, *supra* note 64, at 86; Hu et al., *supra* note 80, at 402.

82 Benjamin J. Abelow et al., *Cross-Cultural Association Between Dietary Animal Protein and Hip Fracture: A Hypothesis*, 50 Calcified Tissue Int'l 14, 16 (1992); *accord.* Fuhrman, *supra* note 64, at 86.

83 *See* Academy of Nutrition and Dietetics, formerly the American Dietetic Association, *Position of the American Dietetic Association: Vegetarian Diets*, 109 J. Amer. Dietetic Ass'n 1266 (2009), *available at* http://www.eatright.org/Media/content.aspx-?id=1233&terms=vegetarian#.UPhofB00V8F.

84 *Id.* at 1267.

85 *See* Academy of Nutrition and Dietetics formerly the American Dietetic Association, *Who Are the Academy's Corporate Sponsors?*, EatRight.org, http://www.eatright.org/corporatesponsors/ (last visited Oct. 11, 2012); Marion Nestle, Food Politics: How the Food Industry Influences Nutrition and Health 126–29 (2002).

86 *See* Benjamin Spock & Robert Needlman, Dr. Spock's Baby and Child Care 381 (9th ed. 2012); Jane E. Brody, *Final Advice from Dr. Spock: Eat Only All Your Vegetables*, N.Y. Times, June 20, 1998, at A1, *available at* http://www.nytimes.com/1998/06/20/us/final-advice-from-dr-spock-eat-only-all-your-vegetables.html?pagewanted=all&src=pm.

87 *See, e.g.*, Kim Willsher, *French Vegans Face Trial After Death of Baby Fed Only on Breast Milk*, Guardian, Mar. 30, 2011, at 23, *available at* http://www.guardian.co.uk/world/2011/mar/29/vegans-trial-death-baby-breast-milk.

88 *See* Campbell & Campbell, *supra* note 2, at 250, 327, 328–29; Caldwell B. Esselstyn, Jr., Prevent and Reverse Heart Disease 3 (2008); Pauline W. Chen, *Teaching Doctors About Nutrition and Diet*, N. Y. Times (Sept. 16, 2010), http://www.

nytimes.com/2010/09/16/health/16chen.html; Kelly M. Adams et al., *Nutrition Education in U.S. Medical Schools: Latest Update of a National Survey*, 85 ACAD. MED. 1537, 1538 (2010).

89 *See* Nina Plank, Op-Ed., *Death By Veganism*, N.Y. TIMES, May 21, 2007, at A19, *available at* http://www.nytimes.com/2007/05/21/opinion/21planck.html; *see also* Sherry F. Colb, *Death By Ignorance*, DORF ON LAW (May 22, 2007, 7:02 AM), http://www.dorfonlaw.org/2007/05/death-by-ignorance.html; John McDougall, *McDougall Reply to New York Times*, DRMCDOUGALL.COM (May 21, 2007), http://www.drmcdougall.com/misc/2007other/nytimes.html.

90 *See Friends: The One With the Fake Party* (NBC television broadcast Mar. 19, 1998); Jessica Carlson, *Natalie Portman Won't Stay Vegan During Pregnancy*, IMPERFECT-PARENT.COM (Apr. 11, 2011), http://www.imperfectparent.com/topics/2011/04/11/natalie-portman-wont-stay-vegan-during-pregnancy/.

91 *See* TRUST FOR AMERICA'S HEALTH & ROBERT WOOD JOHNSON FOUNDATION, ISSUE REPORT: F AS IN FAT: HOW OBESITY THREATENS AMERICA'S FUTURE 9, 101–02 (2010), *available at* http://healthyamericans.org/reports/obesity2010/Obesity2010Report.pdf; Katherine M. Flegal et al., Prevalence and Trends in Obesity Among US Adults, 1999-2008, 303 J. AM. MED. ASS'N 235, 240 (2010).

92 DOUGLAS J. LISLE & ALAN GOLDHAMER, THE PLEASURE TRAP: MASTERING THE HIDDEN FORCE THAT UNDERMINES HEALTH AND HAPPINESS 88–89 (2003).

93 *See id.* at 65, 67; Jonathan Wright, *Wild Animals: Overweight Wild Animals*, ALLEXPERTS.COM (Sept. 14, 2006), http://en.allexperts.com/q/Wild-Animals-705/Overweight-Wild-Animals.htm; Alla Katsnelson, *Lab Animals and Pets Face Obesity Epidemic*, SCIENTIFICAMERICAN.COM (Nov. 24, 2010), http://www.scientificamerican.com/article.cfm?id=lab-animals-and-pets-face-obesity.

94 *See* Ass'n for Pet Obesity Prevention, *Fat Pets Getting Fatter According to Latest Survey*, PETOBESITYPREVENTION.COM (Feb. 23, 2011), http://www.petobesityprevention.com/fat-pets-getting-fatter-according-to-latest-survey/.

95 LISLE & GOLDHAMER, *supra* note 92, at 74; *see also* Mark Bittman, *Hooked on Meat*, N.Y. TIMES: OPINIONATOR (May 31, 2011, 8:30 PM), http://opinionator.blogs.nytimes.com/2011/05/31/meat-why-bother/.

96 LISLE & GOLDHAMER, *supra* note 92, at 90; Corby K. Martin et al., *The Association Between Food Cravings and Consumption of Specific Foods in a Laboratory Taste Test*, 51 APPETITE 324 (2008).

97 *See, e.g.*, JULIE SHERTZER & JAMIE FOSTER, OHIO STATE UNIVERSITY EXTENSION, FACT SHEET: FAMILY AND CONSUMER SCIENCES: NUTRITIONAL NEEDS OF PREGNANCY AND BREASTFEEDING 2 (updated 2008), *available at* ohioline.osu.edu/hyg-fact/5000/pdf/5573.pdf; JOINT STATEMENT BY THE WORLD HEALTH ORGANIZATION, THE WORLD FOOD PROGRAMME AND THE UNITED NATIONS CHILDREN'S FUND: PREVENTING AND CONTROLLING MICRONUTRIENT DEFICIENCIES IN POPULATIONS AFFECTED BY AN EMERGENCY 1 (2007), *available at* http://www.who.int/entity/nutrition/publications/micronutrients/WHO_WFP_UNICEFstatement.pdf.

98 *See* Michela Dai Zovi, *Western Diet Culture*, LIVESTRONG.COM (Sept. 26, 2010), http://www.livestrong.com/article/260131-western-diet-culture/; Carrie R. Daniel et al., *Trends in Meat Consumption in the United States*, 14 PUBLIC HEALTH NUTRITION 575, 579 (2011).

99 *See Docs Want Pregnancy Guidelines Lowered*, MSNBC.MSN.com, (Aug. 14, 2007, 3:34 PM), http://www.msnbc.msn.com/id/20265998/.

100 *See* Committee to Reexamine IOM Pregnancy Weight Guidelines, Institute of Medicine, Weight Gain During Pregnancy: Reexamining the Guidelines 15 (Kathleen Rasmussen & Ann L. Yaktine eds., 2009).

101 *See* Roni Caryn Rabin, *New Goal for the Obese: Zero Gain in Pregnancy*, N.Y. Times, Dec. 15, 2009, at D1, online version *available at* http://www.nytimes.com/2009/12/15/health/15obese.html.

102 Reed Mangels, *Iron in the Vegan Diet*, VRg.org, http://www.vrg.org/nutrition/iron.htm (last visited Oct. 13, 2012); *see also* Fuhrman, *supra* note 64, at 60.

103 *See, e.g.*, Dan McKenna *Myopathy, Hypokalaemia and Pica (Geophagia) in Pregnancy*, 75 Ulster Med.l J. 159 (2006); Ernest B. Hook, *Dietary Cravings and Aversions During Pregnancy*, 31 Am. J. Clinical Nutrition 1355, 1359, tbl.5 (1978).

104 Campbell & Campbell, *supra* note 2, at 232.

105 *Id.*

106 *Id.* at 233.

107 *See id.* at 31; Frances Moore Lappé, Diet for a Small Planet: Twentieth Anniversary Edition 162 (1991); John Robbins, Diet for a New America 170–202 (1998).

108 Campbell & Campbell, *supra* note 2, at 105, 119, 190.

109 *Id.* at 77.

110 *Id.* at 78–79.

111 *Id.* at 79.

112 *Id.*

113 *See id.* app. B at 353–57.

114 *See id.* at 73–74, 80.

115 *See id.* at 80, 88–89.

116 *Id.* at 71.

117 *Id.*

118 *See* Donna L. Hoyert & Jiaquan Xu, U.S. Dep't of Health and Human Services & Centers for Disease Control and Prevention, *Deaths: Preliminary Data for 2011*, 61 CDC Nat'l Vital Stat. Rep., Oct. 10, 2012, at 1, tbl.B at 28, *available at* http://www.cdc.gov/nchs/data/nvsr/nvsr61/nvsr61_06.pdf.

119 *See* Norman Jolliffe & Morton Archer, *Statistical Associations Between International Coronary Heart Disease Death Rates and Certain Environmental Factors*, 9 J. Chronic Diseases 636, 639, tbl.I, 650 (1959).

120 Caldwell B. Esselstyn, Jr., *Is the Present Therapy for Coronary Artery Disease the Radical Mastectomy of the Twenty-First Century?*, 106 Am. J. Cardiology 902 (2010).

121 *Id.* at 902.

122 *See* Esselstyn, *supra* note 88, at 11–12, 67. *Compare Cholesterol Levels: What Numbers Should You Aim For?*, MayoClinic.com (last updated Sept. 21, 2012), http://www.mayoclinic.com/health/cholesterol-levels/CL00001.

123 *See* Esselstyn, *supra* note 120, at 902.

124 Axel Strom & R. Adelsten Jensen, *Mortality From Circulatory Diseases in Norway 1940-1945*, 257 Lancet 126 (1951).

125 *See* Esselstyn, *supra* note 120, at 902.

126 *See* Strom & Jensen, *supra* note 124, at 129; Esselstyn, *supra* note 120, at 902.

127 *See* Strom & Jensen, *supra* note 124, at 129.

128 *See, e.g.*, Yingfen Hsia et al., *An Increase in the Prevalence of Type 1 and 2 Diabetes in Children and Adolescents: Results From Prescription Data from a UK General Practice Database*, 67 Brit. J. Clinical Pharmacology 242 (2009); Anne Fagot-Campagna et al., *Type 2 Diabetes Among North American Children and Adolescents: An Epidemiologic Review and a Public Health Perspective*, 136 J. Pediatrics 664 (2000).

129 *See, e.g.*, U.S. Dep't of Health and Human Services & Centers for Disease Control and Prevention, National Diabetes Fact Sheet: National Estimates and General Information on Diabetes and Prediabetes in the United States 8 (2011), *available at* www.cdc.gov/diabetes/pubs/pdf/ndfs_2011.pdf; Elizabeth H.B. Lin et al., *Depression and Advanced Complications of Diabetes: A Prospective Cohort Study*, 33 Diabetes Care 264 (2010).

130 Campbell & Campbell, *supra* note 2, at 149 (citing Kelly M. West & John M. Kalbfleisch, *Glucose Tolerance, Nutrition, and Diabetes in Uruguay, Venezuela, Malaya, and East Pakistan*, 15 Diabetes 9 (1966)).

131 Campbell & Campbell, *supra* note 2, at 152 (citing R. James Barnard et al., *Response of Non-Insulin-Dependent Diabetic Patients to an Intensive Program of Diet and Exercise*, 5 Diabetes Care 370 (1982)).

132 *See, e.g.*, Neal Barnard, Dr. Neal Barnard's Program for Reversing Diabetes: The Scientifically Proven System for Reversing Diabetes Without Drugs (2007); John A. McDougall, The McDougall Program for a Healthy Heart: A Life-Saving Approach to Preventing and Treating Heart Disease (1998).

133 *See* USDA National Agricultural Statistical Service, Hatchery Production 2010 Summary 1 (2011), *available at* http://usda.mannlib.cornell.edu/usda/nass/HatcProdSu//2010s/2011/HatcProdSu-04-15-2011.pdf; Michael C. Appleby et al., Poultry Behavior and Welfare 184 (2004); *Farming in Season*, FarmForward.com, http://www.farmforward.com/features/spring (last visited Oct. 26, 2011); David Fraser et al., *Farm Animals and Their Welfare in 2000 in* The State of the Animals 2001 87, 90 (Deborah J. Salem & Andrew N. Rowan eds., 2001) (citing USDA National Agricultural Statistical Service, Hatchery Production Summary (1999)).

134 *See* Humane Society of the U.S., An HSUS Report: The Welfare of Cows in the Dairy Industry (2009), *available at* http://www.humanesociety.org/assets/pdfs/farm/hsus-the-welfare-of-cows-in-the-dairy-industry.pdf.

135 *See id.*; HSUS Report (Animals in the Veal Industry), *supra* note 8.

136 *See* HSUS Report (Cows in the Dairy Industry), *supra* note 134; U.S. Department of Agriculture, Food Safety & Inspection Service, Veal from Farm to Table, *available at* http://www.fsis.usda.gov/Fact_Sheets/Veal_from_Farm_to_Table/index.asp.

137 *See generally*, J. Lindsay Falvey, An Introduction to Working Animals 108–12 (1985).

138 American Academy of Pediatrics, *Breastfeeding and the Use of Human Milk*, 115 Pediatrics 496, 498 (2005), *available at* http://pediatrics.aappublications.org/content/115/2/496.full; World Health Organization, *Breastfeeding*, Who.int, http://www.who.int/topics/breastfeeding/en (last visited October 26, 2011).

139 *See* Frances C. Flower & Daniel M. Weary, *Effects of Early Separation on the Dairy Cow and Calf: 2. Separation at 1 Day and 2 Weeks After Birth*, 70 App. Anim. Behav.

Sci. 275, 275 (2001); Susan J. Hudson & M.M. Mullord, *Investigations of Maternal Bonding in Dairy Cattle*, 3 App. Anim. Ethol. 275 (1977).

140 The Encyclopedia of Applied Animal Behaviour and Welfare 636 (Daniel S. Mills et al., eds., 2010).

141 *See* Karen Dawn, Thanking the Monkey: Rethinking the Way We Treat Animals 162 (2008).

142 The Encyclopedia of Applied Animal Behaviour and Welfare, *supra* note 140, at 639; Joanne Stepaniak, The Vegan Sourcebook 39 (2d ed. 2000); John Webster, Understanding the Dairy Cow 114 (2d ed., 1993).

143 *See Pennsylvania Cruelty Case—26 Cows and Calves Rescued*, Farm Sanctuary, http://www.nofoiegras.org/rescue/rescues/past/butler.html.

144 *See Cruelty to Cows*, dairycruelty.com.au, http://www.dairycruelty.com.au/cows.php.

145 *See* Tara Parker-Pope, *Maternal Instinct Is Wired Into the Brain*, N.Y. Times Blog (Mar. 7, 2008, 2:00 PM), http://well.blogs.nytimes.com/2008/03/07/maternal-instinct-is-wired-into-the-brain.

146 *See* HSUS Report (Cows in the Dairy Industry), *supra* note 134; *The Welfare of Cattle in Dairy Production*, Farm Sanctuary, http://thehill.com/images/stories/whitepapers/pdf/DairyCattleWelfareReport.pdf.

147 *See* J.R. Perkins et al., A Study of 1,000 Bovine Genitalia, 37 J. Dairy Sci. 1158, 1159 (1954); D.E.B. Lawton et al., *Farmer Record of Pregnancy Status Pre-Slaughter Compared with Actual Pregnancy Status Post-Slaughter*, 48 N.Z. Vet. J. 160, 162, tbl.I (2000).

148 *See* Ronald M. Nowak, Walker's Mammals of the World 1157 (1999); Baahaus Animal Rescue Group, *Farm Animal FAQs*, Baahaus.org, http://www.baahaus.org/faqs.html.

149 *See* Nicholas D. Kristof, Where Cows Are Happy and Food Is Healthy, N.Y. Times, Sept. 8, 2012, at SR1, *available at* http://www.nytimes.com/2012/09/09/opinion/sunday/kristof-where-cows-are-happy-and-food-is-healthy.html?_r=0

150 *See* H.F. Troutt & B.I. Osburn, *Meat From Dairy Cows: Possible Microbiological Hazards and Risks*, 16 Revue Scientifique et Technique 405 (1997); Jim Bodor & Jacqueline Reis, *How Safe is Our Beef?: Inspectors, Farmers, Brokers Part of Mad Cow Defense*, Worcester Telegram & Gazette, Jan. 18, 2004, at A1.

151 A.W. Nordskog, *Breeding for Eggs and Poultry Meats, in* Animal Agriculture: The Biology of Domestic Animals and Their Use By Man 321 (H.H. Cole & Magnar Ronning eds., 1974); Sidney L. Spahr & George E. Opperman, The Dairy Cow Today: U.S. Trends, Breeding, and Progress Since 1980 8 (1995); *Broiler Chicken Fact Sheet*, Animals Australia, http://www.animalsaustralia.org/factsheets/broiler_chickens.php.

152 The Encyclopedia of Applied Animal Behaviour and Welfare, *supra* note 140, at 95.

153 *See* John Webster, Understanding the Dairy Cow 261 (2d ed., 1993).

154 USDA National Agriculture Library, Entry for "veal calves" in Agricultural Thesaurus and Glossary, NAL Services, http://agclass.nal.usda.gov/mtwdk.exe?k=glossary&l=60&w=7551&n=1&s=5&t=2 (last visited Nov. 2, 2011).

155 Joanna Lucas, *Letter From a Vegan World*, Peaceful Prairie Sanctuary, http://www.peacefulprairie.org/letter.html; Amy, *My Trip to the Stockyard*, Animal Writes

BLOG (July 31, 2009, 10:26 PM), http://studentsforanimalrights.blogspot.com/2009/07/ my-trip-to-stockyard.html; *The Cow Ribbon Campaign*, LIBERATION BC, http://liberationbc.org/projects/cow-ribbon.

156 *See* HSUS REPORT (ANIMALS IN THE VEAL INDUSTRY), *supra* note 8.

157 The Humane Farming Association, *HFA's National Veal Boycott—Campaign Decimating Sales*, HFA.ORG, http://www.hfa.org/vealBoycott.html (last visited Dec. 3, 2011).

158 For photos of a broiler-bred chick beside a layer-bred chick of the same age, see Powered By Produce, *Movie Review: Food, Inc.*, POWERED-BY-PRODUCE.COM (Jan. 28, 2010), http://www.powered-by-produce.com/2010/01/28/movie-review-food-inc (six-weeks-old).

159 *See* THE ENCYCLOPEDIA OF APPLIED ANIMAL BEHAVIOUR AND WELFARE, *supra* note 140, at 96; HUMANE SOC'Y OF THE U.S., AN HSUS REPORT: THE WELFARE OF ANIMALS IN THE CHICKEN INDUSTRY, HUMANE SOC'Y OF THE U.S., 4 (2008), available at http://www.humanesociety.org/assets/pdfs/farm/welfare_broiler.pdf (citing C.G. SCANES ET AL., POULTRY SCIENCE 260 (4th ed., 2004)).

160 *See* Vancouver Humane Society, *Farm Animals: Animal Rescue*, VANCOUVERHUMANESOCIETY.BC.CA, http://vancouverhumanesociety.bc.ca/farmanimals_rescue.html (last visited Nov. 2, 2011).

161 M. N. Romanov & S. Weigend, *Analysis of Genetic Relationships Between Various Populations of Domestic and Jungle Fowl Using Microsatellite Markers*, 80 POULTRY SCI. 1057 (2001), *available at* http://ps.fass.org/content/80/8/1057.full.pdf.

162 United Poultry Concerns, *Chickens: The Egg-Laying Hen*, UPC-ONLINE.ORG, http://www.upc-online.org/chickens/chickensbro.html (last visited Nov. 6, 2011).

163 *See* HUMANE SOCIETY OF THE U.S., AN HSUS REPORT: WELFARE ISSUES WITH SELECTIVE BREEDING OF EGG-LAYING HENS FOR PRODUCTIVITY 1 (2010), *available at* http://www.humanesociety.org/assets/pdfs/farm/welfiss_breeding_egg.pdf (citing A.B. Webster, *Welfare Implications of Avian Osteoporosis*, 83 POULTRY SCI. 184, 188 (2004)); S.C. Bishop et al., *Inheritance of Bone Characteristics Affecting Osteoporosis in Laying Hens*, 41 BRITISH POULTRY SCI. 33 (2000), *available at* http://www.tandfonline.com/doi/abs/10.1080/00071660086376.

164 Conversation with Harold Brown, former animal farmer and founder of FarmKind.org, in Ithaca, N.Y. (October 31, 2010).

165 *See* HSUS REPORT (ANIMALS IN THE EGG INDUSTRY), *supra* note 14, at 7.

166 *See id.* at 1.

167 *See* DAVID EAGLEMAN, INCOGNITO: THE SECRET LIVES OF THE BRAIN 57 (2011).

168 *See* HSUS REPORT (ANIMALS IN THE EGG INDUSTRY), *supra* note 14, at 1. For footage of sorting and disposal of males, see Compassion for Animals, *"Farm to Fridge" by Mercy for Animals: Condensed Version*, YOUTUBE.COM (June 10, 2011), http://www.youtube.com/watch?v=hP3y3OwSHyk.

169 *See* 7 C.F.R. §§ 205.236–205.239 (2010); HUMANE FARM ANIMAL CARE, ANIMAL CARE STANDARDS: EGG LAYING HENS (2009), *available at* http://www.certifiedhumane.org/uploads/pdf/Standards/English/Std09.Layers.2J.pdf.

170 *See* JONATHAN SAFRAN FOER, EATING ANIMALS 109 (2009); *Food Choices*, FARMFORWARD.COM, http://www.farmforward.com/farming-forward/food-choices (last visited Nov. 25, 2011).

171 *See* Institute for Reproductive Health, *Natural Family Planning*, irh.org, http://archive.irh.org/nfp.htm (last visited Nov. 25, 2011).

172 *See* Laurie Zoloth, *"Each One an Entire World": A Jewish Perspective on Family Planning*, *in* SACRED RIGHTS: THE CASE FOR CONTRACEPTION AND ABORTION IN WORLD RELIGIONS 21, 31 (Daniel C. Maguire ed., 2003); DAVID MICHAEL FELDMAN, BIRTH CONTROL IN JEWISH LAW: MARITAL RELATIONS, CONTRACEPTION, AND ABORTION 48 (1968).

173 *Genesis* 3:16 (King James).

174 *See* ABUL FADL MOHSIN EBRAHIM, ABORTION, BIRTH CONTROL & SURROGATE PARENTING: AN ISLAMIC PERSPECTIVE 19 (1989) (Islam); Sandhya Jain, *The Right to Family Planning, Contraception, and Abortion*, *in* SACRED RIGHTS: THE CASE FOR CONTRACEPTION AND ABORTION IN WORLD RELIGIONS 129, 130 (Daniel C. Maguire ed., 2003) (Hinduism); Amirrtha Srikanthan & Robert L. Reid, *Religious and Cultural Influences on Contraception*, 30 J. Obstet. Gynaecol. Can. 129, 134 (2008), *available at* http://www.jogc.com/abstracts/full/200802_WomensHealth_1.pdf (citing B. Gnanawimala, *The Buddhist View: Free to Choose*, ASIAWEEK, Oct. 27, 1993, 54.) (Buddhism).

175 *See Egg Yolk Peritonitis*, AVIANWEB.COM, http://www.avianweb.com/eggyolk-peritonitis.html (last visited Nov. 27, 2011); *Egg Binding*, BIRDVET.COM.AU, http://www.birdvet.com.au/birdcare/EGG%20BINDING.htm (last visited Nov 27, 2011); Merck Veterinary Manual, *Egg-Bound or Impacted Oviducts*, MERCKVETMANUAL.COM, http://www.merckvetmanual.com/mvm/index.jsp?cfile=htm/bc/205803.htm (last visited Nov. 27, 2011); *Prolapsed Cloaca*, AvianWeb.com, http://www.avianweb.com/Prolapse.htm (last visited Nov. 27, 2011).

176 *See Cow*, ANIMAL PLANET (Apr. 22, 2008), http://animals.howstuffworks.com/mammals/cow-info.htm; Jan Sargeant et al., *Clinical Mastitis in Dairy Cattle in Ontario: Frequency of Occurrence and Biological Isolates*, 39 CAN. VET. J. 33, 35 (1998).

177 *See* Ruth C. Newberry et al., *Management of Spent Hens*, 2 J. APPLIED ANIMAL WELFARE SCI. 13, 14 (1999).

178 *See, e.g.*, Blake Morrison, Peter Eisler and Anthony DeBarros, *Old-hen Meat Fed to Pets and Schoolkids*, USA TODAY, Dec. 9, 2009, http://usatoday30.usatoday.com/news/education/2009-12-08-hen-meat-school-lunch_N.htm.

179 *The Dairy Industry*, PETA, http://www.peta.org/issues/animals-used-for-food/dairy-industry.aspx (last visited May 1, 2012); HSUS REPORT (COWS IN THE DAIRY INDUSTRY), *supra* note 134, at 8.

180 *See* Barbara McDonald, *Once You Know Something, You Can't Not Know It: An Empirical Look at Becoming Vegan*, 8 SOC'Y & ANIMALS 1, 4, tbl.1 (2000), *available at* http://www.animalsandsociety.org/assets/library/404_s811.pdf.

181 Francione discusses a "stages" approach to veganism on his blog, Animal Rights: The Abolitionist Approach. *Vegan Mondays?*, ABOLITIONISTAPPROACH.COM, http://www.abolitionistapproach.com/vegan-mondays/ (Apr. 4, 2010).

182 *See* HSUS REPORT (ANIMALS IN THE CHICKEN INDUSTRY), *supra* note 159, at 7.

183 For a video showing a cow awaiting slaughter who exhibits fear and tries to turn around and escape, see *Dans le Couloir de la Mort (Death Row)*, YOUTUBE.COM (Dec. 8, 2008), http://www.youtube.com/watch?v=aHTNq33cXBQ.

184 Farm Sanctuary, *The Dish on Vegetarianism*, VegForLife.org, http://www.vegforlife.org/eats_dish.htm (last visited Dec. 4, 2011); PETA, *Three Reasons to Go Vegetarian*,

PETA.org, http://www.peta.org/tv/videos/psas-vegetarianism/1617808251001.aspx (last visited October 29, 2012).

185 Jo Tyler, *I Say Vegan, You Say Vegetarian, Let's Call the Whole Thing Off*, This-VeganLife.org (Sept. 2011), http://www.thisveganlife.org/i-say-vegan-you-say-vegetarian-lets-call-the.

186 *See* James Oliver Horton, *Safe Harbor: John Brown*, WQLN.ORG, http://www.wqln.org/main/television/original%20productions/Safe%20Harbor/Film/InterviewTranscripts/Horton/JohnBrown.htm.

187 Bowers v. Hardwick, 478 U.S. 186, 188 n.2 (1986).

188 Lawrence v. Texas, 539 U.S. 558, 578–79 (2003).

189 *See* Human Rights Campaign, *Civil Unions*, HRC.ORG, http://www.hrc.org/issues/pages/civil-unions (last visited Dec. 18, 2012); Human Rights Campaign, *Domestic Partners*, HRC.ORG, http://www.hrc.org/issues/pages/domestic-partnerships (last visited Oct. 17, 2012).

190 *See, e.g.*, NORAH VINCENT, SELF-MADE MAN: ONE WOMAN'S JOURNEY INTO MANHOOD AND BACK AGAIN (2006); THOMAS EGELSTON, THE LIFE OF JOHN PATERSON: MAJOR-GENERAL IN THE REVOLUTIONARY ARMY 236–40 (2d ed. 1898), *reprinted in Deborah Sampson: How She Served as a Soldier in the Revolution—Her Sex Unknown to the Army*, N.Y. TIMES, Oct. 8, 1898, *available at* http://query.nytimes.com/gst/abstract.html?res=9402E3D71139E433A2575BC0A9669D94699ED7CF.

191 *See, e.g.*, HENRY LOUIS GATES, JR., *The Passing of Anatole Broyard, in* THIRTEEN WAYS OF LOOKING AT A BLACK MAN, 180–214 (1997).

192 *See, e.g.*, *Statement on Philosophy*, HOMOSEXUALS-ANONYMOUS.COM, http://www.homosexuals-anonymous.com/statement-on-philosophy (last visited Oct. 17, 2012).

193 *See, e.g.*, OUTRAGE (Magnolia Pictures 2009); Eve Conant, *Left Wing: When Gay Bashers Are Gay, Why Do People Just Mock and Turn Away?*, Newsweek.com (May 6, 2010, 2:07 PM), http://www.newsweek.com/blogs/the-gaggle/2010/05/06/left-wing-when-gay-bashers-are-gay-why-do-people-just-mock-and-turn-away.html.

194 *See* Jesse Bering, *Single, Angry, Straight Male . . . Seeks Same?*, SCIENTIFIC AMERICAN, January 2009, *available at* http://www.scientificamerican.com/article.cfm?id=single-angry-straight-male.

195 *See* KENJI YOSHINO, COVERING: THE HIDDEN ASSAULT ON OUR CIVIL RIGHTS 18, 19 (2007).

196 *See, e.g.*, MICHELANGELO SIGNORILE, QUEER IN AMERICA: SEX, THE MEDIA, AND THE CLOSETS OF POWER (2003).

197 *See* Michael Warner, *Introduction, in* FEAR OF A QUEER PLANET: QUEER POLITICS AND SOCIAL THEORY xxi (Michael Warner ed., 1993); The Kinsey Institute, *Kinsey's Heterosexual-Homosexual Rating Scale*, IUB.EDU (last updated Mar. 2009), http://www.iub.edu/~kinsey/research/ak-hhscale.html.

198 *See* JOY, *supra* note 39, at 96–97, 109.

199 *See generally* NICK FIDDES, MEAT: A NATURAL SYMBOL (1991); MICHAEL POLLAN, THE OMNIVORE'S DILEMMA (2006).

200 *See, e.g.*, Heather Timmons & Nikhila Gill, *India's Health Minister Calls Homosexuality 'Unnatural,'* N.Y. TIMES (July 5, 2011), http://www.nytimes.com/2011/07/06/world/asia/06india.html.

201 *See also* JOY, *supra* note 39, at 11-12.

202 Yoshino, *supra* note 195, at 61, 68.

203 For narratives on the emotional lives that animals lead, see Jeffrey Moussaieff Masson & Susan McCarthy, When Elephants Weep (1995).

204 *See* Sherry F. Colb, *Probabilities in Probable Cause and Beyond: Statistical Versus Concrete Harms*, 73 Law & Contemp. Probs. 69, 71–73 n.12 (2010); Karen E. Jenni & George Loewenstein, *Explaining the "Identifiable Victim Effect,"* 14 J. Risk & Uncertainty 235–37 (1997).

205 *See e.g.*, Marlone D. Henderson et al., *Transcending the "Here": The Effect of Spatial Distance on Social Judgment*, 91 J. Personality & Soc. Psychol. 845 (2006).

206 *See e.g.*, Frederick Taylor, Dresden: Tuesday, February 13, 1945 416 (2004).

207 *See* Joy, supra note 39, at 40, 48; John Ezard, *Getting Meat's Image Off the Hook: Butchers Seek to Play Down the Gruesome Image of Their Trade*, Guardian, Nov. 30, 1984; *Labeling Debate: Engaging the Public*, MeatInfo: Online Meat Trades J. (Oct. 15, 2010), http://www.meatinfo.co.uk/news/fullstory.php/aid/11623/Labelling_Debate:_Engaging_ the_public.html.

208 William Neuman, *Gassing Chickens Before Killing Them to Ease Stress*, N.Y. Times, Oct. 22, 2010, at A1, *available at* http://www.nytimes.com/2010/10/22/business/22chicken.html under the title *New Way to Help Chickens Cross to Other Side*.

209 *See, e.g.*, Milton Mills, Physicians Committee for Responsible Medicine, Address at the Annual Conference of the North American Vegetarian Society: Meat Eating and the Biology of Disgust (July 8, 2010); Harold Kudler, *The Limiting Effects of Paradigms on the Concept of Traumatic Stress*, *in* International HandbookOf Human Response To Trauma 5 (Arieh Y. Shalev et al. eds., 2000).

210 *See* American Psychiatric Association, Diagnostic and Statistical Manual of Mental Disorders 467–68 (4th ed., text revision 2000) (shell shock); Rachel M. MacNair, Perpetration-induced Traumatic Stress: The Psychological Consequences Of Killing 32– 34 (2002) (executioners); Gail A. Eisnitz, Slaughterhouse: The Shocking Story of Greed, Neglect, and Inhumane Treatment Inside the U.S. Meat Industry 62 (1997) (slaughterhouse workers); Joy, *supra* note 39, at 82–84.

211 *See* Pachirat, *supra* note 52, at 257–70, 159–61.

212 *See* B.F. Skinner, About Behaviorism 51 (1976).

213 *See* Adam Smith, The Wealth of Nations 57 (1937); John Maynard Keynes, The General Theory of Employment, Interest and Money 292 (1935).

214 Act of Dec. 9, 1999, Pub. L. No. 106-152, 113 Stat. 1732 (codified as amended at 18 U.S.C. § 48 (2006) (amended 2010)), invalidated by United States v. Stevens, 130 S.Ct. 1577 (2010); Animal Crush Video Prohibition Act of 2010, Pub. L. No. 111-294, 124 Stat. 3177.

215 United States v. Stevens, 130 S.Ct. 1577, 1592, 559 U.S. ____ (2010).

216 Brief for the United States at 17–18, United States v. Stevens, 130 S.Ct. 1577 (2010) (No. 08-769) (quoting Punishing Depictions of Animal Cruelty and the Federal Prisoner Health Care Co-Payment Act of 1999: Hearing on H.R. 1887 and H.R. 1349 Before the Subcomm. on Crime of the H. Comm. on the Judiciary, 106th Cong. 126 (1999)).

217 United States v. Stevens, 533 F.3d 218, 220–21 (3d. Cir.2008).

218 United States v. Stevens, No. 04-cr-00051 (W.D. Pa., November 10, 2004), *available at* Petition for Writ of Certiorari at 71a, United States v. Stevens, 130 S.Ct. 1577 (2010) (No. 08-769).

219 John Schwartz, Child Pornography, and an Issue of Restitution, N. Y. TIMES, Feb. 2, 2010, http://www.nytimes.com/2010/02/03/us/03offender.html; Jonathan Turley, Pay Misty for Me: Courts Mull Over Restitution Payments to Victims of Child Pornography From Possessors, JONATHANTURLEY.ORG.BLOG (Feb. 3, 2010), http://jonathanturley.org/2010/02/03/pay-misty-for-me-courts-mull-over-restitution-payments-to-victims-of-child-pornography-from-possessors/.

220 *See, e.g.,* 18 U.S.C. § 2252(a)(2), (a)(2)(A), (b)(1) (2006).

221 For descriptions of the suffering chickens experience at a "processing" facility, see EISNITZ, *supra* note 210, at 165–67 and Factory Farming: Poultry, FARM SANCTUARY, http://www.farmsanctuary.org/issues/factoryfarming/poultry/ (last visited July 11, 2011).

222 *See* GWYNNE DYER, WAR: THE LETHAL CUSTOM 57 (2006); Stephen Evans, How Soldiers Deal with the Job of Killing, BBC NEWS WORLD, June 11, 2011, http://www.bbc.co.uk/news/world-13687796.

223 *See* Ginny Sprang, Post-Disaster Stress Following the Oklahoma City Bombing: An Examination of Three Community Groups, 14 J. INTERPERSONAL VIOLENCE 169, 179–81 (1999).

224 Dave Grossman, Teaching Kids to Kill, NAT'L F., Sept. 2000, at 12; DAVE GROSSMAN, ON KILLING: THE PSYCHOLOGICAL COST OF LEARNING TO KILL IN WAR AND SOCIETY 13 (1995).

225 *See* GROSSMAN, *supra* note 224, at 18–37, 82.

226 A.C. Iverson et al., Risk Factors for Post-Traumatic Stress Disorder Among UK Armed Forces Personnel, 38 PSYCHOLOGICAL MEDICINE 511, 516 (2008).

227 *See* WILLIAM J. DUIKER AND JACKSON J. SPIELVOGEL, WORLD HISTORY: VOLUME I: To 1800 xxii (6th ed. 2010).

228 *See* William C. Donnino, Practice Commentary, Contract Killing, N.Y. PENAL LAW § 125.27 (McKinney 2009).

229 RALPH WALDO EMERSON, Fate, in THE CONDUCT OF LIFE: NINE ESSAYS ON FATE, POWER, WEALTH, CULTURE, WORSHIP, ETC. 1, 5 (1903).

230 Thanks to David Cassuto for suggesting in a conversation with me that consumers eventually become inured to even the most patent displays of violence against animals and that this numbing process may reflect a form of post-traumatic stress disorder.

231 Skinned Alive—Cruel Catfish Slaughter Exposed, YouTube (Jan. 14, 2011), 2:10, posted by "mercyforanimals," http://www.youtube.com/watch?v=sD9M8cjXsL0.

232 *See, e.g.,* Overlooked: The Lives of Animals Raised for Food, YouTube, (Jan. 10, 2008), 5:29, posted by "hsus," http:www.youtube.com/watch?v=Z-cor1uZ2AM; Meet Your Meat PETA Part I, YOUTUBE, (Oct. 23, 2009), 7:45, posted by "OptimisticPessimist," http://www.youtube.com/watch?v=UFNFvOyTJd8.

233 *See, e.g.,* Abortion Pictures, PROLIFEAMERICA.COM, http://www.prolifeamerica.com/Abortion_Pictures.cfm (last visited Aug. 17, 2009).

234 *See* GUTTMACHER INSTITUTE, STATE POLICIES IN BRIEF: REQUIREMENTS FOR ULTRASOUND (Aug. 1, 2011), http://www.guttmacher.org/statecenter/spibs/spib_RFU.pdf.

235 *See* Carol Sanger, Seeing and Believing: Mandatory Ultrasound and the Path to a Protected Choice, 56 UCLA L. REV. 351, 393–94 (2008).

236 *See, e.g.,* Naomi Wolf, *Our Bodies, Our Souls,* THE NEW REPUBLIC, Oct. 16, 1995, at 32; In re Jane Doe, 19 S.W.3d 346, 361 (Tex. 2000).

237 *See* Amy J. Fitzgerald, A Social History of the Slaughterhouse: From Inception to Contemporary Implications, 71 HUMAN ECOLOGY REV. 64 (2010); Lance A. Compa, Blood, Sweat, and Fear: Workers' Rights in U.S. Meat and Poultry Plants, HUMAN RIGHTS WATCH (2004 Report), *available at* http://www.hrw.org/en/node/11869/section/1. For updated labor and employment information on workers in the "animal slaughter and processing industry," see U. S. DEPT OF LABOR, OCCUPATIONAL EMPLOYMENT STATISTICS, May 2011 National Industry-Specific Occupational Employment and Wage Estimates, NAICS 311600 - Animal Slaughtering and Processing, http://www.bls.gov/oes/current/naics4_311600.htm.

238 For image-protection of animal slaughter, see, e.g., Animal Enterprise Terrorism Act, 18 U.S.C. § 43 (2006); H.F. 589, 84th Gen. Assemb., Reg. Sess. (Ia. 2011); H.F. 1369, 87th Leg. Sess. (Mn. 2011).

For image-protection of abortion see, e.g., "buffer" and "bubble" zone laws that limit noise and visual displays near medical facilities and women seeking abortions: Madsen v. Women's Health Center, 512 U.S. 753 (1994); Shenck v. Pro-Choice Network of Western New York, 519 U.S. 357 (1997).

239 *See* Lydia Saad, Americans Still Split Along "Pro-Choice," "Pro-Life" Lines, GALLUP.COM, http://www.gallup.com/poll/147734/americans-split-along-pro-choice-pro-life-lines.aspx; Rich Karlgaard, Rise Up, Vegan Republicans!, HUFFINGTONPOST.COM (March 4, 2010), http://www.huffingtonpost.com/rich-karlgaard/rise-up-vegan-republicans_b_485906.html.

240 *See, e.g.,* Rich Deem, The Bible and Abortion: The Biblical Basis for a Pro-life Position, GODANDSCIENCE.ORG, http://www.godandscience.org/doctrine/prolife.html#human; Steven Ertelt, The Triumph of Peter Singer's Values: Animal Rights More Important Than Human Rights, LIFENEWS.COM, July 28, 2008, *available at* http://www.lifenews.com/2008/07/28/bio-2518/.

241 *See* Susan J. Lee et al., Fetal Pain: A Systematic Multidisciplinary Review of the Evidence, 294:8 JAMA 947, 952 (2005); ROYAL COLLEGE OF OBSTETRICIANS AND GYNECOLOGISTS, FEETAL AWARENESS: REVIEW OF RESEARCH AND RECOMMENDATIONS FOR PRACTICE 11, March 2010, *available at* http://www.rcog.org.uk/files/rcog-corp/RCOGFetalAwarenessWPR0610.pdf.

242 *See, e.g.,* Nebraska Pain-Capable Unborn Child Protection Act, Neb. Rev. Stat. §§ 28-3,102 to 28-3,111 (2010).

243 *See, e.g.,* P.L 193-2011, H.E.A. No. 1210, 117th Gen. Assemb., Reg. Sess. (Ind. 2011).

244 Gonzales v. Carhart, 550 U.S. 124, 125 (2007).

245 *Id.* at 138–39.

246 *See* RESTATEMENT (SECOND) OF TORTS: DUTY TO ACT FOR PROTECTION OF OTHERS § 314 (1965).

247 *Risk of Pregnancy: What is my risk of getting pregnant if I have sex without using contraception or my birth control fails?*, THE EMERGENCY CONTRACEPTION WEBSITE (June 14, 2012 2:42 PM), http://ec.princeton.edu/questions/risk.html.

248 *See, e.g., Birth Control Pills,* PLANNED PARENTHOOD, http://www.plannedparenthood.org/health-topics/birth-control/birth-control-pill-4228.htm (last visited July 25, 2012).

249 *See, e.g.,* The Peta Files, *Vegans Save 198 Animals a Year,* PETA.ORG (Dec. 13,

2010), *available at* http://www.peta.org/b/thepetafiles/archive/2010/12/13/vegans-save-185-animals-a-year.aspx.

250 *See, e.g.*, Mayo Clinic Staff, *Pregnancy Weight Gain: What's healthy?*, MAYOCLINIC.COM, *available at* http://www.mayoclinic.com/health/pregnancy-weight-gain/PR00111; Mayo Clinic Staff, *Third Trimester Pregnancy: What to Expect*, MAYOCLINIC.COM, *available at* http://www.mayoclinic.com/health/pregnancy/PR00009.

251 *See, e.g.,* Peaceful Prairie Sanctuary, http://www.peacefulprairie.org/; Woodstock Farm Animal Sanctuary, http://woodstocksanctuary.org/; Catskill Animal Sanctuary, http://casanctuary.org/; For The Animals Sanctuary, http://www.fortheanimalssanctuary.org/; Farm Sanctuary, http://www.farmsanctuary.org/. For a directory of farm animal sanctuaries around the United States, *see National Shelter List*, http://www.farmanimalshelters.org/links.htm.

252 GARY FRANCIONE & ROBERT GARNER, THE ANIMAL RIGHTS DEBATE: ABOLITION OF REGULATION? (2000).

253 *See* GUTTMACHER INSTITUTE, FACTS ON INDUCED ABORTION IN THE UNITED STATES (Aug. 2011), *available at* http://www.guttmacher.org/pubs/fb_induced_abortion.html.

254 *See, e.g.*, PLATO, CRITO 52a (Cathal Woods & Ryan Pack trans., 2007), *available at* http://ssrn.com/abstract=1023145 or http://dx.doi.org/10.2139/ssrn.1023145; THOMAS HOBBES, LEVIATHAN 88 (J.C.A. Gaskin ed. 1998) (1651); JOHN LOCKE, TWO TREATISES OF GOVERNMENT, Second Treatise § 95, at 348–49 (Peter Laslett ed., 1960) (1689). *But see* TOM REGAN, THE CASE FOR ANIMAL RIGHTS 274 (1983).

255 *See, e.g.*, Craig Howard Kinsley and Kelly G. Lambert, *The Maternal Brain*, SCIENTIFIC AMERICAN, January 2006, at 72.

256 *See Female Bomber's Mother Speaks Out*, BBC NEWS, Jan. 30, 2002, http://news.bbc.co.uk/2/hi/1791800.stm; *An Interview with the Mother of a Suicide Bomber*, MIDDLE EAST MEDIA RESEARCH INSTITUTE (MEMRI) (Special Dispatch No.391), June 19, 2002, http://www.memri.org/report/en/0/0/0/0/0/0/683.htm.

257 Paul Rozin, *Preference for Natural: Instrumental and Ideational/Moral Motivations, and the Contrast Between Foods and Medicines*, 43 APPETITE 147 (2004).

258 *See, e.g.*, *ConAgra Lawsuit: Cooking Oil Giant Sued Over Fishy 'All-Natural' Claims*, HUFFINGTON POST, Aug. 25, 2011, http://www.huffingtonpost.com/2011/08/25/conagra-lawsuit_n_936157.html.

259 *See, e.g.*, Heather Timmons & Nikhila Gill, *India's Health Minister Calls Homosexuality Unnatural*, N.Y. TIMES, July 5, 2011, http://www.nytimes.com/2011/07/06/world/asia/06india.html.

260 *See* CHARLES ZASTROW & KAREN K. KIRST-ASHMAN, UNDERSTANDING HUMAN BEHAVIOR AND THE SOCIAL ENVIRONMENT 497 (7th ed. 2007).

261 Frans B.M. de Waal, *Bonobo Sex and Society*, SCIENTIFIC AMERICAN, Mar. 1995, at 88.

262 *See* GEORGES H. WESTBEAU, LITTLE TYKE: THE TRUE STORY OF A GENTLE VEGETARIAN LIONESS (1986); Adrian Blomfield, *Lioness Who Lay Down with the Antelope*, Telegraph, Jan. 8, 2002, http://www.telegraph.co.uk/news/worldnews/africaandindianocean/kenya/1380783/Lioness-who-lay-down-with-the-antelope.html.

263 Mills, *supra* note 58.

264 *Id.*

265 *Id.*

266 *See* Craig T. Palmer, *Rape in Nonhuman Animal Species: Definitions, Evidence, and Implications*, 26 J. SEX RES. 355, 360–67 (1989).

267 *See* RANDY THORNHILL & CRAIG T. PALMER, A NATURAL HISTORY OF RAPE: BIO-LOGICAL BASES OF SEXUAL COERCION 80 (2000).

268 *See* Sarah Blaffer Hrdy, *Infanticide as a Primate Reproductive Strategy*, 65 American Scientist 40, 43–44 (1977); Anne E. Pusey & Craig Packer, *Infanticide in Lions: Consequences and Counterstrategies*, *in* INFANTICIDE AND PARENTAL CARE 279 (Stefano Parmigiani & Frederick S. vom Saal eds., 1994).

269 *See* DEAN BUONOMANO, BRAIN BUGS: HOW THE BRAIN'S FLAWS SHAPE OUR LIVES 134 (2011).

270 *See id.*

271 *See generally* CULTURAL DIVIDES: UNDERSTANDING AND OVERCOMING GROUP CONFLICT (Deborah A. Prentice & Dale T. Miller eds., 1999).

272 *See* BUONOMANO, *supra* note 269, at 134.

273 *See, e.g.*, Adam Rutland, *The Development of National Prejudice, In-group Favouritism, and Self-stereotypes in British Children*, 38 Brit. J. Soc. Psych. 55, 61 (1999); Jenny Hsin-Chun Tsai, *Xenophobia, Ethnic Community, and Immigrant Youths' Friendship Network Formation*, 41 ADOLESCENCE 285, 287 (2006).

274 *See, e.g.*, VIVIAN GUSSIN PALEY, YOU CAN'T SAY YOU CAN'T PLAY 93–134 (1992).

275 *See* Mills, *supra* note 58.

276 *See id.*

277 *See id.*

278 *See* Andy Lagomarsino, *Food Poisoning Cases Increase During Thanksgiving*, NEW JERSEY NEWSROOM, Nov. 25, 2009, http://www.newjerseynewsroom.com/healthquest/food-poisoning-cases-increase-during-thanksgiving.

279 *See* Mills, *supra* note 58.

280 *See* Press Release, World Cancer Research Fund, Most Authoritative Ever Report on Bowel Cancer and Diet: Links with Meat and Fibre Confirmed (May 23, 2011) (on file with author), *available at* http://www.wcrf-uk.org/audience/media/press_release.php?recid=153; James Meikle, *Study Suggests Link Between Eating Red Meat and Crohn's Disease*, GUARDIAN, July 15, 2005, http://www.guardian.co.uk/society/2005/jul/16/health.food.

281 *See U.S. Could Feed 800 million People with Grain that Livestock Eat, Cornell Ecologist Advises Animal Scientists Future Water and Energy Shortages Predicted to Change Face of American Agriculture*, CORNELL UNIVERSITY SCIENCE NEWS, Aug. 7, 1997, http://www.news.cornell.edu/releases/Aug97/livestock.hrs.html.

282 *See* RICHARD A. OPPENLANDER, COMFORTABLY UNAWARE xi–xii (2011); Joyce D'Silva, *Introduction* to THE MEAT BUSINESS: DEVOURING A HUNGRY PLANET xv (Geoff Tansey & Joyce D'Silva eds. 1999).

283 *See* Mary Beckman, *Crime, Culpability, and the Adolescent Brain*, 305 SCIENCE 596–599 (2004).

284 *See, e.g.*, Matthew S. Stanford et al., *Impulsiveness and Risk-taking Behavior: Comparison of High-school and College Students Using the Barratt Impulsiveness Scale*, 21 PERSONALITY AND INDIVIDUAL DIFFERENCES 1073, 1075 (1996).

285 *See* EAGLEMAN, *supra* note 167, at 158.

286 TOM REGAN, THE CASE FOR ANIMAL RIGHTS 279 (2d ed. 2004); Thomas McPherson, *The Moral Patient*, 59 PHILOSOPHY 171–72 (1984).

287 Mary Midgley, *Duties Concerning Islands*, LX Encounter 36 (1983).

288 *Id.* at 36, 42-43.

289 *See, The Cornwall Declaration on Environmental Stewardship,* THE CORN-WALL ALLIANCE(Oct. 1999), http://www.cornwallalliance.org/docs/the-cornwall-declaration-on-environmental-stewardship.pdf.

290 *See* Regan, *supra* note 286, at 153.

291 *See, e.g.*, Insanity Defense Reform Act of 1984, 18 U.S.C. § 17(a) (2006).

292 Balcombe, *supra* note 51, at 137; *see also* Inbal Ben-Ami Bartal et al., *Empathy and Pro-Social Behavior in Rats*, 334 Science 1427, 1430 (2011).

293 *See* Bekoff, *supra* note 19, at 13; Dale Peterson, The Moral Lives of Animals (2011).

294 Christian the lion—Full ending, YouTube(July 28, 2008), 6:06, posted by "bornfreefoundation," http://www.youtube.com/watch?v=cvCjyWp3rEk.

295 Jennifer S. Holland, Unlikely Friendships: 47 Remarkable Stories from the Animal Kingdom 69–72 (2011).

296 *See* James Barron, *Polar Bears Kill a Child at Prospect Park Zoo*, N.Y. Times, May 20, 1987, http://www.nytimes.com/1987/05/20/nyregion/polar-bears-kill-a-child-at-prospect-park-zoo.html.

297 *See* George P. Fletcher & Luis E. Chiesa, *Self-Defense and the Psychotic Aggressor, in* Criminal Law Conversations 365, 372 (Paul H. Robinson, Stephen P. Garvey & Kimberly Kessler Ferzan eds., 2009); Sherry F. Colb, *Justifying Homicide Against Innocent Aggressors Without Denying Their Innocence, in* Criminal Law Conversations 375 (Paul H. Robinson, Stephen P. Garvey & Kimberly Kessler Ferzan eds., 2009).

298 Eagleman, *supra* note 167, at 208.

299 Tennessee v. Garner, 471 U.S. 1, 3 (1985).

300 *See* Sherry F. Colb, *Why Is Torture "Different" and How "Different" Is it?*, 30 Cardozo L. Rev. 1411, 1458 (2009).

301 Regina v. Dudley & Stephen [1884] 14 Q.B.D. 273 (U.K.); *see* Allan C. Hutchinson, Is Eating People Wrong? : Great Legal Cases and How They Shaped the World 19 (2011).

302 *See* Oppenlander, *supra* note 282, at 27–28.

303 *See generally* Oppenlander, *supra* note 282; Henning Steinfeld et al., Livestock's Long Shadow: Environmental Issues and Options (2006).

304 *See* Maarten J. Chrispeels & David E. Sadava, Plants, Genes, and Agriculture 25–57 (1994); Steinfeld, *supra* note 303, at 23-32.

305 David Pimentel & Marcia Pimentel, *Sustainability of Meat-based and Plant-based Diets and the Environment*, 78 Am. J. Clinical Nutrition 660S, 662S (2003).

306 *Soy Benefits*, Nat'l Soybean Res. Laboratory, http://www.nsrl.uiuc.edu/soy_benefits.html (last visited Oct. 3, 2011).

307 Oppenlander, *supra* note 282, at 36–37.

308 *See Genesis* 1:26–1:31; *Qu'ran* 6:165; Paul W. Taylor, *Are Humans Superior to Animals and Plants?*, 6 Envtl. Ethics 149 (1984) (citing Padmanabh S. Jaini, The Jaina Path of Purification 106–110 (1979)).

309 *See generally* Sam Harris, The Moral Landscape: How Science Can Determine Human Values (2010).

310 *See, e.g.*, Jewish Vegetarians of North America, http://jewishveg.com/torah.

html; The Christian Vegetarian Association, http://www.all-creatures.org/cva/default. htm; Zamir Elhai, *Islam and Vegetarianism*, http://www.godsdirectcontact.org.tw/eng/ news/178/vg_53.htm (last visited Jun. 27, 2012); L.T. Ho-Pham et al., *Veganism, Bone Mineral Density, and Body Composition: A Study in Buddhist Nuns*, 20 OSTEOPOROSIS INTERNATIONAL 2087, 2088 (2009); Sarah Soifer, Note, *Vegan Discrimination: An Emerging and Difficult Issue*, 36 LOY. L.A. L. REV. 1709, 1711 (2003); Jain Vegans, http:// groups.yahoo.com/group/JainVegans/ (last visited Jun. 27, 2012).

311 *See* Françoise-Marie Arouet de Voltaire, *Œuvres de Voltaire 1829, in* ŒUVRES DE VOLTAIRE 48, (Adrien Jean-Quentin Beuchot and Pierre-Auguste-Marie Miger eds., Lefèvre, Paris 1832).

312 *See* QUR'AN, *Sura* 17:33; *Tipitaka* AN 8.39, *Abhisdana Sutta: Rewards*, (Thanissaro Bhikkhu trans.), *available at* http://www.accesstoinsight.org/tipitaka/an/an08/ an08.039.than.html.

313 *Leviticus* 1:2-5 (Jewish Publication Society).

314 *Genesis* 9:1-3 (Jewish Publication Society).

315 *Numbers* 31:17-18 (Jewish Publication Society).

316 *Leviticus* 25:44-46 (Jewish Publication Society).

317 *See* Ner LeElef, *World Jewish Population*, Judaism Online, http://www.simpletoremember.com/vitals/world-jewish-population.htm#_Toc26172077 (last viewed June 20, 2012).

318 *See, e.g.,* ELIEZER BERKOVITS, NOT IN HEAVEN: THE NATURE AND FUNCTION OF HALAKHAH 74 (1983).

319 NORM PHELPS, THE DOMINION OF LOVE: ANIMAL RIGHTS ACCORDING TO THE BIBLE (2002).

320 *Id.* at 15.

321 *Genesis* 1:26-28 (Jewish Publication Society).

322 *See, e.g.,* Rod Preece & David Fraser, *The Status of Animals in Biblical and Christian Thought: A Study in Colliding Values*, 8 SOC'Y & ANIMALS 245, 246 (2000).

323 *Genesis* 1:29-30 (Jewish Publication Society).

324 Norm Phelps draws a similar conclusion from the juxtaposition of these verses. *See* Phelps, *supra* note 319, at 55.

325 *Isaiah* 11:6, 9 (Jewish Publication Society).

326 Richard Schwartz, *The Vegetarian Teachings of Rav Kook*, Jewish Virtual Library, http://www.jewishvirtuallibrary.org/jsource/Judaism/ravkook_veg.html (last visited June 27, 2012) (citing Philip Pick, *The Source of Our Inspiration* 2 (Jewish Vegetarian Society, Paper) (quoting Rav Kook)).

327 *See Leviticus* 11:1-8 (Jewish Publication Society); *Leviticus* 11:9-12 (Jewish Publication Society).

328 *See, e.g., Deuteronomy* 12:21; *Leviticus* 17:10.

329 *See Leviticus* 7:26—27 (Jewish Publication Society); *Leviticus* 17:10—14 (Jewish Publication Society); MISHNEH TORAH, *Sefer Kedushah: MaAchalot Assurot,* at Chapter 6, Halacha 1 (Eliyahu Touger trans.), *available at* http://www.chabad.org/library/article_ cdo/aid/968262/jewish/Chapter-6.htm.

330 *MaAchalot Assurot,* at Chapter 6, Halacha 10—11, *available at* http://www. chabad.org/library/article_cdo/aid/968263/jewish/Chapter-7.htm.

331 *Genesis* 32:33 (Jewish Publication Society).

332 *See Exodus* 23:19 (Jewish Publication Society); *MaAchalot Assurot*, at Chapter 9, Halacha 1, *available at* http://www.chabad.org/library/article_cdo/aid/968265/jewish/Chapter-9.htm.

333 Abraham Chill, The Mitzvot: The Commandments and their Rationale 400 (2000) (quoting Efraim Lunchitz, author of Keli Yakar).

334 *Isaiah* 66:3 (Jewish Publication Society).

335 *Exodus* 23:12 (Jewish Publication Society).

336 *Deuteronomy* 22:6 (Jewish Publication Society).

337 *Deuteronomy* 25:4 (Jewish Publication Society).

338 *Leviticus* 22:27 (Jewish Publication Society).

339 *Leviticus* 22:28 (Jewish Publication Society).

340 *See* Francione, *supra* note 21, at xxxiii.

341 *See, e.g.*, Andrew C. Revkin, *The Troubling Path from Pig to Pork* Chop, N.Y. Times Dot Earth Blog (Feb. 2, 2012, 5:38 PM), http://dotearth.blogs.nytimes.com/2012/02/02/the-troubling-path-from-pig-to-pork-chops.

342 *See* Phelps, *supra* note 319, at 18; *see also* Isaac Bashevis Singer, *The Letter Writer*, *in* The Collected Stories of Isaac Bashevis Singer 250, 271 (1982).

343 *See Meat, Dairy and Pareve*, OK Kosher Certification, http://www.ok.org/Content.asp?ID=63 (last visited June 30, 2012).

344 *Exodus* 23:19 (Jewish Publication Society); *Exodus* 34:26 (Jewish Publication Society); *Deuteronomy* 14:21 (Jewish Publication Society).

345 *See* Frederick E. Greenspahn, *What is the Hebrew Bible?*, *in* The Wiley-Blackwell History of Jews and Judaism 15, 21 (Alan T. Levenson ed., 2012).

346 *See* Strong's Concordance 2102, *available at* http://concordances.org/hebrew/2102.htm.

347 *See, e.g.*, Janzen Family Farms, http://www.janzenfamilyfarms.com/beef.html (last visited Sept. 28, 2012); *Get the Facts: The Destructive Dairy Industry*, Born Free USA, http://www.bornfreeusa.org/facts.php?more=1&p=373 (last visited Sept. 28, 2012).

348 *See, e.g.*, Foer, *supra* note 170, at 113.

349 *See Turkey for Thanksgiving?*, Soc'y for the Advancement of Animal Wellbeing, http://www.saawinternational.org/turkey.htm (last visited Jun. 30, 2012).

350 *See, e.g.*, *Deuteronomy* 14:8 (King James).

351 *See Pig Farming - Here's Your Bacon!*, Soc'y for the Advancement of Animal Wellbeing, http://animalwelfaretaiwan.webs.com/pigs.htm (last visited Jun. 30, 2012).

352 *See Cows*, Soc'y for the Advancement of Animal Wellbeing, http://animalwelfaretaiwan.webs.com/cows.htm (last visited Jun. 30, 2012).

353 *See, e.g.*, Peggy Trowbridge Filippone, *US Lamb Grades: American Lamb is Mild in Flavor*, About.com, http://homecooking.about.com/od/lamb/a/lambgrades.htm (last visited Sept. 28, 2012).

354 Ducks and geese who are not used in foie gras production, for example, may be slaughtered at just seven weeks old. *See Ducks and Geese*, Soc'y for the Advancement of Animal Wellbeing, http://animalwelfaretaiwan.webs.com/geeseandducks.htm (last visited Jun. 30, 2012).

355 *See* Shmuly Yanklowitz, *How Kosher is Your Milk?*, JewishJournal.com (June 7, 2012, 5:16 AM), http://www.jewishjournal.com/socialjusticerav/item/rabbi_herschel_schachters_chumra_on_milk_abuse_in_the_dairy_industry_201206/; Mishneh

Torah, *Sefer Kedushah: Shechitah* at Chapter 10, Halacha 9 (Eliyahu Touger trans.), *available at* http://www.chabad.org/library/article_cdo/aid/971836/jewish/Chapter-10.htm.

356 *See* Yanklowitz, *supra* note 355.

357 *See, e.g.*, Philip Caulfield, *PETA Hopes to Launch Pornography Site, PETA.XXX, to Promote Veganism*, N.Y. Daily News, Sept. 20, 2011, *available at* http://articles.nydailynews.com/2011-09-20/news/30202195_1_peta-lindsay-rajt-graphic-images.

358 In writing this chapter, I wish to acknowledge the support, encouragement, and knowledge of my friend Harold Brown, whose grandmother was a Native American of the Anishinaabe people.

359 *See* Mary Story et al., *Nutritional Health and Diet-Related Conditions, in* American Indian Health: Innovations in Health Care, Promotion, and Policy 201, 212, 213 (Everett R. Rhoades ed., 2000).

360 *See* Marcia Eames-Sheavly, The Three Sisters: Exploring an Iroquois Garden 7 (1993).

361 *See, e.g.*, Linda Murray Berzok, American Indian Food 19, 20 (2005); Colleen Patrick-Goudreau, *Thanksgiving for the Turkeys*, The Compassionate Cook Food for Thought Blog (Nov. 13, 2007), http://www.compassionatecook.com/writings/food-for-thought-writing/thanksgiving-for-the-turkeys.

362 *See, e.g.*, Rita Laws, *Native Americans and Vegetarianism*, Vegetarian J. (Vegetarian Res. Grp. Sept. 1994), *available at* http://www.vrg.org/journal/94sep.htm#native; Berzok, *supra* note 361, at xv.

363 *See, e.g., id.*; Berzok, *supra* note 361, at 172–73.

364 *See* Jordan Paper, Native North American Religious Traditions: Dancing for Life 29 (2007).

365 *See, e.g.*, Atticus, Posting to *Questions from Non-Vegans: "We Have Great Respect for the Animals We Kill,"* The Vegan Forum (Sept. 23, 2005, 5:39 AM), http://www.veganforum.com/forums/archive/index.php/t-5614.html; Susan Bergerstein, *Avatar Will Upset Animal Rights Activists*, Examiner.com (Dec. 19, 2009), http://www.examiner.com/celebrity-headlines-in-indianapolis/avatar-will-upset-animal-rights-activists.

366 Jim Mason, An Unnatural Order: Why We Are Destroying the Planet and Each Other 109 (2005) (internal quotations omitted). I want to express my gratitude to Jeffrey Masson for calling my attention to Jim Mason's quotation of indigenous peoples.

367 *Id.* at 111.

369 *See, e.g.*, Happy Pig Café, http://www.thehappypig.com/, Dancing Pig BBQ, http://www.dancingpigbbq.com/; Angus Taylor, Animals & Ethics: An Overview of the Philosophical Debate 97 (3d ed. 2009); *See also* Suicide Food, http://suicidefood.blogspot.com/.

369 *Saturday Night Live: Cluckin' Chicken* (NBC television broadcast Nov. 21, 1992), *available at* http://www.hulu.com/watch/2317/saturday-night-live-cluckin-chicken.

370 *See* Mason, supra note 366, at 52.

371 *See* USDA Economic Research Service, Obesity (July 30, 2012), *available at* http://www.ers.usda.gov/topics/food-choices-health/obesity.aspx.

372 *See* Patricia Gadsby, *The Inuit Paradox*, Discover Magazine (Oct. 1, 2004), *available at* http://discovermagazine.com/2004/oct/inuit-paradox.

373 *See, e.g.*, Colin Tudge, Feeding People is Easy 54 (2007).

374 *See* Dothard v. Rawlinson, 433 U.S. 321, 345 (1977) (Marshall, J., dissenting). *See generally* Michelle J. Anderson, *From Chastity Requirement to Sexuality License: Sexual Consent and a New Rape Shield Law*, 70 Geo. Wash. L. Rev. 51 (2002).

375 *See* Celia E. Naylor, African Cherokees in Indian Territory: From Chattel to Citizens 2 (2008).

376 Circe Sturm, *Blood Politics, Racial Classification, and Cherokee National Identity: The Trials and Tribulations of the Cherokee Freedmen*, 22 Am. Indian Q. 230, 232 (1998); Tony Seybert, *Slavery and Native Americans in British North America and the United States: 1600 to 1865*, SlaveryInAmerica.org, *archived at* http://web.archive.org/web/20040804001522/http://www.slaveryinamerica.org/history/hs_es_indians_slavery.htm.

377 *See* Karen Anderson, Chain Her by One Foot: The Subjugation of Native Women in Seventeenth-Century New France 207–216 (1993). For a discussion of ways in which the current legal regime under-protects Native American women from violent sexual assault, see Sarah Deer, *Sovereignty of the Soul: Exploring the Intersection of Rape Law Reform and Federal Indian Law*, 38 Suffolk U. L. Rev. 455, 464 (2005).

378 *See, e.g.*, Jill Elaine Hasday, *Contest and Consent: A Legal History of Marital Rape*, 88 Calif. L. Rev. 1373, 1375 (2000).

379 *See generally* Nicolette Hahn Niman, Righteous Porkchop: Finding a Life and Good Food Beyond Factory Farms (2009); Joel Salatin, Folks, This Ain't Normal: A Farmer's Advice for Happier Hens, Healthier People, and a Better World (2011).

380 *See, e.g.*, Ariz. Rev. Stat. § 13-2910.07 (2011) ("Proposition 204"); Prevention of Farm Animal Cruelty Act ("Proposition 2"), Cal. Health & Safety Code, § 25990 (2012); Colo. Rev. State. § 35-50.5-102(a), (b) (2011); Fla. Const. Art. X, § 21 (2012) ("Pregnant Pig Amendment"); Or. Rev. Stat. § 600.150 (2009).

381 *See* A. Mood & P. Brooke, Estimating the Number of Farmed Fish Killed in Global Aquaculture Each Year 19, Table 9 (2012), available at http://fishcount.org.uk/published/std/fishcountstudy2.pdf (includes estimates of land animals as well as marine animals slaughtered).

382 Eric Schlosser, Fast Food Nation: The Dark Side of the All-American Meal 171 (2002).

383 Arizona voters approved Amendment 204 in 2006, for example, but the provision does not become operative until December 31, 2012. *See* Ariz. Rev. Stat. § 13-2910.07 (2011). California's Proposition 2 was approved by voters on November 4, 2008, but it does not become effective until January 1, 2015. *See* Cal. Health & Safety Code, § 25990 (2012). Florida's so-called Pregnant Pig Amendment did not become effective until six years after it was approved by voters. Fla. Const. Art. X, § 21 (2012).

384 *See* U.S. Gov't Gen. Accountability Office, GAO-04-247, Humane Methods of Slaughter Act: USDA Has Addressed Some Problems but Still Faces Enforcement Challenges 4, 5 (2004).

385 *See* Gary L. Francione, *Abolition of Animal Exploitation: The Journey Will Not Begin While we are Walking Backwards*, Animal Equality (2006), http://www.animalequality.net/articles/francione/abolition-of-animal-exploitation.

386 *See generally* Gary L. Francione, Animals as Persons: Essays on the Abolition of Animal Exploitation (2008).

387 *See* Dwight Garner, *The Joys and Pains of Being an Animal*, N.Y. TIMES, Jan. 20, 2009, at C1.

388 *See, e.g.*, OLIVER SACKS, AN ANTHROPOLOGIST ON MARS: SEVEN PARADOXICAL TALES 244 (1996); *We Salute Temple Grandin, A Hero for Animals*, ENCYCLOPEDIA BRITANNICA BLOG (Aug. 3, 2009), http://advocacy.britannica.com/blog/advocacy/2009/08/we-salute-temple-grandin-a-hero-for-animals/; Glenn Whipp, *A Walk in Her Boots*, L.A. TIMES, Aug. 5, 2010, at S12.

389 *See, e.g.*, Alessandra Stanley, *Peering into a Mind That's 'Different, but Not Less,'* N.Y. TIMES, Feb. 4, 2010, at C1.

390 *Id.* at 307.

391 TEMPLE GRANDIN & CATHERINE JOHNSON, ANIMALS IN TRANSLATION: USING THE MYSTERIES OF AUTISM TO DECODE ANIMAL BEHAVIOR 180 (2005).

392 *See Temple Grandin Interview*, GREENMUZE (July 29, 2009), http://www.greenmuze.com/reviews/interviews/1357-temple-grandin-interview.html.

393 *See* TEMPLE GRANDIN, CORPORATIONS CAN BE AGENTS OF GREAT IMPROVEMENTS IN ANIMAL WELFARE AND FOOD SAFETY AND THE NEED FOR MINIMUM DECENT STANDARDS, NAT'L INST. ANIM. AGRIC. (Apr. 4, 2001), *available at* http://www.grandin.com/welfare/corporation.agents.html.

394 *Fresh Air: Temple Grandin On 'The Best Life for Animals,'* NATIONAL PUBLIC RADIO (Jan. 5, 2009), *available at* http://www.npr.org/templates/transcript/transcript.php?storyId=99009110.

395 *See* Bari Weiss, *The Weekend Interview with Temple Grandin: Life Among the 'Yakkity Yaks,'* WALL ST. J., Feb. 20, 2010, at A11.

396 *See* Temple Grandin, Professional Resume, COLO. STATE UNIV., http://lamar.colostate.edu/~grandin/professional.resume.html (last visited Oct. 6, 2012).

397 *See* CHARLES PATTERSON, ETERNAL TREBLINKA: OUR TREATMENT OF ANIMALS AND THE HOLOCAUST 132 (2002).

398 *Id.* at 132–133.

399 *See, e.g.*, FRANCIONE, *supra* note 386, at 69–70.

400 *See, e.g.*, Kim Severson, *Suddenly, the Hunt is on for Cage-Free Eggs*, N.Y. TIMES, Aug. 12, 2007, at A1. Disturbing images and stories of "cage-free" hens are available from Peaceful Prairie Sanctuary. http://www.peacefulprairie.org/freerange1.html (last visited Oct. 6 2012).

401 *See, e.g.*, Jeffrey Davis, *Niman Ranch Raises Meat So Naturally That Even Vegetarians May Want a Taste*, MOTHER NATURE NETWORK (Jan. 18, 2010, 12:14 PM), http://www.mnn.com/your-home/organic-farming-gardening/stories/niman-ranch-raises-meat-so-naturally-that-even-vegetaria.

402 *See, e.g.*, Aaron Kagan, *A Little Slice of Pork Heaven; Upstate New York Business Thrives Raising Heirloom Pigs*, BOSTON GLOBE, Oct. 19, 2011, at 24; Cornell Sun Video, *The Piggery Owners Talk Farming and Pigs*, YOUTUBE (Nov. 9, 2011), http://www.youtube.com/watch?v=fNVt3zDJ7pM.

403 *See, e.g.*, U.S. Office of Mgmt & Budget, *Mobile Slaughter Unit Compliance Guide* (May 24, 2010), *available at* http://www.fsis.usda.gov/PDF/Compliance_Guide_Mobile_Slaughter.pdf; FOER, *supra* note 170, at 115.

404 VICTORIA MORAN, MAIN STREET VEGAN (2012).

405 Victoria Moran, Plenary Address at Vegetarian Summerfest: Your Mission, if You Choose to Accept It (July 11, 2010).

406 *See, e.g.*, Peter Singer, *Cold Turkey: Jonathan Safran Foer's* Eating Animals, THE MONTHLY (Dec. 2009–Jan. 2010), *available at* http://www.themonthly.com.au/books-peter-singer-cold-turkey-jonathan-safran-foer-s-eating-animals-2173.

407 *See* Laura M. Holson, *The New Court of Shame is Online*, N.Y. TIMES, Dec. 23 2010, at ST2, *available at* http://www.nytimes.com/2010/12/26/fashion/26shaming.html?pagewanted=all.

408 *See id.*; CBS, *Woman Who Throws Cat In Trash: 'It's Just a Cat,'* YouTube (Aug. 25, 2010), http://www.youtube.com/watch?v=Bb0Ebo8BeYI.

409 *See* Holson, *supra* note 407.

410 *See, e.g.*, Megan Gibson, *Top 10 Animal Stories: 3. Lady Throws Cat in Dumpster, Unleashes the Rage of the Internet*, TIME SPECIALS (Dec. 9, 2010), *available at* http://www.time.com/time/specials/packages/article/0,28804,2035319_2034893_2034901,00.html.

411 Catherine Burt, *Cats in Trash Bins—The Humane Myth in Action*, IN-A-GADDA-DA-VEGAN (Aug. 26, 2010), http://blogs.standard.net/in-a-gadda-da-vegan/2010/08/26/cats-in-trash-bins-the-humane-myth-in-action/.

412 *Id.*

413 Few reader comments in articles relating to this story discuss the harm done to the cat's rightful owners, but instead express concern for Lola and society. *See, e.g.*, Cryostatic, Comment to *Woman Who Dumped Cat in Trash: 'I Thought It Would Be Funny,'* THE HUFFINGTON POST (Aug. 27, 2010, 12:31 PM), http://www.huffingtonpost.com/2010/08/25/mary-bale-cat-in-trash_n_693933.html.

414 *See generally* KAZUO ISHIGURO, NEVER LET ME GO (2005).

415 *See* AM. VET. MED. ASS'N, AVMA GUIDELINES ON EUTHANASIA 18 (June 2007), *available at* https://www.avma.org/KB/Policies/Documents/euthanasia.pdf.

416 *See, e.g.*, OPPENLANDER, *supra* note 282, at 122-23.

417 *See id.* at 124, 125, 129–30.

418 *See* STEVEN PINKER, THE BETTER ANGELS OF OUR NATURE: WHY VIOLENCE HAS DECLINED 188 (2011). Pinker, however, fails to fully appreciate the implications of a commitment to non-violence for the continuing consumption of animal products. *See* Sherry F. Colb, *A Clash of Justice and Nonviolence*, DORF ON LAW (Nov. 30, 2011, 6:30 AM), http://www.dorfonlaw.org/2011/11/clash-of-justice-and-nonviolence.html.

419 *See supra* note 402.

420 *See More than Four Hundred Years Ago . . .* , NAVAJO-CHURRO SHEEP ASS'N, http://navajo-churrosheep.com/ (last visited Jan. 11, 2012).

421 *See A Traditional Taste of the Past: Carrying the History of Standard-Bred Poultry into the Future*, GOOD SHEPHERD POULTRY RANCH, http://www.goodshepherdpoultryranch.com/ (last visited Jan. 5, 2012).

422 *See* PETER SINGER, ANIMAL LIBERATION 228 (2d ed. 1990); PETER SINGER, PRACTICAL ETHICS 108 (3d ed. 2011).

423 *See, e.g.*, 1 LESLIE STEPHEN, *Ethics and the Struggle for Existence, in* SOCIAL RIGHTS AND DUTIES: ADDRESSES TO ETHICAL SOCIETIES 221, 236 (1896).

424 The Food and Agriculture Organization of the United Nations places the 2010 world population of chickens at over 19 billion. *FAOSTAT: Live Animals*, FAOSTAT, http://faostat.fao.org/site/573/default.aspx#ancor (last visited Jan. 12, 2012).

425 *See Global Livestock Counts: Counting Chickens*, The Economist: Graphic Detail (July 27, 2011, 2:56 P.M.), http://www.economist.com/blogs/dailychart/2011/07/global-livestock-counts (citing Food and Agriculture Organization of the United Nations).

426 *See, e.g.*, Bryan Hodgson, *Buffalo: Back Home on the Range*, Nat'l Geographic, Nov. 1994, at 64, 69–71.

427 Aaron Hass, In the Shadow of the Holocaust: The Second Generation 12 (1996); William B. Helmreich, Against All Odds: Holocaust Survivors and the Successful Lives They Made in America 128 (1992).

428 *See* Jeff W. Tyler & James S. Cullor, *Mammary Gland Health and Disorders, in* Large Animal Internal Medicine 1019 (Bradford P. Smith ed., 3d ed. 2002) (citing William M. Sischo et al., *Economics of Disease Occurrence and Prevention on California Dairy Farms: A Report and Evaluation of Data Collected for the National Animal Health Monitoring System, 1986–1987*, 8 Preventive Vet. Med. 141 (1990)).

429 *See* Carolyn L. Stull et al., *A Review of the Causes, Prevention, and Welfare of Nonambulatory Cattle*, J. Am. Vet. Med. Ass'n. 227, 232 (2007).

430 *See* Hudson &. Mullord, *supra* note 139, at 271, 275.

431 *See* Food & Water Watch, Factory Farm Nation: How America Turned Its Livestock Farms into Factories, v (2010).

432 *See* Lydia Saad, *Plenty of Common Ground Found in Abortion Debate*, Gallup (Aug. 8, 2011), http://www.gallup.com/poll/148880/Plenty-Common-Ground-Found-Abortion-Debate.aspx.

433 Patrick Martins, Op-Ed., *About a Bird*, N.Y. Times, Nov. 24, 2003, at A23, *available at* http://www.nytimes.com/2003/11/24/opinion/about-a-bird.html?src=pm.

434 *See* Press Release, Farm Sanctuary, Farm Sanctuary's "Turkey Whisperer" Shares 10 Fascinating Facts about Turkeys (Nov. 23, 2011), *available at* http://www.adoptaturkey.org/aat/media_center/pr_2011_turkey_facts.html.

435 *See* Colin C. Whitehead et al., *Skeletal Problems Associated with Selection for Increased Production, in* Poultry Genetics, Breeding and Biotechnology 29, 47 (William M. Muir & Samuel E. Aggrey eds., 2003); Martins, *supra* note 433, at A23; Sabri Ben-Achour, *The Evolution of the Thanksgiving Turkey*, American University Radio News (Nov. 23, 2011), http://wamu.org/news/11/11/23/the_evolution_of_the_thanksgiving_turkey (quoting Julie Long, poultry researcher at the U.S. Dep't of Agric.'s Agric. Research Center).

436 *See* Farm Sanctuary, *supra* note 434.

437 *See* Humane Soc'y of the U.S., An HSUS Report: The Welfare of Animals in the Turkey Industry 3 (2009); *Heidi's Hens°—The Certified Organic, Range Grown Turkey*, Diestel Turkey Ranch, http://www.diestelturkey.com/products_the_hh.htm (last visited Feb. 19, 2012).

438 *See* Matthew Mulcahy, Hurricanes and Society in the British Greater Caribbean, 1624–1783, 96–97 (2006); David Patrick Greggus, Haitian Revolutionary Studies 56 (2002).

439 *See Global Livestock Counts: Counting Chickens, supra* note 425.

440 Endangered Species Act of 1973, 16 U.S.C. §§ 1531–1544 (2006).

441 *See* 16 U.S.C. § 1538(a)(1)(B).

442 *See* Ian Sample, *Wide Roaming Animals Fare Worst in Zoo Enclosures*, TheGuardian, Oct. 2, 2003, http://www.guardian.co.uk/uk/2003/oct/02/environment.science;

Ros Clubb & Georgia Mason, *Animal Welfare: Captivity Effects on Wide-ranging Carnivores*, 425 NATURE 473 (2003).

443 *See* Georgia J. Mason, *Stereotypies: A Critical Review*, 41 ANIM. BEHAV. 1015 (1991).

444 *See* P.H. Cransberg et al., *Sequential Studies of Skeletal Calcium Reserves and Structural Bone Volume in a Commercial Layer Flock*, 42 BRITISH POULTRY SCI. 260, 263 (2001); J. S. Rennie et al., *Studies on Effects of Nutritional Factors on Bone Structure and Osteoporosis in Laying Hens*, 38 BRITISH POULTRY SCI. 417, 421 (1997) ("[T]he modern hybrid laying hen is highly susceptible to osteoporosis.").

445 *See* C.M. Dwyer, *Environment and the Sheep, in* THE WELFARE OF SHEEP 41, 52 (Cathy M. Dwyer ed., 2008).

446 *See* CLIVE PHILLIPS, THE WELFARE OF ANIMALS: THE SILENT MAJORITY 125 (2009).

447 *See Sheep*, ANIMAL LIBERATION VICTORIA, http://www.alv.org.au/issues/sheep. php (last visited Mar. 17, 2012).

448 *See* U.S. Dep't of Agric., Animal and Plant Health Inspection Serv., *Wildlife Damage Management*, USDA: APHIS, http://www.aphis.usda.gov/wildlife_damage/ (last visited Mar. 11, 2012).

449 For data on how many animals Wildlife Services killed or euthanized in 2010, see WILDLIFE SERVICES' PROGRAM DATA REPORTS, ANNUAL TABLES FY 2010: TABLE G. ANIMALS TAKEN BY WILDLIFE SERVICES—FY 2010 (2011), *available at* http://www.aphis. usda.gov/wildlife_damage/prog_data/2010_prog_data/PDR_G/Basic_Tables_PDR_G/ Table%20G_ShortReport.pdf.

450 *See* OPPENLANDER, *supra* note 282, at 27–28.

451 *See* WORLD WILDLIFE FUND, SOY EXPANSION—LOSING FORESTS TO FIELDS 2 (2003), *available at* http://awsassets.panda.org/downloads/wwfsoyexpansion.pdf; JASON CLAY, WORLD AGRICULTURE AND THE ENVIRONMENT: A COMMODITY-BY-COMMODITY GUIDE TO IMPACTS AND PRACTICES 475 (2004); World Wildlife Fund, *Environmental Impact of Beef: Habitat Conversion*, WWF GLOBAL, http://wwf.panda.org/what_we_do/ footprint/agriculture/beef/environmental_impacts/habitat_conversion/ (last visited Apr. 29, 2012).

452 *See, e.g.*, CATTLEMEN'S BEEF BOARD, FACT SHEET: THE ENVIRONMENT AND CATTLE PRODUCTION, MYBEEFCHECKOFF.COM, http://www.beefboard.org/news/files/factsheets/ The-Environment-And-Cattle-Production.pdf (last updated Oct. 2007); AMERICAN MEAT INSTITUTE, AMI FACT SHEET: CLIMATE CHANGE AND ANIMAL AGRICULTURE 2 (2009), *available at* http://www.meatami.com/ht/a/GetDocumentAction/i/52379.

453 Ed Hamer, *Fallow and Fertile*, ECOLOGIST (June 20, 2008), http://www.theecol-ogist.org/blogs_and_comments/commentators/other_comments/269443/fallow_and_ fertile.html; Levente Czeglédi & Andrea Radácsi, *Overutilization of Pastures by Livestock*, 3 GYEPGAZDÁLKODÁSI KÖZLEMÉNYEK 29, 34 (2005), *available at* http://www. agr.unideb.hu/kiadvany/gyep/2005-03/06Czegledi.pdf.

454 *See* OPPENLANDER, *supra* note 282, at 28–32; World Wildlife Fund, *Environmental Impact of Beef: Habitat Conversion*, WWF GLOBAL, http://wwf.panda.org/what_ we_do/footprint/agriculture/beef/environmental_impacts/habitat_conversion/ (last visited Apr. 29, 2012).

455 *See* Ori Herstein, *Why 'Nonexistent People' Do Not Have Zero Well-Being but No*

Well-Being at All 12 (Cornell Law School, Working Paper No. 95, 2012), *available at* http://scholarship.law.cornell.edu/clsops_papers/95.

456 The author credits Michael C. Dorf for proposing this hypothetical scenario in a conversation.

457 *See* Herstein, *supra* note 455, at 3.

458 *See* Steve Graham, *Animal Ingredients in Home Improvement Products*, NETWORX (July 26, 2011), http://www.networx.com/article/animal-ingredients-in-home-improvement-p.

459 Andy Lamey, *Food Fight! Davis versus Regan on the Ethics of Eating Beef*, 38 J. Soc. Phil. 331 (2007), *available at* http://animalrights.aresistance.net/readings/Andy%20Lamey%20-%20Food%20Fight!%20Davis%20versus%20Regan%20on%20the%20Ethics%20of%20Eating%20Beef.pdf; Stephanie Ernst, *Are Vegans Responsible for More Deaths in the Fields? No Way*, CHANGE.ORG (Oct. 31, 2009), *reprinted at* http://www.all-creatures.org/articles/ar-field.html. For a discussion of how harvesting particular crops can destroy habitats on which animals depend for survival, see ELLIE BROWN & MICHAEL F. JACOBSON, CENTER FOR SCIENCE IN THE PUBLIC INTEREST, CRUEL OIL: HOW PALM OIL HARMS HEALTH, RAINFOREST & WILDLIFE (2005), *available at* http://www.cspinet.org/palm/PalmOilReport.pdf.

460 *See, e.g.*, *No Such Thing as a Vegan*, WE KNOW MEMES (Mar. 2, 2012), http://weknowmemes.com/2012/03/there-is-no-such-thing-as-vegan/.

461 *See, e.g.*, Annie B. Bond, *Top 10 Eco-Friendly Reasons to Buy Organic Meat & Dairy*, CARE2, http://www.care2.com/greenliving/why-buy-organic-dairy-meat.html (last visited Oct. 9, 2012).

462 *See* CAROL J. ADAMS, THE SEXUAL POLITICS OF MEAT: A FEMINIST-VEGETARIAN CRITICAL THEORY 40 (1990); JOY, *supra* note 39, at 21.

463 *See* PIRKEI AVOS, ETHICS OF THE FATHERS: A NEW TRANSLATION WITH A CONCISE COMMENTARY ANTHOLOGIZED FROM THE CLASSICAL RABBINIC SOURCES 6 (Mesorah Publications, 1984).

464 *Id.* at 23.

465 *See* JAMES OLIVER HORTON & LOIS E. HORTON, SLAVERY AND THE MAKING OF AMERICA 83 (2005); 2 JOHN ASHWORTH, SLAVERY, CAPITALISM, AND POLITICS IN THE ANTEBELLUM REPUBLIC: THE COMING OF THE AMERICAN CIVIL WAR 1850–1861, 162 (2007).

466 *See* 1 A. Glenn Crothers, *Free Produce Movement, in* ENCYCLOPEDIA OF ANTI-SLAVERY AND ABOLITION 266–68 (Peter Hinks & John McKivigan eds., 2007); Margaret Hope Bacon, *By Moral Force Alone: The Antislavery Women and Nonresistance, in* THE ABOLITIONIST SISTERHOOD: WOMEN'S POLITICAL CULTURE IN ANTEBELLUM AMERICA 275, 278–79 (Jean Fagan Yellin & John C. Van Horne eds., 1994). Rather than support the institution of slavery, some Quakers refused to buy cotton products altogether. *See* MARGARET H. BACON, THE QUIET REBELS: THE STORY OF THE QUAKERS IN AMERICA 100–01, 105 (1969).

467 *See generally* ANNE FARROW ET AL., COMPLICITY: HOW THE NORTH PROMOTED, PROLONGED, AND PROFITED FROM SLAVERY (2005).

468 *See* FARM FOUNDATION, THE FUTURE OF ANIMAL AGRICULTURE IN NORTH AMERICA 7 (Nov. 2004), http://www.farmfoundation.org/projects/documents/Initial-WhitePaperNovember04.pdf.

228 *Endnotes*

469 *See* Jenny Hall & Iain Tolhurst, Growing Green: Organic Techniques for a Sustainable Future 2–3 (2006).

470 Veganic Agriculture Network, http://www.goveganic.net/ (last visited Sept. 28, 2012).

471 *See Veganic Fertility: Growing Plants from Plants*, Veganic Agriculture Network (Aug. 25, 2012), http://www.goveganic.net/spip.php?article205.

472 *See, e.g.*, Model Penal Code § 210.1 (1985); *Murder: An Overview*, Legal Information Institute (Aug. 19, 2010, 5:20 PM), http://www.law.cornell.edu/wex/murder#model_penal_code.

473 *See* Model Penal Code § 210.3 (1985); *Manslaughter*, Legal Information Institute (Aug. 19, 2010, 5:19 PM), http://www.law.cornell.edu/wex/manslaughter.

474 *See, e.g.*, Cal. Penal Code § 195 (2011), *available at* http://www.leginfo.ca.gov/cgi-bin/displaycode?section=pen&group=00001-01000&file=187-199.

475 *See, e.g.*, Gary Null et al., Death by Medicine (2011), *available at* http://www.lef.org/magazine/mag2004/mar2004_awsi_death_01.htm; 3 Gilbert Lau, *Iatrogenic Injury: A Forensic Perspective, in* Forensic Pathology Reviews 351, 353 (Michael Tsokos ed., 2005).

476 *See* National Center for Statistics and Analysis, National Highway Traffic Safety Administration, Fatality Analysis Reporting System Encyclopedia, http://www-fars.nhtsa.dot.gov/Main/index.aspx (last visited Oct. 2, 2012).

477 *See generally* CDC, Alcohol and Public Health, http://www.cdc.gov/alcohol/ (last updated Sept. 14, 2012).

478 *See* Colleen Patrick-Goudreau, The 30-Day Vegan Challenge: The Ultimate Guide to Eating Cleaner, Getting Leaner, and Living Compassionately 8–9 (2011).

479 Gaverick Matheny, *Least Harm: A Defense of Vegetarianism From Steven Davis's Omnivorous Proposal*, 16 J. of Agric. & Envtl. Ethics 505, 506 (2003), rebutting Steven L. Davis, *The Least Harm Principle May Require That Humans Consume a Diet Containing Large Herbivores, Not a Vegan Diet*, 16 J. of Agric. & Envtl. Ethics 387, 388 (2003).

480 *See* Jeanne Yacoubou, *Is Your Sugar Vegan?*, The Vegetarian Res. Group (2007), http://www.vrg.org/journal/vj2007issue4/2007_issue4_sugar.php.

481 *See, e.g.*, Eric C. Mussen, *Impact of Honey Bees on the California Environment*, Univ. Cal. Bee Briefs, Feb. 2, 2002, *available at* http://ucanr.org/sites/entomology/files/147620.pdf.

482 *See* Alexei Barrionuevo, *Honeybees Vanish, Leaving Keepers in Peril*, N.Y. Times, Feb. 27, 2007, *available at* http://www.nytimes.com/2007/02/27/business/27bees.html?pagewanted=all.

483 *See, e.g.*, Ingrid H. Williams, *Insect Pollination and Crop Production: A European Perspective, in* Pollinating Bees: The Conservation Link Between Agriculture and Nature 36 (Peter G. Kevan & Vera L. Imperatriz-Fonseca eds., 2002), *available at* http://www.webbee.org.br/bpi/pdfs/livro_02_willians.pdf.

484 *See* Dennis Craven, *Vegan Sweeteners*, SlashFood (Aug. 25, 2006, 6:10 PM), http://www.slashfood.com/2006/08/25/vegan-sweeteners/.

485 *See* Searchable Vegan Beer, Wine and Liquor Guide, Barnivore, http://www.barnivore.com/liquor?vfilter=Vegan# (last visited Oct. 2, 2012).

486 *See Honey Bee Basics: Bee Senses*, Sonoma Cnty. Beekeepers' Ass'n, http://www.sonomabees.org/html/honey_bee_basics.html (last visited Oct. 2, 2012).

487 *See, e.g.*, Singeli Agnew, *The Almond and the Bee*, S.F. CHRONICLE, Oct. 12, 2007, *available at* http://www.sfgate.com/cgi-bin/article.cgi?f=/c/a/2007/10/14/CM2S-S2SNO.DTL.

488 *See Pesticide Issues in the Works: Honeybee Colony Collapse Disorder*, EPA, May 15, 2012, http://www.epa.gov/pesticides/about/intheworks/honeybee.htm.

489 *See Re-Queening*, THE BEE WORKS, http://www.beeworks.com/informationcentre/requeening.html (last visited Oct. 2, 2012).

490 *See* Gary L. Francione, *Commentary #4: Follow-Up to "Pets" Commentary: Non-Vegan Cats*, ANIMAL RIGHTS: THE ABOLITIONIST APPROACH (Aug. 17, 2009), http://www.abolitionistapproach.com/follow-up-to-pets-commentary-non-vegan-cats/.

491 *See* FRANCIONE, *supra* note 21, at 175–76; Dana Goodyear, *Eating Bugs to Save the Planet*, THE NEW YORKER, Aug. 15, 2011, at 38.

492 *See supra* note 22, and accompanying text.

493 *See* Howard H. Erickson, *Animal Pain*, 56 J. APPLIED PHYSIOLOGY 1135 (1984).

494 *See* David DeGrazia & Andrew Rowan, *Pain, Suffering, and Anxiety in Animals and Humans*, 12 THEORETICAL MED. & BIOETHICS 193 (1991).

495 *See* Alan Dawrst, *Can Insects Feel Pain?*, UTILITARIAN-ESSAYS.COM (July 2012), http://www.utilitarian-essays.com/insect-pain.html.

496 *See, e.g.*, Debbie Hadley, *Do Insects Feel Pain?*, ABOUT.COM, http://insects.about.com/od/insects101/f/Do-Insects-Feel-Pain.htm (last visited Oct. 2, 2012).

497 *See, e.g.*, Douglas Fox, *Consciousness in a Cockroach*, DISCOVER MAGAZINE, Jan. 10, 2007, http://discovermagazine.com/2007/jan/cockroach-consciousness-neuron-similarity.

498 *See* JONATHAN BALCOMBE, THE EXULTANT ARK: A PICTORIAL TOUR OF ANIMAL PLEASURE 13 (2011).

499 *See* EISNITZ, *supra* note 210, at 273; James McWilliams, *PTSD in the Slaughterhouse*, TEXAS OBSERVER, Feb. 7, 2012, http://www.texasobserver.org/eat-your-words/item/18297-ptsd-in-the-slaughterhouse.

500 Claude Steel, WHISTLING VIVALDI (2010).

501 *See* Jeffrey Masson, *Does "Humane Meat" Exist?*, YOUTUBE (Dec. 2, 2011), http://www.youtube.com/watch?v=D4GvVmoJlwk.

502 *See id.* at 2:20.

503 Water boils at 212 degrees Fahrenheit.

504 *See,* Michael D.A. Freeman, *"But If You Can't Rape Your Wife, Who[m] Can You Rape?": The Marital Rape Exemption Re-examined*, 15 FAM. L.Q. 1, 9–10 (1981) (citing MATTHEW HALE, HISTORIA PLACITORUM CORONAE 636 (1736)); Joanne Schulman, *State-by-State Information on Marital Rape Exemption Laws*, in DIANA E.H. RUSSELL, RAPE IN MARRIAGE 375, 375–81 (1982).

505 *See, e.g.*, FOER, *supra* note 170, at 241; Catherine Clyne, *Singer Says: The* Satya *Interview with Peter Singer*, SATYA, Oct. 2006, *available at* http://www.satyamag.com/oct06/singer.html; JEAN KAZEZ, ANIMALKIND: WHAT WE OWE TO ANIMALS 178–80 (2010).

About the Author

SHERRY F. COLB is Professor of Law and Charles Evans Hughes Scholar at Cornell University Law School, where she teaches courses in animal rights, evidence, and criminal procedure. She is a graduate of Columbia College and Harvard Law School, and a former law clerk to the late Supreme Court Justice Harry A. Blackmun. Colb lives in Ithaca, New York, with her husband, two daughters, and two mixed-breed dogs.

About the Publisher

LANTERN BOOKS was founded in 1999 on the principle of living with a greater depth and commitment to the preservation of the natural world. In addition to publishing books on animal advocacy, vegetarianism, religion, and environmentalism, Lantern is dedicated to printing books in the U.S. on recycled paper and saving resources in day-to-day operations. Lantern is honored to be a recipient of the highest standard in environmentally responsible publishing from the Green Press Initiative.

CPSIA information can be obtained at www.ICGtesting.com
Printed in the USA
BVOW07s1953090114

341258BV00001B/1/P

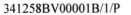